INDUSTRIAL PORT DEVELOPMENT

INDUSTRIAL PORT DEVELOPMENT

WITH CASE STUDIES FROM SOUTH WALES AND ELSEWHERE

R. E. TAKEL, M.Sc., F.R.I.C.S., M.C.I.T.

Estate Surveyor, British Transport Docks Board, South Wales

With a Foreword by

SIR HUMPHREY BROWNE, C.B.E.

Chairman of the British Transport Docks Board

BRISTOL: SCIENTECHNICA (Publishers) LTD.

1974

ISBN 85608 010 1

PRINTED IN GREAT BRITAIN BY HENRY LING LTD.,
A SUBSIDIARY OF JOHN WRIGHT AND SONS LTD., AT THE DORSET PRESS, DORCHESTER

TO MY WIFE

\

PREFACE

THE years since the Second World War have witnessed the greatest revolution in port development and operation for over a century. This revolution is seen in part in Britain, particularly in cargo handling methods and in scattered and sometimes isolated sites providing for big ship development. It is seen more completely on the Continent of Europe and elsewhere, with examples of fully integrated port and industrial areas on a scale not known before.

Although ports are expensive structures, and the results of faulty design and management will have correspondingly great effects on finances, there is a relative lack of technical literature on many aspects of port development. This book represents the attempt of a surveyor to fill part of the vacuum by providing guidelines for port development, particularly in relation to his specialist role in land economy, land use and control, and physical planning. Since the profession of surveyor is sparsely represented in ports, it may be that this work will introduce some new approaches to a difficult problem, particularly for those who are unfamiliar with this specialization.

The work commences with a discussion of the factors leading to the current transformation of the ports, the conception of industrial ports, and the characteristics which decide whether an area would be a suitable site for industrial port development. A case study is given, which may be used as a model for similar studies of other areas. European port systems are described and some of the lessons which might be of significance in the event of new industrial port development are considered.

Some technical aspects of industrial port development are dealt with in Part II, covering the principles of ownership of port and industrial areas, and of land use. The principles discussed include aspects which might be of relevance to many types of port, including purely transit ports, and the whole should cover maritime techniques of general interest to town planners, geographers, and serious students of maritime affairs. Techniques for land use analysis and the assessment of land requirements are described, together with the principles applicable in port land planning and valuation. Examples are taken from actual cases and many recent port plans are discussed.

Part III discusses the long-term prospect and the factors which might affect that prospect, and advocates optimism and a positive approach towards industrial port development. Whatever the defects of this book, the author has enjoyed the best of both worlds. The valuable help and advice of the Department of Maritime Studies, University of Wales Institute of Science and Technology, have influenced the academic content. In the practical world, years of experience and contact with leading figures of the port world, particularly those of the British Transport Docks Board, past and present, have influenced the practical side. Any merits come from those sources; the defects are the author's alone.

Finally, I should emphasize that the views expressed in this book are my own and not necessarily those of the British Transport Docks Board.

ACKNOWLEDGEMENTS

I am grateful to the British Transport Docks Board and the Port Director, South Wales, Mr. T. S. Roberts, J.P., for making it possible for me to undertake the research and the writing for this book and to my friends David M. Evans and Sidney Evans for their encouragement to place on record the results of experience.

I am indebted to Professor A. D. Couper of the Department of Maritime Studies, University of Wales Institute of Science and Technology, for his advice and encouragement, as well as to members of staff of the Department who have been of great assistance.

I am also indebted to a very large number of officers and staff in the British Transport Docks Board who have been unfailingly helpful.

Invaluable help and advice has been received from maritime industries, ports, and traders in South Wales and elsewhere; from the Secretary of Newport Harbour Commissioners, Mr. W. J. Slade; from the Port Authorities of Rotterdam, Antwerp, Le Havre, and Rouen, and from the officials of the Ministre d'Équipement et Logement, Paris. Especial thanks are due to Lt. Col. R. H. Edwards, lately Civil Engineer, South Wales Ports, for generous help with copies of his many papers on port matters, historic photographs, and diagrams, as well as a great deal of valuable advice.

Kind permission to reproduce several illustrations from other sources is gratefully acknowledged. In particular, the Council of the Institution of Civil Engineers for the use of *Figs.* 18, 25, 28, 33, and The National Ports Council for the use of *Fig.* 5 and Appendixes VI, VII. *Fig.* 26 is used with the permission of the Controller of Her Majesty's Stationery Office.

Every professional career is influenced by the example of other members of the profession. In particular I would like to record the debt I owe to an early mentor, J. R. C. Honey, F.R.I.C.S. and examination medallist, for his advice on methodology, and to C. W. Parker, A.R.I.C.S., A.M.I.Mun.E., a pioneer in evolving techniques for New Town development.

I also wish to thank the publishers, particularly Mr. L. G. Owens and his assistant Mrs. B. Vowles, for their help and skill in handling a complex manuscript.

My gratitude is due to Tom Hughes and Richard Clarke for their work in turning sketches into excellent drawings and maps and to Miss Joy Grant for producing the final typescript, Mrs. M. Fuller for typing the early drafts, and Mrs. E. Morgan for helping with the tables.

Cwmbran, 1972   R. E. T.

INTRODUCTION

There is a tide in the affairs of men
Which, taken at the flood, leads on to fortune,
Omitted, all the voyage of their life
Is bound in shallows and in miseries.
On such a full sea are we now afloat,
And we must take the current when it serves,
Or lose our ventures.
WM. SHAKESPEARE,
Julius Caesar, Act IV, Scene III.

BRUTUS's famous words seem appropriately nautical in flavour to be quoted here. Critics of such an optimistic view of the future of British ports might point to the unhappy result of Brutus's desire for battle. Unfortunately for Brutus, good general advice was applied to bad circumstances. The account which follows tries to show how the economic battlefield exemplified by Britain differs from Phillipi.

All port activities are industrial, in an etymological sense, but the ports of the future will differ from the traditional image of a port by combining the cargo interface with related manufacturing industry to a far greater extent than in the past. This has come about because of the need to import increasing quantities of Britain's raw materials, both for energy and manufacture. Transport of raw material is an expensive matter in the twentieth century and the more this cost can be reduced, the more competitive industry becomes. From this simple fact emerges the need of industry for a port location. The need increases in direct relationship to three factors: bulk of raw material in relation to value; extent of reduction of bulk or weight during processing; and the difficulty and cost in handling the raw material from ship to industry. The industries which feel the strongest attraction are the prime industries, but more and more these will tend to attract subsidiary or secondary industry using their products or servicing their plants. Some experts imply that coastal attraction for industry is negligible, but this argument has not impressed their counterparts in Japan, although the distance factors are similar.

The trend will inevitably make the port a much more complex system, integrated with other aspects of the British economy. Hence its development will require considerably more thought than in the past, not least because of the impact on the environment.

There are a large number of studies of ports in Europe. That by Professor James Bird (*The Major Seaports of the United Kingdom*, Hutchinson, 1963) is considered to be the most comprehensive of its type, dealing not only with descriptive aspects but also establishing comparative patterns of growth from the earliest harbours. It is not intended that this book should be in any way compared with such a study. The work that follows has been conceived as a study of the need for a positive approach to industrial port development and its problems.

The study has three principal aims: The first is to describe trends affecting seaports and their effect on related industry. The second is to discuss the economic and physical factors which could make future growth in ports an important part of value-added economies like that of Britain. The third deals with part of the process which follows acceptance of the conception of an industrial port, developing techniques necessary for translating conception into reality.

These aims perfectly supported would provide a mammoth task; one which requires the attention of a large range of disciplines. The limitations of the study are, therefore, the limitations of the individual. As a port surveyor for many years, the author has been obliged, as a matter of course, to deal with port land development in the existing economic environment. Many detailed studies, some of which were published, led to the conclusion that the attraction of ports for manufacturing industry, which has existed for some hundreds of years, was increasing at a considerable pace. Because this was of vital importance to the already industrialized port areas of South Wales, thought had to be given to the problems that the scale of modern industry created, and their effect on port development policies. The same rationale is applicable to other ports of Britain, and it is because these problems and their solutions are not confined by national boundaries that the publication of this work has been suggested. In preparing it, South Wales has been used to provide case studies only where it is necessary to obtain analyses in depth, or where a detailed example is preferable to a mere description of methodology. Similar techniques could be applied universally, and not only to industrialized ports. Examples from other parts of Britain and Europe are used wherever possible.

Ports, as a whole, fall into various categories, but all will contain the same problems of handling goods at the interface between sea and land. Some will be purely transit ports, acting as a staging post at some point between origin and destination of cargo. Others will be purely industrial in character, with berth and manufacturing industry in close proximity. These may be suitable for deep drafted or smaller vessels, or both. More frequently, it is suggested, ports will combine the transit and industrial functions, or will need to do so if they are to survive as important economic units, insulated against competition by the captive trade which port-related industry implies.

In dealing with the problems of industrial ports for the 1980s and beyond, the greater includes the lesser. The concept examined is the combined port, with both transit and industrial functions. It is, therefore, presented with the hope that it may contribute something of value to all ports which are concerned with their future, as well as to those whose interests are bound up, directly or indirectly with the general prosperity which a port and its trade can bring.

The work which follows is capable of further development, but in extending the study it is essential to widen the disciplines involved. It would be impertinent to stray too far into the realms of intellectual discussion belonging to other professions. On the other hand, the available research in port development is not extensive and this account may suggest a number of fields in which further research is worth while. The work may be said, therefore, to have a further hidden aim: to stimulate the study and research necessary to develop a new port system worthy of a maritime trading nation.

Throughout the history of ports runs the thread of communications; of rivers and estuaries; of packhorse trails, turnpike roads, canals, railways and motorways and ultimately of air freight; of the changes in vehicle which alter the scale of those communications, but not the principle. Growth has been fastest when these have met the needs of the day. When economic changes have wrought a temporary decline, failure to keep communications up to date has accentuated the difficulties. Even with modern communications, some seem to draw the wrong conclusions. One view qualifies the opportunity for the future by pointing out that a motorway crossroads on the port boundary is necessary to a transit port. This ignores the lessons of history. Nations in war and peace, throughout the ages, have sought control of crossroads of one sort and another but, as any General would point out, no captured crossroads should be sterilized by his ordnance depot. Intersections in communications must be kept clear to speed the traffic flow.* Modern vehicles and roads which place ports close to major intersections in time/distance and within easy reach of markets, will be the real basis on which future hopes rest.

As for the third aim; while some nations, including Britain, still investigate the advantage of port-related industry, there is little written information on the techniques necessary to give practical effect to opportunity. This work tries to identify some of the practical problems which will arise, to draw lessons from Europe, and to provide at least a start in evolving techniques. Of necessity these are restricted, since every witness observes an event differently. Almost every major skill is involved in the industrial port process. The problems must be approached from a number of points of view.

It is to be hoped that such investigations will not long be delayed, for time is short if a maritime nation is to take the current when it serves.

---

* *Severnside: A Feasibility Study*, para. 5.61. H.M.S.O., 1971.

xi

CONTENTS

FOREWORD

by Sir HUMPHREY BROWNE, C.B.E.

Chairman of the British Transport Docks Board

I AM very pleased to be invited to write a Foreword to this book since I believe that it will make a major contribution to the literature available on port development.

Since I joined the British Transport Docks Board early in 1971 I have been impressed by the high standard of management and by the quality of functional skills in the organization. Mr. Takel, as Estate Surveyor for the South Wales ports, has a wide knowledge of ports, as this book will demonstrate.

There is no doubt that Mr. Takel has provided a useful book. I wish it every success.

PART I
THE CHANGING PORT

CHAPTER I

TRENDS IN MARITIME INDUSTRIAL RELATIONSHIPS

RÉSUMÉ OF INDUSTRIAL TRENDS

PORTS have evolved since early times, although the greatest changes in developed countries came about in the period during and following the industrial revolution of the eighteenth century. The prosperity of ports like those of South Wales was based on vast supplies of coal for energy in close proximity to the coast. This raw material contributed to the growth of heavy industry, but the greatest proportion of the trade of the ports consisted of exports of coal to feed industry and steam transport all over the world.

The decline in importance of coal can be said to have started as a result of the investigation into the properties of oil and the invention of the internal combustion engine.

The first modern investigation was made in 1847 by James Young and Lord Playfair.* The first publicized results were for candles of paraffin wax and these proved a godsend to the poor, who had previously relied on tallow. The real advance lay in the discovery of a process of distillation. From this followed the discoveries of the properties of the other distillation products, but development of machinery to utilize these took another 50 years.

The effects of the decline in importance of coal were also delayed by the capital invested in steam propulsion and industrial steam plant, and the need for heavy capital investment programmes for the plant and machinery developed for oil. Acceleration of development after World War I was also slowed again by the years of recession and by the need to conserve shipping space in World War II, but thereafter the change of energy sources has moved apace. By 1969, oil provided 49·8 per cent of the world's energy requirements, the remainder being provided (in order of importance) by coal, natural gas, and hydro-electric and nuclear power.

With the displacement of coal by oil, the industrial centre of gravity moved to the oil refinery. In a country without appreciable inland oil reserves, this has meant, in Britain, a move towards the coast. In effect, the port of 1970 takes the place of the pithead of 1870, as the energy source for an industrial nation.

A second trend influenced the movement of industry towards coastal locations. This was created by an increasing reliance on imported raw materials, particularly of ores. Since bulk is reduced by prime industrial processing, prime

* KAY, F. GEORGE (1952), *Pioneers of British Industry*, p. 51. London: Rockliff.

industry had always been sited in the most economic location for transport costs. Such a characteristic was represented at Swansea for centuries in connexion with copper production. With the gradual exhaustion of home ores and the discovery of richer or larger sources overseas, the second trend has reinforced the arguments for a move to the coast.

The change forced on Britain by these two factors has already gone a very long way. In South Wales, for example, Dowlais Works, Cardiff, was established on the basis of imported ores in 1891; Llandarcy oil refinery at Swansea was established, as the first in Britain, in 1917; small steelworks sprang up in Port Talbot (1902 and 1916); Newport, followed by East Moors, Cardiff (1934); Ebbw Vale (1938); Margam (1947); and Spencer Works, Llanwern (1962).

These are major developments, but other important industries have also grown up near ports; examples include petrochemicals, chemicals, aluminium, processing of timber and timber products, other non-ferrous metals, and cereals.

Location of suitable industry in the vicinity of ports has considerable economic importance in offsetting the effects of change in older industry, and in providing a base for new and healthy growth. Although there has been massive contraction in the mining industry, employment in the ports of South Wales (excluding Milford Haven) and port-related industries is 75,000 (*Table I*).*

Table I.—TRAFFIC FLOWS THROUGH SOUTH WALES PORTS AND RELATED EMPLOYMENT (EXCLUDING MILFORD HAVEN)

Traffic Flow	Tonnage	Employment
Iron ore (Iron and Steel) (inc. tinplate)	8,617,000	52,100
Oil/Petroleum (inc. storage chemicals)	6,321,000	2,750
Petrochemical/Chemical	164,000	4,940
Aluminium/Bauxite	252,000	7,700
Zinc/Lead	164,000	850
Nickel	76,000	1,200
Cereals	142,000	500
Timber	278,000	1,000
	16,014,000	71,040
Employees of British Transport Docks Board and registered dock workers		4,000
Total employed		75,040

(*Source*: G. Hallett and P. Randall, 1970.)

The stabilizing effect of maritime industry on port trade is borne out by the Martech Study for the Port of London (1966) on the origin and destination of exports and imports. This pointed out that the South Wales ports were

* HALLETT, G., and RANDALL, P. (1970) Maritime Industry and Port Development in South Wales, p. 106. Cardiff: University College.

relatively invulnerable to competition from London and Liverpool. The main reason was the existing relationship between heavy industry and the ports.

TRENDS IN SHIPPING

The trends noted with industry have been affected by developments in shipping. Increasing capital and operational costs, great competition in the industry, particularly from flags of convenience, and exploitation of natural resources in more distant locations, have all contributed to the pressures for research into ship design and size.

The length of time spent by ships in port represents a loss of earning capacity, which can be of critical importance in economic ship operation, and so there has been parallel research into cargo handling and port layout and design.

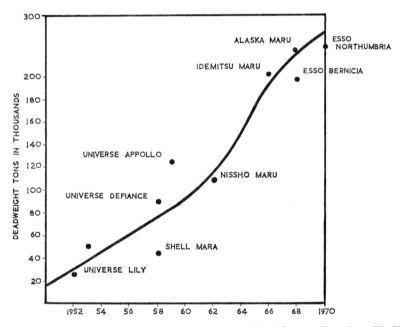

Fig. 1.—Progress of maximum tanker sizes, 1951–1968. (*Source*: Based on H. Shinto (1968), *Ships*, Vancouver.)

The process of change—which is still continuing—has produced a number of important developments. Ships have increased in size and sophistication, with the emergence of mammoth carriers, container vessels, LASH (Lighters aboard ship) and BOB (Barges on Board) systems, and ship-based cranes replacing the older derricks. Ports have had to provide berths for an increasing range of vessel size; handling equipment to deal with cargo delivered in new forms such as unit loads and containers, bulk packages, or just plain bulk; new layouts of

Table II.—Cost per Cargo Ton—Tankers (in Dollars)

Vessel Size	Port Days			
	4	7	10	14
A. 5,000 miles				
25,000	2·27	2·59	2·92	3·36
50,000	1·49	1·71	1·93	2·22
75,000	1·19	1·37	1·55	1·78
100,000	1·02	1·17	1·33	1·53
150,000	0·84	0·97	1·09	1·26
200,000	0·75	0·87	0·98	1·13
300,000	0·66	0·76	0·86	1·00
B. 10,000 miles				
25,000	4·14	4·48	4·81	5·25
50,000	2·71	2·93	3·15	3·44
75,000	2·16	2·34	2·52	2·76
100,000	1·85	2·01	2·16	2·36
150,000	1·51	1·64	1·77	1·94
200,000	1·36	1·47	1·59	1·74
300,000	1·19	1·29	1·39	1·53
C. 15,000 miles				
25,000	6·07	6·40	6·74	7·19
50,000	3·95	4·17	4·39	4·69
75,000	3·15	3·33	3·51	3·75
100,000	2·69	2·85	3·00	3·21
150,000	2·20	2·33	2·46	2·63
200,000	1·97	2·08	2·20	2·35
300,000	1·72	1·82	1·92	2·06
D. 25,000 miles				
25,000	10·05	10·40	10·74	11·20
50,000	6·49	6·72	6·94	7·25
75,000	5·16	5·34	5·53	5·77
100,000	4·40	4·56	4·72	4·92
150,000	3·58	3·71	3·84	4·02
200,000	3·20	3·32	3·43	3·59
300,000	2·79	2·90	3·00	3·14

(*Source*: Trevor D. Heaver (1968) *The Economics of Vessel Size*, National Harbours Board of Canada.)

Table III.—World Fleet of Large Tankers, 1 January, 1970

Size Group	No.	Gross tons dwt.
60– 80,000	243	16,941,000
80–100,000	157	14,075,000
100–150,000	96	11,027,000
150–200,000	31	5,464,000
200–250,000	54	11,410,000
250,000+	9	2,727,000
Total	590	61,644,000

(*Source*: Fearnley & Egers Chartering Co. Ltd., *see* footnote, p. 7.)

quayside land to speed ship turnround; and industrial facilities for port-related industry.

In a physical and capital sense, the major changes have taken place in connexion with the carriage of crude oil and ores.

OIL TANKERS

In 1944, a 23-year old record for tanker size was beaten when the 23,000 dwt. *Phoenix* was completed. Since that date there has been a steady progression in tanker size (*Fig. 1*).

A tentative increase in size began to take advantage of greater draughts provided at ports such as Antwerp and Rotterdam. By doing so, it became possible to reduce per ton costs for carriage, principally because increasing size meant no corresponding increase in crew size and, at the same time, large ships are cheaper per ton to build. In simple terms, a 200,000 dwt. (dead weight tons) vessel carries 8 times as much as a 25,000 dwt. ship, costs about 5 times as much to build and has the crew size increased by 25 per cent or less.

The attitude to large ships was greatly affected by the Suez War of 1956 and the closure of the Canal. This imposed on tankers bringing oil to Europe from the Middle East an additional voyage distance from Aden of 5,457 sea miles.

The interruption in oil supplies to a continent heavily committed industrially taught a lesson which will not easily be forgotten. Not only did research indicate that further increases in size would result in lower per ton costs of carriage, but the uncertain politics of the Middle East showed that the Suez Canal should not again be relied upon as a corridor of trade. Development in ship size reached, and then exceeded, the capacity of the canal and, when this was deepened by Egypt, exceeded it yet again. The justification for increase has been emphasized by the further closure after the 1967 war.

The table of cargo costs prepared by Trevor D. Heaver (*Table II*) shows that whilst there is a saving, even for comparatively modest increases in size, the greatest savings accrue to the greatest increases and the greatest distances.

In 1969 the tanker fleet had a size distribution as shown in *Table III*. By 1969 tankers of over 60,000 dwt. were moving 402 million tons of oil shipments. At the end of 1969, 90 tankers of above 150,000 dwt. were trading; 45 ships in the 200,000 dwt. range were commissioned, and delivery of another 60 was expected in 1970. The new building under construction or ordered will mean a growth in the world tanker fleet of almost 50 per cent over the next four years.*

BULK CARRIERS (ORE)

The most dramatic increases in ship size have taken place in tankers, with vessels such as the 326,000 dwt. *Universe Ireland* plying regularly between

* Fearnley & Egers Chartering Co. Ltd. (1969), *Review.*

Table IV.—Bulk Carrier Shipments, 1960–1969
(Vessels over 18,000 dwt.)

	1960	1961	1962	1963	1964	1965	1966	1967	1968	1969
In million metric tons:										
Iron ore	31	38	47	54	80	98	107	127	151	181
Grain	1	3	7	14	16	17	25	29	40	36
Coal	3	6	12	18	25	30	34	39	48	60
Bauxite and Alumina	3	5	6	8	10	12	13	15	16	19
Phosphates	—	—	—	1	1	2	4	7	12	12
Other Bulk Cargoes	—	1	1	3	6	12	24	41	59	61
Total	38	53	73	98	138	171	207	258	326	369
Total World Seaborne Trade (main bulk)	228	239	246	269	308	327	340	352	384	419
In thousand million ton/miles:										
Iron ore	98	123	149	184	278	356	424	514	653	822
Grain	5	17	38	74	90	95	151	188	233	218
Coal	13	29	59	87	121	146	167	203	269	347
Bauxite and Alumina	6	9	11	14	18	21	26	35	39	54
Phosphates	—	—	—	2	4	6	12	29	56	50
Other Bulk Cargoes	—	2	4	9	19	35	98	199	295	305
Total	122	180	261	370	530	659	878	1,168	1,545	1,796
World Total (main bulk)	746	833	854	956	1,146	1,260	1,360	1,465	1,614	1,833

Increase in trade 84 per cent. Increase in ton/miles 146 per cent.

(Source: Fearnley & Egers Chartering Co. Ltd.)

Kuwait and Bantry Bay, Ireland. There has also been a spectacular increase in sizes of bulk carriers, principally for iron ore. Some of these are combined carriers, available for oil or ore, or for return loads of other cargo such as motorcars and steel products (*see Table IV*).

The causes of this change differ from those affecting tanker size. Firstly, ore is less easily handled than oil and requires a more elaborately equipped berth. This has tended to relate ship size to existing port facilities. Secondly, much ore has been imported from sources such as Sweden, Spain, and North Africa, comparatively close to European steelworks. *Fig.* 2 illustrates the cost curves for varying distances and ship sizes. The short-distance curves are much flatter than the others. This, together with limits on berthing facilities in some ore ports, has tended to keep down vessel size.

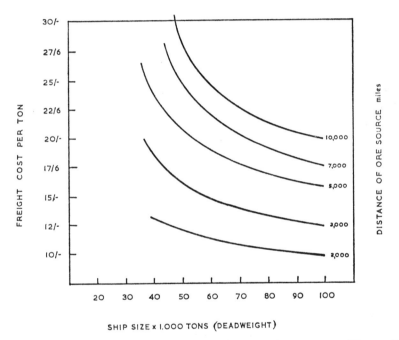

Fig. 2.—Freight cost related to ship size and distance of ore source. (*Source*: W. G. Meredith and C. Wordsworth (1966), *Journal of the Iron and Steel Institute*.)

Tables V, VI contrast the size distribution of existing bulk carriers and carriers on order in July, 1970.

Orefields had been opened up over a long period in distant locations, such as Canada and Venezuela, but more recently Australian orefields have been developed. The vast increase in voyage distance has underlined the force of economic argument in favour of larger vessels.

Table V.—Size Distribution of Existing Bulk Carriers, July, 1970
(Figures in '000 dwt.)

Size of Vessel in '000 dwt.	Ore C.	Comb. C.	Other Bulk C.	Total Bulk C.
10–18	1,313	191	7,500	9,004
18–25	1,264	435	10,684	12,383
25–30	667	200	6,669	7,536
30–40	1,114	347	7,635	9,096
40–50	370	650	6,039	7,059
50–60	1,740	1,228	5,253	8,221
60–80	1,197	4,211	3,862	9,270
80–100	181	3,928	331	4,440
100+	543	3,200	414	4,157
World	8,389	14,390	48,387	71,166

(*Source*: Oslo: Fearnley & Egers Chartering Co. Ltd.)

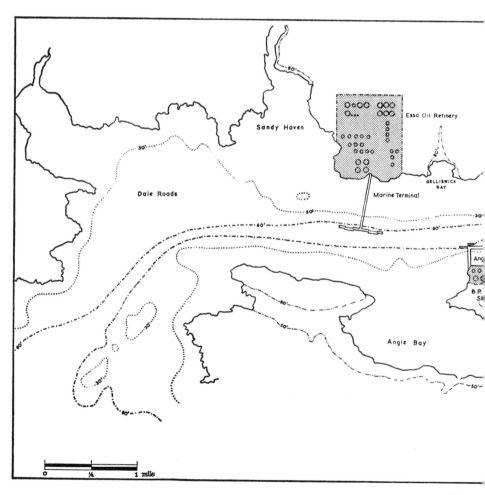

Fig. 3.

Table VI.—SIZE DISTRIBUTION OF BULK CARRIERS ON ORDER, JULY, 1970
(Figures in 'ooo dwt.)

Size of Vessel in 'ooo dwt.	Ore C.	Comb. C.	Other Bulk C.	Total Bulk C.
10–18	—	—	443	443
18–25	23	—	1,958	1,981
25–30	100	—	2,881	2,981
30–40	32	—	2,429	2,461
40–50	—	145	618	763
50–60	111	—	1,916	2,027
60–80	152	207	1,884	2,243
80–100	264	2,266	241	2,771
100–150	923	3,995	2,814	7,732
150+	318	11,526	151	11,995
Total	1,923	18,139	15,335	35,397

(*Source*: Oslo: Fearnley & Egers Chartering Co. Ltd.)

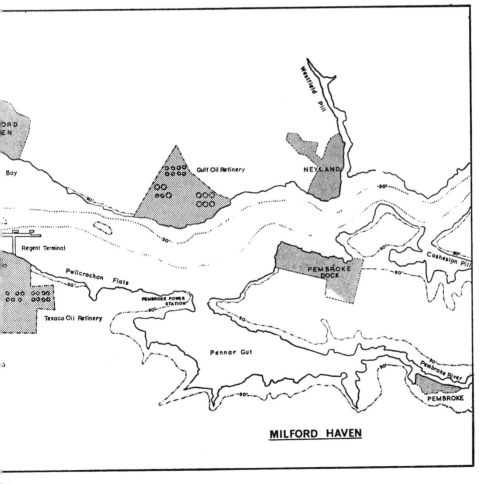

MILFORD HAVEN

Haven.

Construction of accommodation for increasing ship size in Britain did not start on any scale until after Suez and, even so, has been on a fragmented basis, with uncontrolled port investment before 1964, a conservative port outlook, and competitive investment by oil companies (*Fig. 3*).

THE INDUSTRIAL PORT CONCEPT*

The new industrial strategy and the increased size of bulk vessels has greatly altered the approach to port development. The consequent changes, illustrated by European ports, such as Rotterdam, Antwerp, and Le Havre, have hardly begun in Britain. Port facilities have been provided for tankers in such natural harbours as Milford Haven and the Clyde, but the fact that Port Talbot Tidal Harbour (opened 1970) is the largest new harbour work in over 50 years—and cost approximately the same as the new lock at Le Havre—shows the low level of industrial port investment in Britain, compared with Europe.

The European examples all show important port/industrial complexes. Rotterdam is already 25,000 acres in extent, whilst Antwerp and Le Havre also plan growth to this size. Other developments exist at Wilhelmshaven, Hamburg, Zeebrugge, Dunkirk, Marseilles, Genoa, Taranto, Leghorn, and even Augusta in Sicily.

The intense competition in Europe is explained by the growth attracted by industrial ports and by the fact that ports are considered part of navigation and, therefore, are outside the Rome Treaty.

THE NATIONAL PORTS COUNCIL AND M.I.D.A.s

Following a visit to Europe in 1966 by officials of the National Ports Council, the Council made the following recommendation in its 1966 Annual Report:—

Maritime Industrial Development Areas:
32. Despite these natural advantages offered by the geography of Great Britain, however, it must be recognised that to meet the port requirements of importers of bulk material by the development of separate facilities for each user may not, in all cases, be economic. This is particularly the case where the industry is sensitive to the size of the immediately adjacent market. As can be seen from the map (p. 20) there are very few areas where deep water frontage (or potential deep water frontage) coincides with undeveloped land near main population groupings. Major port installations for single users in such areas might be too expensive for such individual users. Alternatively, such individual developments might, if permitted, pre-empt unduly large parts of these scarce resources.
52. As noted at paragraph 32 above, there are very few areas left in this country where deep water and ample land for industrial development coincide in the vicinity of major population areas. This relates, of course, to the import of bulk materials

* M.I.D.A.s (or Maritime Industrial Development Areas) is the name given by the National Ports Council to the industrial port concept. In order to make the text easier to read this will be printed as M.I.D.A.s where appropriate.

for processing and in this context the Council consider that 'deep water' must mean not less than 40 feet of water (at low water ordinary spring tides). In some areas this problem could be eased by large scale land reclamation such as has been carried out with marked success on the Tees. In the Low Countries, in particular, a policy of land reclamation has been carried out with great success for many years and, in the Council's view, it is arguable that this country may have neglected this aspect of long term land use planning.

53. Certainly the competition for land near deep water and major population areas is intense. Apart from urban requirements, which extend beyond housing, schools, etc., to sewage disposal and the electricity supply industry (for which the sea, even where fuel is not moved by water, forms a convenient and inexpensive cooling pond), there are many other pressures, including amenity, on the land available.

54. The Council, therefore, taking the view that land of the type described is a scarce national resource, have decided that a primary long term planning effort must be the identification of sites where long term new port development and associated industrial development could most advantageously take place. At such sites, it would be possible to bring large bulk carriers to berths immediately against the plants that would use or produce the cargoes which the vessels would carry. The comparative economy of large vessels compared to smaller ones would result in smaller costs of ocean carriage and the absence of land transport costs for the bulk goods would be an added gain. Such Maritime Industrial Development Areas, as they might be termed, could have considerable attractions for industries, particularly those using materials that could be imported in large bulk carriers but which individually might be unable to support the cost of independent facilities. The Council consider it significant that several Continental countries are constructing port facilities in such a way that they give access for large vessels to extensive areas of land available for industrial development. The competitive advantages of industry so sited might be considerable.

55. Clearly, studies into this problem would extend to fields beyond the Council's sphere. The Council naturally, however, maintain close liaison with industries and organizations, such as Regional Economic Planning Councils, concerned with port developments and, in this case, they have proposed to the Ministry of Transport that studies should be put in hand to examine places at which deep water facilities could be made available adjacent to areas of land suitable for industrial development; to assess the costs, and the prospects that such sites might attract industries requiring facilities of this nature; and to assess the extent to which the national economy might benefit. It is clear that many considerations additional to those relating to transport planning will be involved but the Council hope, in conjunction with the Ministry, to explore the best means whereby cooperative studies in this field by appropriate bodies could be instituted. The Council would naturally be anxious to play their proper part in such studies.

As a result, the Government and the National Ports Council initiated studies in 1967 to identify potential sites for Maritime Industrial Development Areas (M.I.D.A.s). Although the report (by Sir William Halcrow and Partners) was not released, statements in Parliament and in the National Ports Council

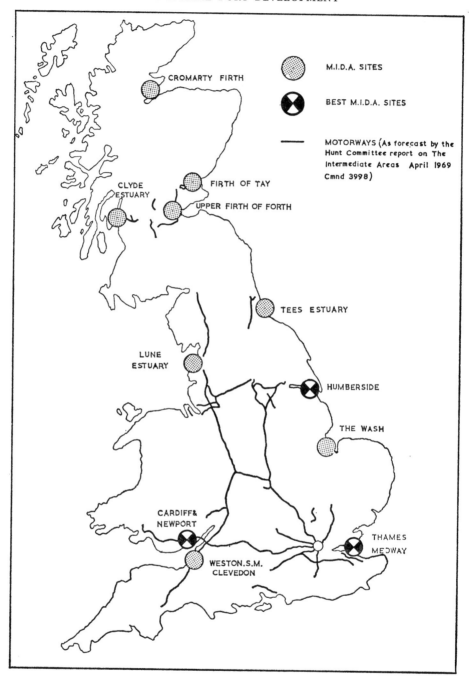

Fig. 4.—Possible M.I.D.A. sites. (*Source*: G. Hallett and P. Randall, 1970.)

progress reports have shown that the first physical examination defined three sites—Severn/South East Wales, Thames Medway, and North Humberside—as having outstanding characteristics, and a further seven sites—Cromarty Firth, Outer Firth of Tay, Upper Firth of Forth, Tees Estuary, Lune Estuary, the Wash, Weston-super-Mare/Clevedon—as worthy of further examination (*Fig. 4*). In the physical examination the criteria for consideration were*:—

1. Nearness to deep water (50–60 ft. MHWN without excessive dredging). The N.P.C. also feels that potential depths beyond 60 feet would be very desirable for M.I.D.A.s.

2. Availability of at least 5,000 acres of level land reasonably near the deep water, suitable for heavy industrial development with or without reclamation, together with substantial further contiguous and backland areas.

3. Favourable broad economic geography of the location, including such factors as population, industry, inland communications, and relation to markets and to other overseas ports.

The Council points out that the most obvious sites have already been largely exploited (though not necessarily in the best way), not only in such estuaries as the Mersey, but also in natural deep water harbours such as Milford Haven. Planning problems also affect Milford Haven and other areas because they have exceptionally high amenity value (*see Fig. 5*) or are remote from existing centres of population.

The Council regards these problems as well worth tackling, because it considers M.I.D.A.s a planning concept of the greatest significance, to a trading nation with an expanding population, in relation to any attempt to control the developing environment. It says: 'The aim of M.I.D.A.s is to provide optimum as opposed to *ad hoc* solutions, both for those industries which ought to be able to support necessary port developments themselves, but even more for those which cannot separately do so. . . . The cost of such development should be lower than the aggregate cost of a series of piecemeal approaches'.

DEFINITION OF INDUSTRIAL PORT DEVELOPMENT

M.I.D.A.s can, therefore, be defined as a planned and co-ordinated port and industrial complex to achieve the following objects:—

1. *Economies of Ship Transport Costs for Bulk Raw Materials.*—The sites require sea access for bulk carriers of sufficient depth to enable the most economic ship size to be used, particularly in the trades of crude oil and iron ore.

2. *Economies of Cargo Handling Costs for Raw Materials.*—This implies an industrial location close to the point of transhipment. The exact location will depend on such factors as the bulk/value ratio, the effect of reduce bulk processes, and the ease of handling. In the first case, the lower the value in relation to the

* National Ports Council (1969), *Ports Progress Report*, chap. VII.

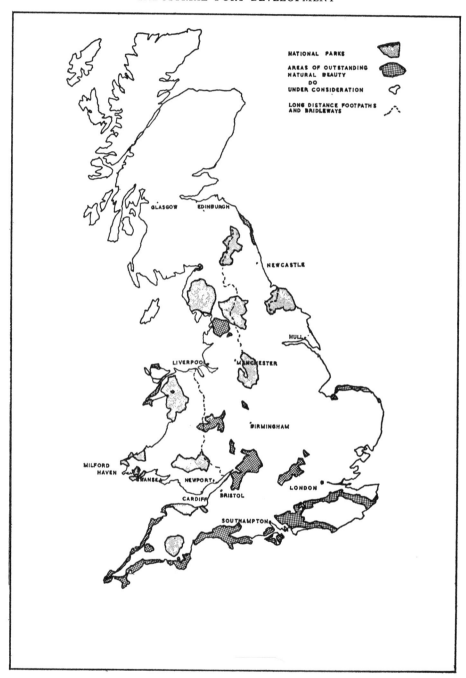

Fig. 5.—Map showing areas of national parks. (*Source*: National Ports Council.)

unit of bulk, the higher would be the effect (in percentage terms) of transport on total cost of raw material delivered. The second and third factors, whilst also being linked with the bulk/value consideration, are also important in deciding locations. Handling costs are higher for dry bulk as against liquid bulk cargoes. Temperature requirements for 'difficult' cargoes, such as liquid sulphur, asphalt, and liquefied natural gas (L.N.G.) are also relevant. The importance of such considerations is due to the competition which might arise for sites. The problem is dealt with later in connexion with planning, but proper economy in dock construction will mean zoning of industries according to the economies of handling their particular cargoes.

3. *Economies of Scale.*—The present situation in Britain displays a scattered pattern of deep water facilities (*Fig.* 6) which must have had a spiralling effect on the total capital employed as well as on transport costs. The creation of planned complexes should enable port investment to be kept at an economic level and the cost of infrastructure to be reduced in National terms.* New maritime development on the present basis necessarily leads to pressure for public expenditure at widely dispersed points in such fields as communications, housing, social and educational services, and amenity. The concentration of such developments in a limited number of centres will reduce the overall investment necessary. If placed where infrastructure already exists, the savings will be even greater.

In considering the capital outlay on new dock works, reference is made later to the extent of subsidization of Continental ports, and to the way in which entrepôt trade can affect the future development of British ports. British ports no longer receive the 20 per cent Port Modernisation Grant for new facilities under the Harbour Act, 1964. In these circumstances it would seem that the best trading results would accrue to Britain only if existing suitable infrastructure were to form an important part of new port development.

4. *Control and Amenity.*—The unspoiled coastline of Britain is diminishing every year. The result has been an increase in awareness of the extent to which this has been and is taking place. Equally, the landward aspect of maritime development is causing concern.

CONSERVATION

Organizations like Operation Neptune have as their goal preservation of the unspoiled lengths of coastline. It is an obvious truism that coastline will be spoiled to a much greater extent by sporadic and uncontrolled development than by intensive development of small zones.

For example, five major developments of about 1,000 acres each will occupy one single area of $7\frac{1}{2}$ sq. miles, e.g., $2\frac{1}{2}$ m. × 3 m., or could be spaced at 5-mile

* P.I.A.N.C. 22nd International Navigation Congress, Paris (1969), Miss Susan W. Fogarty, D. J. Bright, D. C. Coode, D. G. McGarey, N. N. B. Ordman, and J. T. Williams, Paper No. 6 on 'Land for Port Development', para. 4.8.

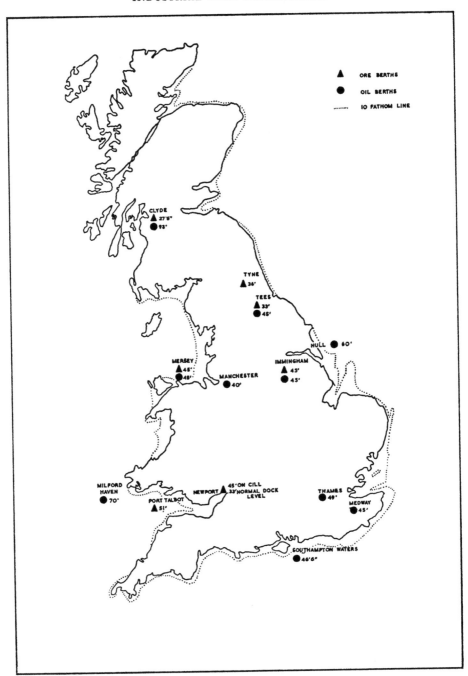

Fig. 6.—Map showing the scattered nature of deep water ports, Great Britain, 1970.

intervals—within sight of each other—and affect 20 miles of coast (e.g., Milford Haven) or have even more widespread effect if one were placed in each of five estuaries.

A site of 1,000 acres has a perimeter of, say, 5½ miles (4,000 ft. × 10,000 ft.) and five similar sites 27½ miles if separately located. In concentration (2½ m. × 3 m.) the perimeter would be 11 miles (*Fig.* 7).

Concentration in one zone with landscaping and tree screening and careful location could mitigate the effect to a considerable degree. Such concentration

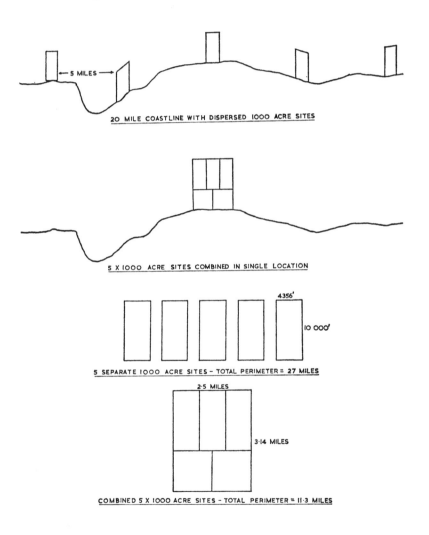

Fig. 7.—Effect of coastal development.

will also provide sufficient revenue by means of local taxation to make such amenity treatment even more effective.

These considerations have been emphasized (in 1970) by the difficulties experienced in gaining planning consent for refineries by Murco and Chevron in Scotland and Amerco in Milford Haven.

An example, late but effective, of what can be done, is given by the amenity treatment of Brielsemeer, adjacent to Europort in Rotterdam. This area provides a lake with adjoining woodlands and facilities for sailing, bathing, and picnicking. It includes yacht marinas, beaches, picnic areas, and walks of considerable attraction, and has become extremely popular, although, like Europort, it has only recently been completed. On the human scale, industry, apart from the tops of a very few stacks, is invisible; and yet Europort is hardly more than a stone's throw away.

CONTROL OF POLLUTION

A major problem created by modern industry is that of pollution, both liquid and atmospheric. Maritime industry has attracted a great deal of criticism on this score, principally because of the atmospheric pollution at Rotterdam. Undoubtedly, this occurred because of the way in which growth exceeded all expectations. Concentrations of oil refining and chemical plants in early post-war developments occurred close to much older residential areas. Lacking experience of the problems created by such industrial growth these residential areas were also expanded with high density housing to accommodate the new workers and the pollution problems were thus intensified.

In fact, the creation of a maritime industrial area affords a way of improving control over pollution. The site can be located to avoid affecting residential areas or other sensitive features. It gives an opportunity for smaller industries to share the cost of constructing and operating treatment and precipitation plants and the concentration eases the task of supervising pollution control. The existence of an overall authority also helps, since these authorities can include anti-pollution provisions in contracts, including leases. They would not be bound by the limitations of general pollution legislation and could plug any gaps.

In Holland, Dutch law prescribes standards which must be observed both in atmospheric and other pollution. Currently, control is being improved considerably. A refinery of Shell has existed since 1929 but is now being provided with a 230-metre stack with filters and precipitators. Similar installations must be provided at newer plants.

Antwerp controls pollution by means of a Pollution Commission. It operates a flexible system and, where a high pollution industry is established, a much more stringent control is applied to adjacent areas to bring down the overall level. Industry is carefully located according to its problems, the effect on adjoining areas, and the prevailing winds. A close watch is always kept on the global effect.

In Le Havre, also, there is a local control applied by the Port Autonome. This insists on standards higher than those applied by law and includes provisions in contracts and leases. The port authority also carries out examinations to ensure that standards are being observed.

ASSESSMENT OF MARITIME INDUSTRY FOR BRITAIN

BRITAIN AND THE NETHERLANDS

Industrial port development has had dramatic effects in Europe. In 1967, for example, the 'Consultation Organization for Seaport Development in South-West Netherlands' was formed as a result of the continued growth of Rotterdam, the pressures on land created by this growth, and the anticipated spread of industrial 'spin-off' to the adjoining provinces.

By January, 1968, this organization had presented a report to the Dutch Government.* The report recommended further study on the various problems arising from Rotterdam's growth. These problems, which are not inconsiderable, flowed from the way in which growth had exceeded all expectations. In recommending study, the report presented an extremely optimistic picture of the economic effect of Rotterdam development. It began with an opinion that national economic development 'must be stimulated by the powerful injections the seaport activities will be able to supply'.

Table VII shows the annual growth of selected industries in the Netherlands and is taken from the report. It is of significance that the fastest growth is shown in port-related industry, which is compared with the general industrial average.

Table VII.—ANNUAL GROWTH OF SOME DYNAMIC INDUSTRIES IN THE NETHERLANDS
(together representing 11·6 per cent of the national production in 1965)

	1955/60	*1960/65*	*1965/70**
Chemical industry	9·6	12·4	11·9
Petroleum refining	10·5	8·6	6·8†
Metal industry	12·5	9·6	6·0
Electrotechnical industry	11·9	9·7	8·7
Total industrial production	4·6	5·1	5·3

* Central Plan Bureau estimate.
† This will be higher following the construction of the oil channel.

In the years 1960–1965 seaport industrial activities at Rotterdam showed an average annual growth of 9 per cent compared with the Netherlands average of 5–6 per cent.†

* Report of the Consultation Organization for Seaport Development in South-West Netherlands (1968).

† Rotterdam City Council (1969), *Plan* 2000+.

An important feature of Dutch seaport development is illustrated by the fact that port investment has attracted private industrial investment in the ratio of 8:1 (*see* p. 31).

Continental ports are dealt with in greater detail later but it is important to observe that the success of ports like Rotterdam and Antwerp has inspired the creation of similar enterprises in almost every country in Europe. Indeed, the influence of Dutch thinking is now worldwide and the shape of the seaport has been irreversibly altered by their example.

It is necessary to point out that the hinterland situation in Britain is different to that in Europe. With a coastline well over 2,000 miles in length and a population of 55 million, most areas of Britain are within one-day return distance from the sea. Inland water transport has only limited significance and the total United Kingdom trade is conditioned by the population size.

On the other hand, Western Europe, excluding Scandinavia, has a population of over 250 million. The coastline is that of a large land mass with only one or two nations having access to the sea in a way at all comparable with Britain (e.g., Italy, Spain, Denmark). Barge traffic is able to travel large distances—1,000 miles and more inland—and a substantial population lies over 250 miles from the sea. However, the conditions supporting the Land Bridge argument, discussed in Chapter III, and Common Market membership, could permanently alter the situation and Britain should be prepared.

THE BRITISH PROBLEM

Whether or not Maritime Industrial Development Areas are to be created in Britain is a matter for Government, and consent of Government is essential because of the scale of capital investment required. The Harbours Act, 1964, makes it necessary for Government approval to be given to all development schemes in excess of £1,000,000, and the use of this curb is essential to prevent gross over-provision in ports facilities.

In examining the potential of likely areas, the value of a completely objective examination cannot be overlooked. Similarly, the danger of a political decision altering the result of the economic examination cannot be overstressed. The chosen areas must be soundly based in economic terms. This is not to say that the social cost and benefits of maritime development should be ignored in any cost benefit analysis, since support action in difficult areas has already cost the Government many hundreds of millions of pounds. Regional Employment Premium alone is said to have cost about £100 million a year. The abolition of investment grants is claimed to save £670 million by 1974–75, but other provision, such as tax allowances, may preserve roughly the same advantages for Development Areas. Saving in social expenditure is a valid benefit which could accrue to M.I.D.A.s development. Social factors are extremely relevant in assessing total economic benefits. Furthermore, the population of this country is growing—one estimate gives a population of 70 million for England and

Wales by A.D. 2000.* Other emergent nations are forcing the pace of competition with their industrial growth. In order to provide a healthy economy and environment for future generations, Britain must bring its own industrial efficiency to the highest level and this means, in part, the reduction of transport costs to the lowest possible level. The effect of this pressure has been called the 'March to the Coast'.

There is therefore a need for maritime industrial development in Britain, though not on the scale of Rotterdam, and this view is supported by evidence of the benefits arising from similar policies in ports like Antwerp and Le Havre. French official policy is to use port investment to stimulate industrial growth in selected areas. The evidence suggests that the policy, which really is to treat a port as a vital if sophisticated part of communications, is at the heart of modern industrial growth.

Britain has failed, so far, to achieve more than a fragmented approach to the physical creation of a new ports system, although she has moved slowly towards establishing a policy. The National Ports Council's proposals of 1966, had, by 1970, resulted in the publication of the 'study of a study'.†

In the same period Rotterdam had obtained a number of major economic reports on the same topic, but it must be recorded that a cost benefit analysis of M.I.D.A.s for Britain was approved in 1970. On 18 February, 1971, *Lloyds List* reported that the Government appeared to have abandoned any chance of proceeding with the concept since the Under-Secretary for Trade and Industry had revealed that the cost benefit study was not under way. Instead a reduced study was proposed (*Lloyd's List*, 23 February, 1971) into the needs of the bulk industries.

This can only be a temporary setback since economic pressures will ultimately force British industry into adopting a comprehensive maritime policy. It would be a much less sombre picture, however, if a central direction could be shown to exist, even if this did not extend to active participation. The reduced study must keep in mind the development of sites capable of being expanded into a M.I.D.A. when the appropriate time comes.

The slowness of British investigations has been criticized.‡ In Graham Hallett's opinion, owing to the absence of effective planning, either by national government or local authorities, 'the United Kingdom is well on the way to producing a pattern of maritime industry which is bad from the point of view of amenity, expensive in terms of investment, and inefficient in terms of operating costs'.

* *Western Mail*, 8 September, 1970, extract from Registrar General's Report on Population Trends.
† PESTON, M. H., and REES, R. (1970), *Maritime Industrial Development Areas: Feasibility Study of a Cost Benefit Assessment of Maritime Industrial Development Areas*. National Ports Council.
‡ HALLETT, G. (1970), '*How not to plan M.I.D.A.s*', *Loughborough Journal of Social Studies*.

COLLEGE OF EUROPE: CONFERENCE ON PORTS, 1970

In these circumstances it is perhaps appropriate to refer to the College of Europe Conference on the future of European ports (Bruges, April, 1970). This conference was admirably wound up by the summary of Professor Rudolf Regul of the College of Europe.

It was estimated that by 1990 European trade would have multiplied threefold. Of the new total, three-quarters would be bulk cargo and two-thirds of maritime exports would consist of oil products, fertilizers, and metallurgical and manufactured goods. The increased trade would call for additional harbour facilities of a capital intensive nature, concentrated in a few areas.

The functions of harbours would be amplified by the coastal migration of input-dependent industry and the diffusion effects may be widespread. It was generally agreed that the processes were irreversible. The decision making processes should be based on economic criteria and the principal questions to be answered are:—

1. Where shall projects be effectuated?
2. How shall investments be carried out?
3. When should they be undertaken?*

It was necessary to evaluate the desirability of providing a new port or of improving an old one, estimating the benefits both for the immediate and the ultimate hinterland.

Cost benefit analysis gives rise to many unsolved questions, such as the measurement of benefit, and might well be combined with discounted cash flow analysis of the public sector. In this case, the forecast port charges should relate to the ship facilities actually used and to the port time used.

In the investigation it is essential to examine the relationship between ports and industries showing, first of all, the ports and their industry as an entity before distinguishing between the social, national, and private benefits brought by maritime development. Secondly, investigations should be made into the effect of ports on regions and their role in the total system.

It was suggested that evaluation should be made first on a regional basis; if this showed a benefit, then a wider evaluation would be justified.

Competition is artificially affected by investment decisions in ports and by differing approaches to commercial targets. There is, therefore, a need to examine ports on a national, and sometimes, international basis and to improve the basis of maritime statistics and methods of discovering trade and economic trends.

All this may appear to be a case for further prolonged investigation and delay, but delay could be fatal in a British context. In the absence of a national port plan for Britain, or control inside the Common Market, decisions might be

* Goss, R. O. (1970), 'The Size of Ships', *Report of the Conference on the Future of European Ports*, Bruges. College of Europe.

taken by individual authorities without even the limited investigation contained in this study. Distortions and mistaken investment will both have an unfortunate effect on this highly developed island. Control of maritime development in an enlarged market could make Britain the laggard in perpetuity. The first steps have already been taken towards establishing this control.*

Similar considerations affect decisions in France. Gallic logic has perceived that although tools to quantify port investments have not been developed fully (p. 46 et. seq.) decisions must be made. These decisions are being made on the basis of existing theory and the developments are being extended as the techniques are enlarged. This might well be an example for Britain to follow.

The answer to the problem would appear to be to identify the best sites for a M.I.D.A., bearing in mind the need, from an economic viewpoint, for extension as growth proceeds. Suitable sites could be first reserved for this purpose and then planned so that development could proceed by stages as the demand occurs.

* Vleugels, R. (1973). 'Port Economy in the European Economic Community', *Chartered Institute of Transport Journal*, March.

Chapter II

MARITIME INDUSTRIAL COMPARISONS

DEVELOPMENT TOWARDS MARITIME INDUSTRY IN EUROPE

In order to assess the likely benefits of maritime development, it is advisable to examine the continental trend. For this purpose, a description of Rotterdam and Antwerp, as well as the French system, seems appropriate. In general, it should be emphasized that industrial growth in Europe has tended to concentrate around those ports which have provided big ship facilities. In 1962–63, it was estimated that 10 per cent of the population of the European Economic Community lived in the metropolitan area of a seaport.* This tendency has been used as an argument for extensive port construction at a large number of locations. Today, ports from Augusta in Sicily to Wilhelmshaven in Germany are pressing claims for predominance.†

The use of European examples should not be taken as an argument for scattered investment in Britain. On the other hand, it would be equally wrong to consider that only one new industrial port is necessary. There are a number of natural M.I.D.A.s such as Milford Haven, the South Wales ports, Clyde, and Immingham in the present unplanned system. If the principle is accepted and planned bulk facilities can be provided, it is reasonable to contemplate development in differing degrees in each of the potential M.I.D.A.s bridges (*see Fig.* 14) but it would be wrong to go ahead in the 1970s with new deep-water installations on sites which are unsuitable, by reason of size or location, with the expectation of expansion into a M.I.D.A.s, when a programme is ultimately accepted.

Important lessons for the future are to be learned from the Continent of Europe, where, despite the competition, the haphazard influence of port growth in economic locations has been harnessed into planned development, creating immense areas of maritime industry.

The basis of European M.I.D.A.s development is the world growth in trade in oil. Provision of facilities for the import of crude oil has resulted in the establishment of refineries and petrochemical complexes. These, in turn, attract other industries using prime manufactures and by-products. Similarly, steelworks

---

* VLEUGELS, R. (1969), 'The Economic Impact of Ports and the Regions they serve and the Role of Industrial Development', Conference of the International Association of Ports and Harbours, Melbourne.

† *Report of the Conference on the Future of European Ports*, Bruges, April, 1970. College of Europe.

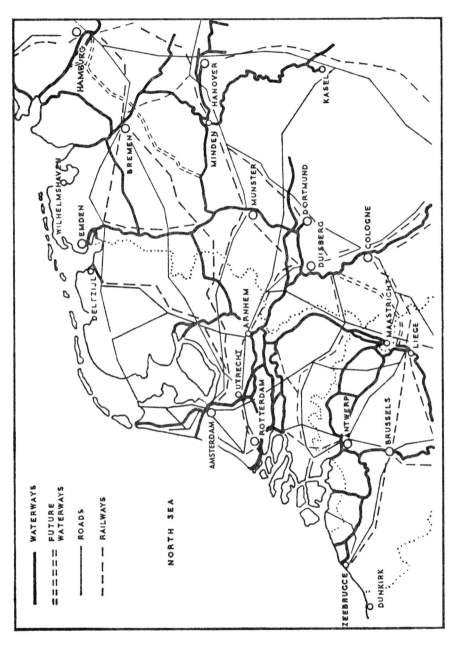

Fig. 8.—Inland transport links in the Low Countries. (*Source: The Amsterdam Port Areas,* 1970. Inbucon B.V. Amsterdam, and Port of Amsterdam)

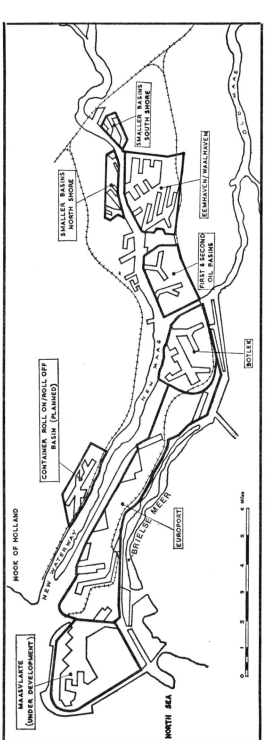

Fig. 9.—Map of the port areas, Rotterdam.

AREA IN ACRES

PORT AREA	Total Area	Water	Transportation Facilities	Leasable Sites
Maasvlakte under development	6,400	2,225	800	3,375
Europoort	9,050	2,675	1,863	4,512
Botlek	3,125	750	500	1,875
Container, roll on, roll off, basin planned	1,150	365	135	650
First and second oil basin	1,800	260	240	1,300
Eemhaven/Waalhaven	2,800	1,165	485	1,150
Smaller basins, south shore	435	275	40	120
Smaller basins, north shore	385	195	40	150
Total	25,145	7,910	4,103	13,132

and metal industries attract secondary industry, although this trend can be obscured by commercial pricing policies, as with steel in Britain. The creation of self-generating growth areas in prime manufactures becomes an attraction for industry of all types. However, precise location of secondary industry is often less important than with heavy industry because of the effect of the bulk/value ratio on transport costs. Hence small, high-value manufactures (e.g., cosmetics and radios) can be sited in quite remote positions to aid in solving social and economic problems. Furthermore, the ability to pump crude oil by pipeline enables refineries to be established in the least harmful positions, or located, within limits, in areas where industrial growth is needed.

ROTTERDAM

The builders of this modern port once chose as their slogan a statement of priorities: 'The quay must exist before the ship calls'. This would not excuse port development in bad locations and, indeed, the position of Rotterdam, astride one of Europe's main inland waterways, is unrivalled (*see Fig. 8*). In considering United Kingdom developments in a M.I.D.A.s context, it should be remembered that the potential hinterland of Rotterdam with its waterway connexions, contains 150 million people. This considered, it would seem that the main difference would be one of scale. In view of the present-day vastness of Rotterdam (*Fig.* 9), and taking into account its competitors, this would still seem to justify *planned* maritime development of considerable size in Britain.

Rotterdam has had a long history as a port. The town took its name from a dam built on the River Rotte in A.D. 1270. In the seventeenth century the small fishing port of Rotterdam was expanded when Johan van Oldenbarnevelt initiated the construction of a commercial port on the right bank of the river. By 1620 this port was in use but was later affected by sand accumulation in the approaches. The Voorne channel was constructed in 1830 in an attempt to improve the position, but it was not a complete success.

The Act of Mannheim guaranteed all countries with a Rhine bank free passage along the river and its tributaries and this led to the growth of important transit trade in ore, coal, timber, phosphates, pig iron, and wheat. By 1870 new facilities had to be provided on the left, or south, bank.

Rotterdam owes its present importance to Dr. P. Caland. His conception was of an unobstructed route to the North Sea through the sand dunes. The original channel, now called Nieuw Waterweg (New Waterway), was 3 miles long and was first used by two fishing smacks in March, 1872. It had been started as the reconstruction of an old shipping channel called the 'North Hole'.

The improvement to the port approaches which the reconstruction of the channel brought about, has enabled the municipally controlled port to carry out a continuous programme of harbour improvements by deepening and widening the Nieuw Waterweg. The port authority is able to construct new port facilities along the banks without the expense of locks, and salt water is prevented from contaminating the upper reaches of Rotterdam's waterfront at the Hartel Locks system where a curtain of air bubbles prevents mixing.

The size and trade of Rotterdam was much smaller before 1939. In 1938 trade amounted to 42,371,000 metric tons (imports 24,504,000 tons; exports 17,867,000 tons) and was carried in 15,360 vessels.

Before 1939 work had been started on Petroleumhaven, a new harbour on the south side of the New Waterway, to serve Shell and other refineries. Work was delayed by the Second World War, but this time-lag enabled revisions to be made to the plan and, when the work was completed in 1955, water depths had been provided up to 39 ft. The harbour has a capacity for vessels up to 40–50,000 deadweight tons.

Construction of Eemhaven, another harbour on the south bank, started during the war. It was the first harbour to be completed after 1945 and has a water depth of 33 ft. Continuous improvements have been made to layout and facilities since completion and the harbour now occupies 1,171 acres—approximately the size of Cardiff Docks—of which 725 acres are land.

In 1947 Rotterdam took a fresh decision to 'provide the quays' by embarking on the Botlek project. Site work commenced in 1954 and the harbour, again on the south bank, accepted ships from 1957. After improvements in depth, the harbour is able to take vessels up to 80,000 deadweight tons. It has a total area of 3,125 acres, of which 2,375 acres are land.

This harbour, with its capacity to accept large vessels and the availability of sites, has proved to be of immense interest to the rapidly growing oil refining industry. It has attracted refineries with petrochemical and chemical plants, as well as other bulk industries based on borax, liquid sulphur, aluminium, iron ore, fertilizers, and grain. This has brought about self-generating growth which continues to add to the industrial strength of Rotterdam. Improvements have been made to the main road and rail communications to cope with the increase in traffic.

The provision of berths for large bulk carriers resulted in an increase in the number of ships of 65,000 dwt. and over. Rotterdam, therefore, decided to build an even larger harbour south of the New Waterway in 1957. It has achieved world fame as Europort and is notable for its canal shape. The water area is known as the 'Caland Canal' and the banks consist of slopes rather than continuous walls, with berths and jetties where needed. The first ship entered in 1960. The total area of Europort is 9,050 acres, of which water covers 2,675 acres. Industrial sites, amounting to 4,512 acres, are included in the total area. By 1967 the harbour was able to accept ships up to 200,000 dwt. and later improvements have increased the capacity to accept 250,000 dwt. vessels with draughts up to 62 ft. Industrial and commercial berth development is only possible on one side of the canal for most of its length. The narrow strip on which Europort lies does not permit double frontage development by industry. On the other hand, it has been necessary to separate large bulk carriers, which have to manoeuvre towards berths, from the busy main channel of the New Waterway. For this reason, the port authority has been obliged to leave a 'training bank' between the Caland Canal and the New Waterway.

The continuing pressures to provide yet more port facilities have brought into being the port's latest extension—Maasvlakte (Meuse Shallows)—where construction is still proceeding. This harbour, containing 6,400 acres, lies on the coast and requires extensive sea protection works. The port authority plans to provide berths for vessels up to 500,000 or even 700,000 dwt. The harbour is intended to accommodate ore preparation and steel plants as well as oil installations.

A container port is planned for the north bank of the New Waterway.

Rotterdam now looks forward to the year A.D. 2000 and has commissioned a number of studies to provide a basis for planning. The proposals emerging from these studies envisage a vast extension, broadening the belt of port and industry which now exists. The present areas of the port (*see Fig.* 9) amount to 25,145 acres in all and it is possible that this area will increase over the next thirty years by another 100,000 acres (gross).*

The industrial growth at Rotterdam has meant great prosperity. Definitions of port-related industry differ, but one unofficial estimate suggests that up to 700 industries have been attracted to the port by the provision of ship facilities. These industries have not been deterred by a piling depth for construction of up to 70 ft.

Apart from industrial growth, trade has increased so that Rotterdam now handles the largest tonnage in the world and proudly displays a telegram from the Port Authority of New York recording the year when it overtook that port's position. Trade growth had been interrupted by the second World War and tonnage did not reach the 1938 figure again until 1953. In 1968, 32,145 ships called at the port carrying 156,882,000 tons of cargo (imports 119,109,000 tons, exports 37,773,000 tons). No less than 132,240,000 tons of the total consisted of bulk cargo. The 1972 tonnage is about 260,000,000 tons.

So great has been the attraction of new port facilities at Rotterdam that in one case a mere decision to carry out development—the tanker channel, costing 150 million guilders—produced private industrial investment decisions within six months totalling 1,200 million guilders—that is, eight times the port investment.†

The entire Nieuw Waterweg (sometimes called 'Nieuw Maas') and a tributary (the Koningshaven) are State owned and controlled. Europort lies partly outside the city boundaries but is owned and operated by the port authority as well as Maasvlakte, which is completely outside the city boundary.

* RUITER, R. (1970), 'Seaport Development in the Netherlands', *Report of the Conference on the Future of European Ports*, Bruges. College of Europe.

† Report of the Consultation Organization for Seaport Development in South-West Netherlands, 1968.

31

The management of the port is headed by the Managing Director (Dr. Postuma), appointed by the City Council, and he controls a separate municipal undertaking. The City Committee, under which the Managing Director operates, consists of an Alderman, six members of the Corporation, and four nominated members from citizens of Rotterdam. From 1956 to 1971 the Alderman responsible for port matters was the Burgomaster.

The State bears the costs of maintenance of the Nieuw Waterweg. The cost of improvements is shared between the State and Municipality, the latter bearing one-third.

Development of the port land area is mainly in the hands of private enterprise. Although the City operates some wharves and transit sheds, most of the port land area, as well as quays, has been leased to private enterprise. The further development of the quays and land areas is therefore carried out by lessees and, apart from management of shipping, maintenance, and new port extensions, the port management's principal interest is that of landlord of an industrial port estate.

The Dutch Government has encouraged the establishment of an oil refinery at Amsterdam (Mobil), served from Rotterdam, in order to produce the industrial prosperity and 'spin-off' which Rotterdam has enjoyed. Growth and prosperity in the Netherlands has resulted in hourly wages in industry moving ahead from a position 11 per cent below Britain in 1957 to a level 10 per cent higher in 1965.* No doubt this is in large measure due to the annual seaport/ industrial growth rate of 9 per cent referred to in Chapter I. It is also partly due to labour shortages which have arisen.

Experience in Rotterdam shows that employment in port-related industrial development is matched by an equal employment proportion in the service industries. By 1990, 160,000 workers are estimated to be required in the port/ industrial area. Average employment density in the petroleum industry is 10 per hectare (2·5 acres) and only 1–2 per hectare in port storage areas, owing to high mechanization.

ANTWERP

Like Rotterdam, Antwerp is of ancient foundation and is also owned by the Municipality. After the Battle of Valmy (1792) the French Revolutionaries sought to expand their influence over neighbouring countries. The National Convention declared that the Scheldte was open to commerce, no doubt in the hope that Antwerp might rival, if not oust London as the centre of world trade.† Having conquered the Austrian Netherlands the five Directors turned their

* Report of the Consultation Organization for Seaport Development in South-West Netherlands, 1968.

† FULLER, J. F. C. (1970), *The Decisive Battles of the Western World, 1792–1944*, p. 59. London: Paladin.

attention to the conquest of Britain, assembling ships and flat-bottomed boats. It was in this period of trade expansion and threatened invasion that Napoleon Dock was built at Antwerp and from that time the port has grown to occupy a major position in Europe.

The port was saved from much battle damage in the Second World War by the dash of British troops, but subsequently it was heavily damaged by V2 rockets and repairs cost £60 million.

Its position, in relation to the Rhine, is rather less favourable than that of Rotterdam but good water connexions, notably the Albert Canal, exist and more are planned to the Rhine and Maas waterways. It is connected to the sea by the Scheldte estuary. The highest lock lies some 90 kilometres from the sea and the lowest (Zandvliet), 70 kilometres. The lower reaches of the port approaches lie in Dutch territorial waters.

The trade of Antwerp in 1937 was 28·3 million tons. By 1950 it had again reached 21·5 million tons and the first post-war development, built with foreign aid, was a petroleum dock, Marshall-dok. This dock provided berths for the largest bulk oil carriers then in use. Refineries of S.I.B.P. and Esso settled there, immediately followed by the first petrochemical plant (Petrochim) in 1951. Oil and oil products have become the principal trade as a result. Iron ore is also imported in quantity and carried to Liege and Charleroi by barge and to Luxembourg by rail.

In 1956 financial votes (5,000 million B.Fr.) enabled a start to be made on a 10-year port extension scheme which has completely altered the shape and potential of the port (*Fig.* 10). The new facilities enable ships of considerably increased size to reach the new berths. Previously, the limit was 35,000 dwt. or 35 ft. draught. The Scheldte has been dredged to provide for 42 ft. draught (70,000 dwt.). In dock, the post-1956 docks have a depth ranging from 50–55 ft.; parts of the earlier docks have also been increased in depth up to 55 ft., with access along the new Kanaldok from Zandvliet lock farther downstream, having a depth of 57·4 ft. Further works are planned to the Scheldte to take advantage of the lock and dock size.

The major new work, Kanaldok, which was opened in 1967, consists of a long canal-like dock flanked by large industrial areas. The dock, provided by the Port Authority, will have no quays or jetties until these are provided by developing industries, but any structures provided by private enterprise will revert to the port at the end of the leases granted. The shape of the water area provides a large potential frontage for port-related industry and water frontage is increased by a small number of inset docks. Because Kanaldok was planned to link up with existing docks the industrial area between Kanaldok and the River Scheldte is quite shallow. The lock (Zandvliet) measures 500 metres by 57 metres and is 18·48 metres deep and 100,000-dwt. ships can be handled once channel improvements are completed. In 1967 139 vessels of 50,000 dwt. or more called at the port.

Table VIII.—ANTWERP. INDUSTRIES IN THE PORT AREA SINCE 1951
(Position at 1 January, 1969)

Industry	Annual Production	Employees	Acres	Investment Equivalent	Per Acre	Future Expansion Area	Future Expansion Investment
Oil refining	24,700,000	2,455	1,200	£122,000,000	102,000	67	£6,800,000
Petrochemical	1,061,000	2,388	468	£104,000,000	221,000	960 * (reserve)	
Basic chemical	2,250,000	2,205	1,847	£89,000,000	48,000	622	£20,500,000
Motors (units)	420,000	13,000	580	£61,000,000	105,000		
Ship repair		4,500	170	£15,000,000	88,000		
Port electricity			22	£23,000,000	88,000	317	£120,000,000
	28,000,000	24,500	4,300	£414,000,000	91,000	1,866	£147,300,000

Table IX.—ANTWERP. GENERAL STATISTICS, 1958/68

	1958	1968
Surface of port area	13,200 acres	26,260 acres
Water surface of docks	1,470 acres	3,580 acres
Length of quays	35 miles	61 miles
Covered storage	1·6 million sq. yds.	2·5 million sq. yds.
Tank storage	1,253 million cu. ft.	2,556 million cu. ft.
Industrial sites	320 acres	5,800 acres
Maritime cargo turnover	35·2 million metric tons	72·4 million metric tons

(Source: Antwerp Port Authority.)

The attraction of industry by these developments has produced imposing statistics. Between 1950 and 1968 the port area increased from 12,050 acres to 26,260 acres. The proportion let to industry has increased even more dramatically. In 1958 industrial sites totalled 320 acres. In 1967, the year Kanaldok opened, 5,000 acres were used by industry. In 1968 the area reached 5,800 acres (*Tables VIII, IX*). By May, 1969, the Port Authority had 17 new industrial applicants which it was unable to accommodate in the existing docks. A highly selective approach to site allocation for industry prevailed throughout this growth. The industrial growth was accompanied by a large increase in traffic. Since 1950 trade has grown by more than 50 million tons to a 1968 total of 72,213,000 tons (imports 48,638,000 tons; exports 23,575,000 tons). Bulk cargo accounted for 50,251,000 tons.

Looking head, the Port Authority plans new developments in the fairly short term on the west bank of the Scheldte, where a net area of 10,000 acres (17,125 acres gross) is available. Three petrochemical companies started production on this site in 1971.

The port has experienced difficulty owing to the large increases in size of bulk oil carriers. At the present time, 250,000-dwt. vessels, with crude oil for Antwerp, dock at Rotterdam, whence the oil is pumped overland for a distance of 40 miles. The new dock facilities on the left bank of the Scheldte are planned with, ultimately, a new connecting channel to a lower point on the estuary in order that larger vessels can be admitted once technical problems are overcome. The new channel would need to pass through Dutch territory and negotiations are proceeding between governments. At the end of 1970 Antwerp was seeking tenders for a new lock on the left bank, 1,170 ft. long by 162 ft. wide and catering for an average draught of 57 ft. Construction started in the summer of 1971 and the new lock will be one of the four largest in the world. Agreement in principle has been reached between the Belgian and Dutch Ministers of Public Works on the construction of a further, even larger, lock at Balhoek for vessels up to 150,000 dwt. In addition, offshore island projects are being studied to berth even larger vessels.

Other negotiations concern a more direct canal link to the Rhine from Kanaldok—important since 60,000 barges enter the port each year. Equal attention has been paid, as at Rotterdam, to the improvement of road and rail communications. The latter are of relatively greater importance to Antwerp than to Rotterdam. A considerable amount of heavy industry lies in rail-served areas which are mainly in the French-speaking parts of Belgium. The need for a heavier rail network in the port does create great difficulties in achieving a satisfactory plan. It also adds to the cargo handling problems by increasing the number of alternative land vehicles to which any one cargo might be loaded.

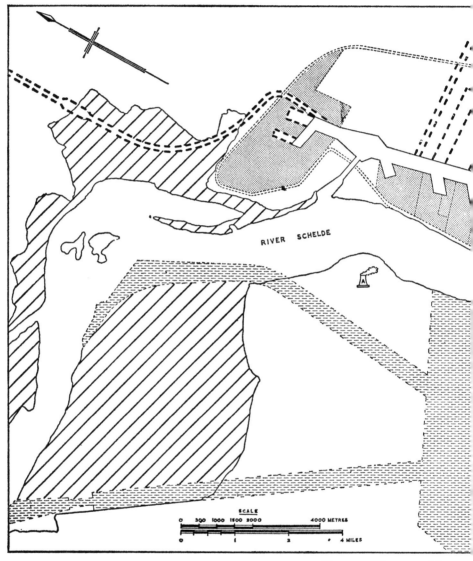

RIVER SCHELDE

SCALE

Fig. 10.—The port of Antwer

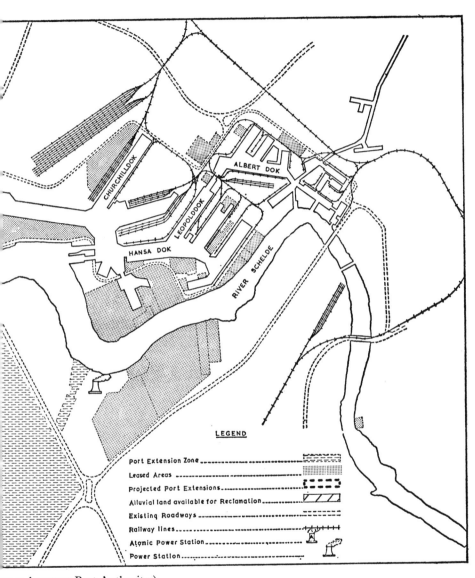

LEGEND

Port Extension Zone
Leased Areas
Projected Port Extensions
Alluvial land available for Reclamation
Existing Roadways
Railway lines
Atomic Power Station
Power Station

rce: Antwerp Port Authority.)

THE FRENCH PORT SYSTEM

The French port system is an evolved system with a considerable amount of central control over investment in the 110 ports which exist today. Because the ports of France are regarded as having an important role to play in the realization of national planning policies, they are organized into a 'total' system within the boundaries of France. This national characteristic of the organization of French ports could have an important influence on the shaping of a future British policy. In any event it is wise to consider the French system as a whole before examining the growth of any individual port.

The system seems to have evolved from the administration which was created immediately after the French Revolution in 1789.

EVOLUTION OF THE SYSTEM

In the nineteenth century the French State provided its ports with major engineering works such as breakwaters, locks, and quays, leaving the exploitation of these works to bodies like the local Chambers of Commerce. These bodies financed the equipment of the civil engineering works with cranes, warehouses, and other facilities and services, deriving income from tolls levied on ships, goods, and passengers.

By the beginning of the twentieth century the State had assumed responsibilities for:—

Construction and maintenance of basic engineering works.
Aids to navigation, except harbour lights.
Allocation of berths through the Harbour Master.
Levying of 'quay dues' for the benefit of the National budget.

Chambers of Commerce or, occasionally, the Municipalities were authorized to collect tolls, but in turn had to contribute towards the cost of basic engineering works to the extent of 50 per cent of the cost, or in smaller ports 75 per cent. The Chambers provided sheds and cranes and were permitted to operate auxiliary services, e.g., fire-fighting, lighting, and salvage. They also sometimes contributed to the cost of dredging.

The port area was regarded as public land earmarked for port use, and development was handled by the State Estate Administration. Government Departments and Local Services were responsible for numerous other matters. Such a situation of divided responsibilities created a need for co-ordination and improvement. The first attempt to provide this resulted in an Act dated 12 June, 1920, and an Order in Council of 1921, which was intended to create new independent port authorities. Unfortunately, for the success of the Act, only Le Havre and Bordeaux requested the new status.

Minor improvements and alterations to the system were effected over succeeding years, but it was not until 1965 that a statute was enacted which again attempted to create a logical and acceptable system. The aims of this Act were to provide a framework for adapting port installations and facilities speedily to the rapid evolution in maritime trade practice and to establish heavy industries at the ports. The incentive for the act was the increasing demand for investment everywhere as a result of the success of Rotterdam. Because of the limited amount of capital available for port investment, the State felt it necessary to take steps to channel funds into what were considered to be the most worthwhile developments. In this it had regard to a general industrial and social policy as well as maritime matters. This philosophy seems particularly relevant to the situation in Britain today.

The new system created six independent ports, or 'Ports Autonomes' (Dunkirk, Le Havre, Rouen, Marseilles, Bordeaux, and Nantes/St. Nazaire) which were intended to form an important part of State economic policy (*Fig.* 11). In order to support this policy, the new authorities were vested with wide powers and responsibilities, but in turn were subjected to a considerable degree of supervision by the State.

SMALL PORTS

Although the statute gives powers to the Minister of Equipment and Housing to entrust the new independent ports with the operation of adjoining smaller ports and inland navigation, the majority of French ports lie outside the new 'independent port' system.

In these 'minor ports' the situation is in some respects similar to that applying before 1965. The State continues to carry out construction and maintenance of harbour works such as dredged channels, locks, and quays. The superstructure can be provided either by local bodies, such as a Municipality or a Chamber of Commerce, or by the State. In the case of a local body a contract is drawn up between the State and the developer to cover the concessions enjoyed. The State may also give permission to commercial companies to construct facilities such as cranes.

The administration of minor ports in matters of construction and maintenance is centralized in Paris. In addition, a Port Manager is appointed who must hold the status of Chief Engineer (Bridges and Roads). This manager may be wholly engaged on port management or, in the smallest ports, may also have jurisdiction over bridges and highways in the adjoining Department (or County).

The entry into port management is normally by a well-defined civil service route, beginning with selection from Polytechnic and two years training in the School of Bridges and Roads (École des Ponts et Chaussées). The numbers trained are closely related to the forecasts of manpower planning. The manager exercises authority over the maritime services of his port, which are all staffed by civil servants; and is responsible for general action on Ministry Services, including roads and railways, and co-ordination of other administrations extending into the port, such as land, police, Municipality, Department, and the Chamber of Commerce.

Centralization of the State administration is limited by the establishment of two committees set up by a decision of the Prefect of the Department in all

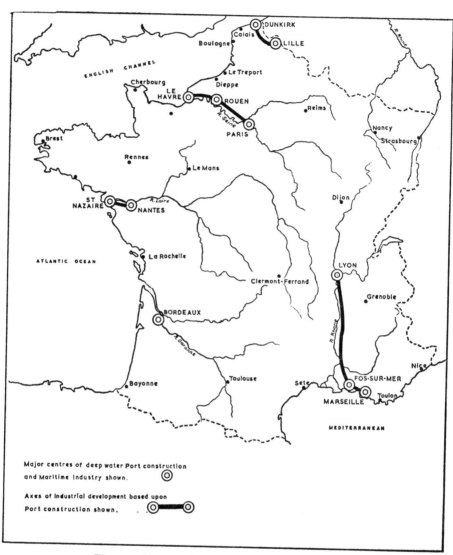

Fig. 11.—France, showing industrial port strategy.

but the smallest ports. The first, or Consultative Committee, is composed of five members nominated by the Chamber of Commerce, two by local authorities (one from the town, one from the Department) and two by chief port users. This committee is consulted on exploitation, maintenance, and improvement. It gives financial advice and discusses new projects.

The second committee is the Permanent Committee of Enquiry, composed of the nine members of the Consultative Committee with a further four representatives of the chief port users. Its function is to advise on works, port dues, and tariffs. In addition, a separate structure is based on a National Committee and consists of a local Nautical Committee which includes the Chief of the County Marine Service and four members from main port users, appointed by the Prefect of the Department. The national and local committees are *ad hoc* committees; only the chairmen are permanent, and other members are appointed because of their qualifications in relation to specific matters. These committees are consulted on maritime works, such as lights and beacons, and on important infrastructure works.

Exploitation is decentralized in that the State grants concessions covering the construction and exploitation of superstructures, e.g., sheds, wharves, and cranes. These grants are effected by ministerial decision; under law in the case of smaller works, or by special decree for major proposals. All important decrees are controlled by the State Council.

There is a standard contract for grants of concessions for terms up to 50 years. The function and application of grants is similar to the leasehold system used in British ports, with similar controls. The terms of grants control the nature of structures to be provided; their use, maintenance, and alteration; and also provide for reversion of the structures to the State at the end of contract. 'Public' concessions are also created in these ports, for which equipment is provided by the Chambers, but which, theoretically, belongs to the State. Provision is made for the Chamber to receive revenues based on its investment. In the case of a private concession the equipment provided does not revert to the State, but the owner must make it available for use when required.

The finance of minor ports is, in theory, provided by the State for infrastructure and by the Chamber of Commerce for superstructure, but in practice the Chamber contributes additional funds in every case. There is no fixed rule and the grants applicable in autonomous ports do not apply. The State may pay up to 50 per cent of the cost of new infrastructure and usually pays one-third. The Chamber provides the remainder, generally borrowing from public sources. The Local Authority may also be persuaded to assist financially.

In superstructure development the Chamber usually obtains funds for minor works from local sources, having recourse to public and other funds for major expenditures.

Once development is carried out, the State maintains the infrastructure, with Chambers sometimes contributing towards the cost of maintaining shipping access as well as paying for maintenance of the superstructure. Port employees who are civil servants are paid by the State, whilst others (auxiliaries) are paid by the Chambers or private employers.

REVENUE

Before 1967 there were many dues fixed by the State which were standard throughout the French ports and were credited to the State. Amongst these were quay dues paid by ships. Other dues were received by Chambers of Commerce and Local Authorities, sometimes consisting of a fixed rate for a specific investment. Revenue from land was a State receipt.

Since an Act of 28 December, 1967, a system has operated under which a new series of dues is levied on ships, goods, and passengers.

Ships' dues are based on net registered tonnages and vary according to class of vessel, destination, and whether vessels are dealing with whole or part cargo. These dues are paid by the ship. Dues on goods are based principally on weight and type and are not strictly *ad valorem*. High-value goods are charged an increased due, but this is not calculated on a percentage basis. Dues on goods are paid by owners or agents for cargo. A national standard due is payable on each passenger, based on the distance of the ship's journey.

All dues are collected by Customs and credited either to the Port Autonome or, in smaller ports, to the owners of concessions, such as the Chamber of Commerce.

Changes in port charges are initiated either by the Port Autonome or, in the case of minor ports, by the Prefect, and are subject to control by the Minister of Finance and the Minister of Equipment and Housing. Sometimes control is delegated by the latter to Local Authorities. By regulation, all proposed increases must be notified to users and a local inquiry may be held before final approval by the Minister.

CENTRAL PLANNING, MAJOR PORTS, AND MARITIME INDUSTRIAL DEVELOPMENT

The controversy over recent proposals to nationalize British ports gives a special interest to the centralized organization of port control in France. Most major British Port Authorities opposed nationalization (or rationalization!) and seemed to prefer a situation which enables a Port Authority to persuade a Ministry of the logic of its own proposals without reference to a national ports plan. It is difficult to escape the conclusion that the underlying reason was the desire of an authority to secure a larger share of national investment than it might otherwise be given. The French reorganization of 1965 had the specific aim of avoiding the dissipation of investment which such a system threatens. Whilst all developments in Britain over £1,000,000 require ministerial approval and National Ports Council vetting, the latter body has a purely advisory function and a political decision can easily be inserted at a later stage. No major refusals seem to have been publicized apart from that of Portbury (Bristol), and even this scheme was recommended by the Council. In addition, many of the smaller 'major port' authorities do not have in their employ all of the wide range of expertise required in modern port development. In these circumstances the value of the case for development that is made depends on the calibre and experience, real or claimed, of the outside advisers retained.

French ports are overseen by the Minister of Equipment and Housing, who has a research department constantly looking at the whole port scene. It seems, from the author's discussions at the Ministry of Equipment and Housing, that in France powers and functions relating to ports, which in Britain have been scattered among several Government departments, are concentrated in one Ministry. The recent creation of a Department of the Environment might be instrumental in achieving better co-ordination of port affairs in Britain, if lessons can be usefully applied from French practice.

The basic concept of economic planning under the National Planning Commissariat is the controlling feature of the French system of port organization. In this framework, modern port investment is seen as an important factor in inducing industrial growth, particularly in modern growth industries, such as oil and petrochemicals.

The Commissariat works on a five-year plan and allocates finance to the Minister for port investment for the period. Each minor port manager or independent port authority makes proposals in accordance with the port and harbour development plan. The Ministry defines the yearly amount available for investment and, on the basis of a central examination of proposals, allocates funds to ports for a series of projects. In addition to this central financial control, there is also positive central planning. On the results of research, the Ministry will point out to ports the fields which deserve investigation and development. The funds for the five-year period commencing 1966/67 amounted to 2,300 million F for public investment and 80–100 million F per annum for maintenance, including dredging, or almost five times the Belgian grant for the ten-year development programme at Antwerp.

The examination of proposals for major works will always take into account the following factors:—

1. National benefit, including growth injection in problem areas.
2. National loss, e.g., destruction of amenities.
3. Social and local economic benefits.

In short, there is a national approach to port investment with positive planning and positive financial control.

The investment policy in ports is guided by a series of hypotheses and principles:—

1. French ports do not generally have the large industrial and population concentrations found behind those in Germany and elsewhere.
2. Before 1965 the large number of competing ports meant dissipation of investment in a number of unrelated areas without outstanding growth in any single area.

43

3. Membership of the Common Market has made a wider development of the economy necessary. The new system of association with other Common Market countries and the removal of customs barriers now makes it possible for France to import for other Market members. The impetus to the economy given by European Economic Community membership also makes for an increase in raw material imports. As a Common Market member France has no wish to have its own industry at a cost disadvantage with other Common Market countries.

In view of the necessarily limited total funds and the conditions ruling industrial growth, major investment has been restricted to carefully chosen localities in order to assure success. The rules for choice are similar to those suggested by the National Ports Council for its M.I.D.A.s proposals:—

1. *Physical.*

   a. Capacity for development for accommodating ships up to 260,000 tons at reasonable cost.

   b. Land availability for industrial development or reclamation possibilities at economic cost.

2. *Economic.*

   Nearness to market.

The Ministry is of the opinion that it is better to develop around an existing growth than to start in virgin areas, on the basis that present growth proves an economic attraction and reduces infrastructure expenditure. This thinking has led to the conclusion that areas with the greatest potential for growth lie at three points in France—namely, Dunkirk, Le Havre/Rouen, and Marseilles (*Fig.* 11).

Whilst it may be said that developments like Golfe de Fos, Nantes/St. Nazaire, and Bordeaux do not appear, at first sight, to conform to the criteria, they do form part of a recognizable pattern. The development of the three major sites selected has been visualized in the form of a series of industrial axes, to create a maritime basis for new industrial growth, with inland water routes so far as they can be provided. The developments on the west coast are necessarily smaller and have been decided upon as government action in the nature of economic aid for a 'difficult' area. Each of the axes is radial in direction, leading inland at approximately right angles to the adjacent coast.

It should be pointed out that France has a continental outlook and its port philosophy contains reasoning which links it with the rest of Western Europe. This may apply to Britain in relation to the Midas Bridge and Common Market affiliations to a greater or lesser degree. What is relevant is that France is able to afford three major M.I.D.A. projects and even one of the small ones—Bordeaux—is two-and-a-half-times the size of the N.P.C. minimum.

Major Industrial Axes

The reasoning behind the selection of the three principal areas may be summarized:—

Le Havre/Rouen. This development will form the deep sea part of the Le Havre, Rouen, Paris axis since Le Havre is regarded as the sea approach to the Paris Region, with which it is connected by the River Seine. Rouen, approximately midway between Le Havre and Paris, lies 120 kilometres inland and can accept ships up to 20,000 dwt. fully laden and up to 30,000 dwt. on spring tides. Proposed dredging work in the Seine will enable the port to take vessels around 60,000 dwt. (*International Freighting* 16 May, 1973). Such a ship capacity gives a good indication of the navigability of the River Seine and of the maritime development possible along its banks. Le Havre, at the estuary of the Seine Valley, has excellent shipping access, plentiful land and labour, with the Paris market region behind. Additional land suitable for maritime industry exists in quantity up to Rouen and beyond (*Fig.* 12). The existing infrastructure of road, rail, canal, public services, and pipelines justifies further the economic selection of the area. Finally, the Seine Valley can provide good conditions of work and amenity along an axis representing a two-hour rail journey, equal in time to the Newport–London rail service.

Marseilles/Golfe de Fos/Lyons. The South of France is a popular holiday and amenity area but the French Government is concerned about the relative lack of industry there. In this sense the Rhône Valley is underprovided and there is a resulting social problem. An axis for development—Marseilles/Golfe de Fos/ Lyons—has, therefore, been selected. Marseilles/Golfe de Fos is the key to the project and it is hoped that new port construction, with associated industry, will trigger off the growth needed for improving the economic situation of the hinterland. The low employment density of prime industries should be in contrast to the employment created by secondary industries following in their train. As an example, the car industry should be attracted by a concentration of steel, rubber, plastics, aluminium, and other prime producers. Time alone will prove the basic reasoning, but the developments which have been forecast are already taking place.

It was considered that not enough new industry, in employment terms, could be associated with the old port and so Golfe de Fos was selected for the principal new development involving port construction. Fos is considered to be a prime site, with good sea access and ample industrial land. The very small tidal ranges in the neighbourhood make locks unnecessary. The new industrial area is located in what was near desert land and, therefore, acquisition costs were low. A refinery (Esso) has been completed and there is a 'continental' scale pipeline, 490 miles in length, to Karlsruhe. A new steelworks is under construction and will be completed shortly. The absence of a tidal problem has made it possible to dredge three separate channels and harbours, one for each of the main categories of port trade, as well as to provide jetties for crude oil tankers (*see Fig.* 35). The trade of Marseilles in 1964 was 47 million tons, of which 36 million tons was oil and oil products. By 1968 trade had increased to 56 million tons, although Fos had not then begun to make its impact.

45

Dunkirk/Lille. First of the new style ports, with a 1962 steelworks, Dunkirk and the adjoining area also meet the physical criteria. Dunkirk is the major port for the old industrial hinterland of North-East France to which it is linked by waterway. This hinterland, once based on a coal economy, has been suffering the same sort of decline as development areas of Britain, with old industries and falling employment in mining.

The Dunkirk/Lille axis has, therefore, been conceived to give a maritime impetus to new growth. The prospect of growth is based on prime industry, using imported raw materials, with steelworks and aluminium reduction, in addition to oil-based industry. A lock of 125,000 dwt. capacity was completed by 1971, whilst the new port area will eventually have access for vessels of 200–300,000 dwt. Other new industry (e.g., Renault) will be based along the canal, which will extend maritime industrial growth towards the hinterland.

Whilst it would seem that France has moved nearer to a national ports policy than any other major country, the Minister of Equipment and Housing considers that at the French level of choice, the tools to quantify results have not yet been developed fully. It is considered, however, that greater dangers will ensue from delay in physical development than from errors of judgement arising from unknown factors.

At the same time, it should be emphasized that the dangers of overcentralization are realized. For this reason local enterprise in seeking development is encouraged and the Port Autonome is seen as a good system for securing local involvement. Private industry is also encouraged to invest in ports and maritime industrial areas, with differential grants to persuade industry against over-development on the best sites. Private quays are leased to industry, with public quays provided for other cargo. As an example of the level of land allocation, the following figures indicate the scale of present planning provisions:—

Dunkirk—5,000 HA (12,500 acres)
Marseilles/Fos—(1st stage) 7,000 HA (17,500 acres) with reserve of 8,585 HA (21,500 acres)
Le Havre—6,000 HA plus 4,000 HA of reclamation (25,000 acres)
Tancarville (Seine Valley)—1,000 HA (2,500 acres)
(Total area Le Havre/Rouen—18,000 HA or 45,000 acres).
(*See also Table X*).

In spite of the lack of planning 'tools', the record of expansion represented by Le Havre—even now in the early stages of development—provides imposing statistics of the benefits of maritime development. A short account of this port might, therefore, be of interest.

Development of Le Havre. Le Havre (=The Harbour), lying at the mouth of the Seine, was founded in 1517 as a naval base and trading port. Its naval significance has now been lost. It is the second port of France and the leading Atlantic port.

After the Normandy invasion and the breakout from the beachhead, Le Havre, in common with other Channel ports, was defended by the Germans in order to deny its use to the Allies. As a result, the port was almost totally destroyed. Reconstruction began immediately after the war and the port has now embarked upon a programme of expansion (*Fig.* 12). Its situation, like that of Southampton, is on the main Channel route to Belgian, Dutch, and German ports. It is connected by canal (the Tancarville Canal) and the river Seine to Rouen and thereafter to inland parts of France. The Tancarville Canal, which has a direct connexion to the dock system of Le Havre, can accommodate 4,000-ton lighters, 2,000-ton barges, and 4,000-ton ocean-going vessels to Gonfreville. The port is partly tidal and partly enclosed.

Le Havre is administered by an autonomous port authority first created in 1925. The State exercises supervision over administrative and financial matters in the port.

The 1925 system was altered in 1966 under the statute of 1 June, 1965, and the Director of the Port is a civil servant. The majority of the staff, numbering

Table X.—FRENCH PORTS—AREAS OF PORT INDUSTRIAL ZONES

	HA	
Dunkirk		
Petite Synthe/Grand Synthe	264	
Saint Pol sur Mer	20	
Zones Portuaires	2,500	
Bourbourg	'no limit'	
(provisional)	5,000	(12,500 acres)
Le Havre/Rouen/Basse Seine		
Le Havre	10,000	
Basse Seine (Tancarville, Port Jerome, Caudebec, Anneville, Rouen)	8,000	
	18,000	(45,000 acres)
Marseilles/Golfe de Fos		
Zones Portuaires	15,585	(39,000 acres)
Bordeaux		
Bassens	815	
Grattequina	2,000	
Ambes	1,500	
Paullac St. Estephe	270	
Verdon	1,500	
	6,085	(15,200 acres)
Nantes/St. Nazaire		
Chevire	200	
extension	150	
Donges	400	
	750	(1,875 acres)

(*Source: Les Ports maritimes et Fluviaux français* (1970). Paris: Cerex.)

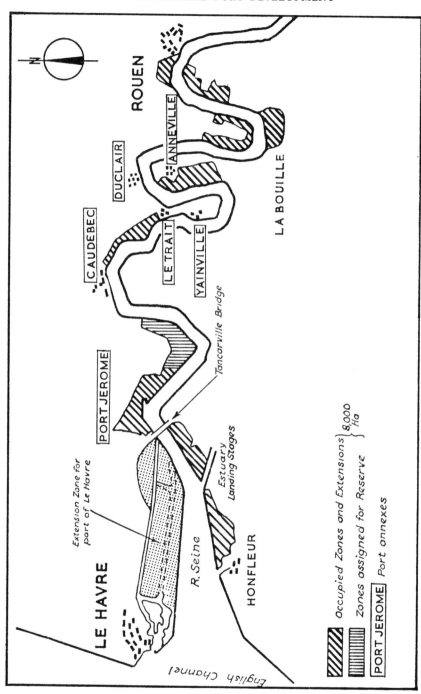

Fig. 12.—Le Havre and maritime industrial zones to Rouen. (*Source: Les Ports maritimes et Fluviaux français*, 1970. Paris: Cerex.)

about 2,000, is employed by the port authority and not by the state. The port authority provides a budget on a five-year basis for approval of infrastructure development and decides superstructure development itself. After approval, the Port Director is able to transfer money from one project to another, giving a certain flexibility in investment. The port authority is not permitted to retain profits, which must be returned to the state. Depreciation, previously charged on an historic cost basis, is being changed to a replacement cost basis. Increases in port charges must be approved by the Government and rent for land leased may be periodically reviewed by reference to the changes in price of the lessee's product. The port derives half its revenue from dues, one-quarter from hire of equipment, and one-quarter from rent. The authority's policy is to keep dues as low as possible in order to encourage shipping to use the port.

The trade of Le Havre in 1938 was 6,688,000 tons, similar in volume to the trade of Swansea in 1968. Despite the wartime destruction, this had grown by 1950 to 9,906,000 tons. A relatively gradual growth then took place, with trade rising from 13 million tons in 1951 to 16·6 million tons in 1960. Since that date, growth has taken place at a much faster rate, reaching 37 million tons in 1967 and about 60 million tons in 1970. This trade was carried in 13,243 vessels.

The principal import is crude oil (27·6 million tons in 1967) and exports of refined oil products (2·2 million tons). Coal, imports and exports, totalled 1·5 million tons. No other traffic exceeded 500,000 tons.

The cause of this growth has been the provision of berths for deep-draughted ships. Despite a 27 ft. tidal range, there is a minimum depth of 37·7 ft. at low water spring tides in the outer harbour, and part of this harbour has been deepened to allow for draughts up to 59 ft. The major part of the oil port comprises eight berths leased to Compagnie Industrielle Maritime, two of 20,000 tons, three of 45,000 tons, two of 90,000 tons (upgraded from 45,000 tons), and one of 200,000 tons completed in 1966. These berths served five existing refineries, with three more opened in 1969. Oil is carried by pipeline from the berths to the refineries; a pipeline also carries refined products to Paris.

The number of tanker berths in the port has been increased from 13 in 1936 to 20 in 1968. The original port area, 1,116 acres, is now being extended to provide more port facilities and large industrial areas. The proposed expansion —by more than 20,000 acres—is as impressive as that which has taken place at Rotterdam. The port facilities will include a tidal basin increasing the area of the southern tidal dock by 296 acres, with quays and container facilities. At the inner end a lock is under construction to take vessels up to 250,000 dwt. (dimensions 400 m. × 67 m.) at a cost of 200 million F, with room for two more locks alongside. Inside the lock a central maritime canal is planned, driving through the industrial areas, with a link to the Tancarville Canal. When completed, in about 1985, the total port area will be about 10,000 HA (25,000 acres), of which 3–4,000 HA (7,500–10,000 acres) will have been reclaimed from alluvial

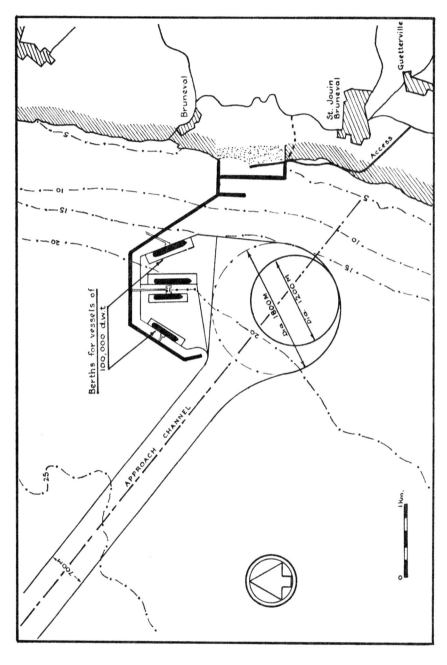

Fig. 13.—Le Havre Antifer terminal. Final stages of coastal port project. (*Source:* Port autonome du Havre.)

flats at the Seine mouth. In fact, the old cliff face (which will create pollution problems for that part of the town lying above it), lies a considerable distance from the present river.

Road and rail improvements have been and are being made and, with the new canal, should provide the efficient transport links to exploit the port's potential. A fifth of the total area of 25,000 acres—approximately 5,000 acres—will be port 'operational' land. The remainder will be let to industry. The port authority will reclaim and charge 9 per cent of costs of reclamation and preparation as rent on 50-year leases.

Land for operations and 'port related' industry is available on an average basis of 60 HA (150 acres) per berth at present, but this will vary in future according to industry and trade. If economy in berth construction is possible in the extensions, it is likely that the ratio of land to water frontage will increase substantially. The present calculations include a number of berths of traditional or purely operational type. The expected employment level is 7–8 per hectare.

Le Havre, although successful in terms of growth, is at a relatively early stage of M.I.D.A. development and is, therefore, of great interest in a British context. The State makes grants (*inter alia*) of 80 per cent for port infrastructure and 60 per cent for superstructure, and these have enabled very ambitious works to be contemplated. The State also provides the port authority with land at a nominal charge and the port is responsible only for the cost of reclamation.

In addition to normal port land-based activities, such as warehousing, handling containers and bulk goods, and operating passenger terminals, there has been considerable growth in port-related industry. As well as oil refining installations, chemical, non-ferrous metal reduction, and car assembly plants have been established in the port. In order to provide energy for the expected growth, further power station capacity is being constructed in stages, 850 MW having been added by 1969.

In the long term the port envisages trade changes based on factors arising from the congestion in the English Channel and the position of the 20-fathom isobath (submarine contour). These forecast changes, affecting access for large ships to those ports approached through the narrow and shallow parts of the Channel, which may also benefit South Wales, have led the port to explore the possibility of an offshore island for 500,000-ton ships off Ouistreham or a tidal harbour at Antifer (*Fig.* 13). The berths provided would be connected by pipe-line to buffer storage installations and thence to French and Low Country industry. The coastal project at Antifer has now been selected and design studies are proceeding.

DEVELOPMENTS IN EUROPE AND LESSONS FOR BRITAIN

Modern European port development presents a vast and complex picture. It has been brought about because Western Europe, like Britain, needs to import most of its raw materials. Like Britain, it is also an advanced industrial society and the growth in demand fostered by a high standard of living has received further impetus from the creation of the European Economic Community.

The reasons why European seaport growth has taken its present form have already been discussed in Chapter I and the type of port which has evolved is fundamentally different from that of the past. Whilst the early changes took place without preceding experience to guide port developers, the stimuli and processes have become much better understood and there has been a steady improvement in the standard of European developments providing lessons and examples for new projects elsewhere. Almost every aspect of development will illustrate principles, either by example or default, which should be adopted, and this is the great merit of studying existing installations. The worldwide interest shown in Rotterdam, Antwerp, Le Havre, and others, indicates the extent to which such industrial ports are regarded as demonstrating principles for new projects.

Some of these principles are identified below:—

1. Apart from demonstrating the likely economic benefits of maritime development, the principal fact demonstrated in Europe is that of scale. The scope for M.I.D.A.s development in Britain has been a subject of much consideration and a little study, but the still prevalent tendency to suggest that only one area is needed should be judged in relation to *Table XI*.

Table XI.—Areas of Major European Industrial Ports

European M.I.D.A.s Projects	Existing Areas (acres)	Projected Growth (where known) (acres)
Rotterdam	25,000	100,000 (gross)
Antwerp	26,000	17,125 (gross)
Dunkirk	12,500*	10,100 (net)
Le Havre/Rouen	45,000	
Marseilles	39,000	
Bordeaux	15,200	
Hamburg	31,000*	
	193,700	127,225

* Report of the Consultation Organization for Seaport Development in South-West Netherlands.

The gross area for present designated sites, 193,700 acres, does not include those of Genoa, Taranto, Leghorn, Bremen, and other important ports. With a Western European population of approximately 250 million people, even these incomplete figures represent an average provision of 40,000 acres for each 50 million population. If the other port areas and future projections are included, it is possible that the total will be multiplied threefold: yet the population of Britain exceeds 50 million persons today and would seem to justify maritime industrial areas in excess of 40,000 acres and perhaps 120,000 acres by A.D. 2000.

For this reason, current comment implying that only one maritime industrial area is needed is difficult to comprehend.*

France has deemed it essential to create three major axes of port-stimulated industry; the Netherlands has the major complex at Rotterdam and is trying to stimulate more growth at Amsterdam; Belgium has a major centre of growth at Antwerp with further areas at Zeebrugge/Bruges and at Ghent. Germany and Italy each have three important industrial port centres.

Fig. 14 shows three possible belts of industrial growth in Britain which would be stimulated by maritime industrial development on the Western coast, particularly in the Severn estuary. One additional advantage Britain would possess from the creation of these M.I.D.A.s Bridges arises from the flexibility given by the existence of port facilities at each end of each Bridge. The continental ports serve interior industrial areas, the products of which must again be returned to the coast for export outside the European Economic Community. The size of the Western European land mass implies greater land transport costs for industrial manufacturers as a result.

2. Important general lessons can be learnt from a study of French port policy. Practice relating to minor ports is probably irrelevant in the British situation but the philosophy and guiding principles for major port development seem to be based on the most carefully thought out and logical, in a national sense, of all European practice.

Undoubtedly, seaport development in the Netherlands would, under national guidance, have taken the same general course as that being followed, but this would have ensued from the economic advantages of location at one of the mouths of the Rhine. There would probably have been detailed differences of layout. The situation in Britain is not quite so clear-cut as in the Netherlands and the claims of individual port authorities require impartial assessment. Control of a much more positive kind than that exercised with the assistance of a purely advisory and representative National Ports Council is necessary to avoid draining resources and to channel investment into the best sites. Because of the length of coastline, and the consequent large number of sites where port facilities can be physically located, the need is even greater than in France.

3. France has taken the course of applying a unified National policy. Whilst other European countries may not have applied a central control, almost all developments have, at the very least, a unified estuarial control. In the same way, it would seem important to regard estuaries, like the Clyde and the Severn, as a whole. This is of great importance for master planning. The Rochdale Committee reported (para. 112) 'a single estuarial authority is more likely to produce a master plan for the future than a number of independent and

* BLACK, J. N., 'Potential Aspects of Development—Seaport', Foulness Conference, 1970, p. 4. Thames Estuary Development Co.

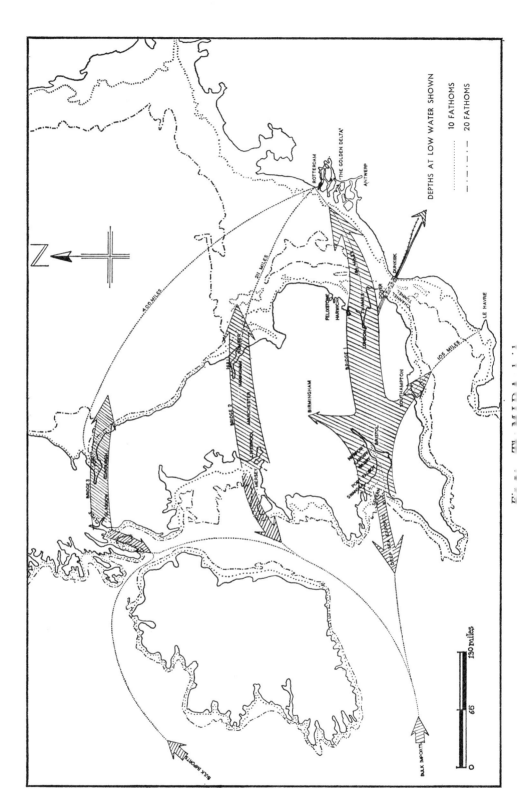

N

DEPTHS AT LOW WATER SHOWN
.... 10 FATHOMS
—··—··— 20 FATHOMS

ROTTERDAM
'THE GOLDEN DELTA'
ANTWERP

211 MILES

400 MILES

FELIXSTOWE
HARWICK
DUNKIRK
DOVER
CHANNEL TUNNEL
105 MILES
LE HAVRE

BRIDGE 3
EDINBURGH
GLASGOW
BRIDGE 2
HUMBER
HULL
HUMBER
LEEDS
MANCHESTER
MERSEY
BIRMINGHAM
BRIDGE 1
BRISTOL
SOUTHAMPTON
PORTSMOUTH
SEVERN

BULK IMPORTS

BULK IMPORTS

0   65   190 miles

competing undertakings'.* Other projects will also be more easily carried out by a unified authority. The construction and operation of an expensive tidal model, necessary for research on alternative port developments, is one example.

4. Future large-scale industrial growth depends upon the establishment of maritime industry from which secondary industry, both port-related and general, will arise. The agglomeration effect, whereby the products of one industry become the raw materials of another, plays a particularly important part in this growth. It also seems that maritime industrial employment will be matched by an equal number in service employment. Maritime industry is, in the main, capital intensive and requires replacement plant at relatively short intervals. Production of this plant causes growth in engineering industry. The largest growth industry has been oil refining and its associated industries, from which a wide range of end uses can follow, as shown by *Table XII*.

Some European ports underestimated the extent of growth in secondary industry. Because of this, Rotterdam, for example, is now paying especial attention to locations for secondary industry in its expansion programme, including some sites with port facilities. In general, however, secondary industry has a much less critical need for port locations.

5. The provision of port facilities for the new ranges of bulk carriers has in all cases been the first step in attracting growth. Industry requiring these facilities for new plants is always looking for suitable locations. Today, decisions to site new industrial plants are often announced on the heels of proposals to build bulk carrier facilities.

It is desirable that a new port should cater for all classes of vessel. One of the disadvantages of recent development in Britain is the isolated nature of many new port facilities or the restricted nature of the design. A comprehensive approach is needed so that agglomeration effects can be port served without the need for re-appraisal of schemes or *ad hoc* solutions.

The way in which port facilities are provided must be controlled by the need for economy, particularly in lock construction. The number of potential ship calls is reduced in direct ratio to the increase in size of vessels. The largest class, the tanker, may average 250,000 dwt. or more, but the biggest vessels bring problems, including the physical one of handling $\frac{1}{2}$–1 million tons in one cargo. It may be possible to provide unloading facilities at lower cost for these very large vessels by utilizing offshore buoy moorings or jetties. Since oil can be carried by pipeline for considerable distances, the mooring can be sited some distance from the maritime industrial area in order to obtain the best anchorage and the deepest water. It is important to assess the relative costs and advantages of lock or mooring. In particular, the possibility of native oil reserves, as in the

* *Report of the Committee of Inquiry into the Major Ports of Great Britain*, Cmd. 1824 (1962). London: H.M.S.O.

North or Celtic seas, can affect the decision. North Sea oil is light oil, more suitable for gas, petrol, and kerosene production, and this implies continued importation of heavier oils for products such as lubricants. If North Sea reserves can supply the capacity of East Coast refineries, a strategy is suggested

Table XII.—Some Products derived from Oil

Primary Derivatives	Typical End Uses
Carbon black	Tyres, plastics
Synthesis gas	Explosives, fertilizers, wood adhesives, animal feeds, nitrogen fertilizers, paint resins, anti-freeze, synthetic fibres (polyesters)
Methane	Shower curtains, toys, pipes, adhesives, plastics, synthetic rubber, solvents, refrigerants, fire extinguishers, pharmaceuticals, rayon, fumigants
Ethane	Toiletries, acetic acid, anti-freeze, detergents, paints, plastics, packaging, housewares, toys, tubing, polyvinyl chloride (*see* 'Methane' above), foam insulation, packaging
Propane	Gasketings, seals, solvents, epoxy resins, detergents, insulation, paints, plastics, synthetic rubber, synthetic fibre (acrylics), housewares, auto interiors
Butane	Nylon, plastics, synthetic rubber, lacquer solvents, tyres, windows, oil additives, adhesives
Benzene	Resins, pharmaceuticals, nylon, detergents, boats, auto parts, dyestuffs, synthetic rubber, insecticides
Toluene	Nylon, explosives, paint solvents
Xylenes	Paint solvents, paint resins, reinforced plastics, phthalic anhydride, fibres (polyesters)
Naphthalene	Dyestuffs, insecticides

(*Source*: Tugendhat, C. (1968), *Oil: The Biggest Business.* London: Eyre & Spottiswoode.)

for deep sea importation to be routed to West Coast refineries. Refineries using supplies from sea wells which cannot be piped only need ship facilities for vessels up to 50,000 dwt. This limit is dictated by the difficulties of handling very large ships at moorings in the open sea. In fact, within reason the size of vessel below this limit could be matched to existing port capacities.

Crude oil is now pumped from Rotterdam to Antwerp, 40 miles distant and to Amsterdam 35 miles away. Rotterdam also imports oil for Duisberg, 125 miles away, and Frankfurt, 280 miles inland. The closer the oil terminal lies to the refinery, the greater is the range of products which can be manufactured. The Duisburg and Frankfurt refineries are principally concerned with high-demand products, such as fuel oils and petrols. Dry bulk cargoes, such as ores, require vessels up to 100–150,000 dwt. at the present time, but there are reports of ore carriers of 200,000 dwt. or more.

6. To achieve the fullest economies in port construction costs the dock/industrial area must be of sufficient depth on berth to permit the establishment

of industry in parallel zones. Pipeline served industry can lie farther back from berths, leaving the intermediate area for industry and trades with greater handling problems. The restriction of depth of industrial areas at Europort for political and other reasons has meant oil refineries being established at the waters' edge, thereby sterilizing considerable lengths of water frontage. A typical square refinery site of 400 acres has sides just over 4,000 ft. long and might be adequately served from one 1,500 ft. berth.

7. Great attention must be paid to social and planning requirements. Choice of location, construction of plant, provision of reserve areas, and landscaping or screening require careful attention to marry the essential demands of economics and environment. Much new (and old) housing development at Rotterdam has proved to be too close to industrial areas and measures to control or prevent pollution have been found to be paramount. In Britain greater control than that possible with existing legislation is necessary, although the improved control proposed by the Ministry of Housing and Local Government (*Guardian*, 17 September, 1970, p. 28) is to be welcomed. Rotterdam's practice is to specify permitted limits of contamination by atmospheric or liquid effluent, only granting sites to industrialists prepared to conform to the rigid provisions. It is claimed that tree belts around industrial zones will help to reduce atmospheric pollution. At Antwerp, a pollution committee of experts examines each proposal in relation to the total effect on the atmosphere or water areas (*see* pp. 20, 21, and 171).

Provision of amenities for workers and for residential areas is of considerable importance. Continental ports have had considerable recent success in this field and reference has been made to Brielsemeer on the fringe of Europort (p. 20). Antwerp is also providing attractive staff buildings and a small adjacent river and lake for water sports. The greater leisure time provided by increasing prosperity requires planned facilities for the benefit of the population.

8. In the light of accepted membership of the E.E.C. the financing of port construction needs consideration, if only to prevent British maritime trade being reduced to the status of feeder services. Compared with the 20 per cent Port Modernization Grant in Britain, which has now disappeared, Antwerp has received 100 per cent of the basic cost of construction of Kanaldok, including locks and dredging, and 60 per cent of the cost of superstructure works, such as quay surfaces and sheds. In France, the respective grants were (1970):—

- a. Maintenance of port approaches, including outer harbours and breakwaters—100 per cent of cost.
- b. Maintenance and operation of access locks—100 per cent of cost.
    Construction and/or renewal of breakwaters, access locks, dredging new docks, dredging and extending or improving access channels—80 per cent of cost.
- c. Construction of other works, such as quay walls, wharves, and graving docks—60 per cent of cost.

The Port of Rotterdam Authority denies that any subsidy is received, but discussions with other competing ports suggest that the State pays two-thirds of the cost of deepening the river and building sea dykes. In addition, the port itself pays no 'rates' and the State Railways pay for half the cost of providing main lines in the port area. The National Ports Council commissioned a study on this aspect of European port development because of the possible future effects on British ports.*

In addition to consideration of port finance in relation to continental practice, it is considered to be desirable that, within Britain, a common financial and accounting practice should apply between port and port. The lack of a common practice is a frequent cause of disagreements between nations in Europe but almost all have a common policy within their boundaries. A similar policy in Britain would have additional value in preventing distortions of the system and in ensuring that comparisons are made on a logical basis (*see* p. 24 et seq.).

9. Land for port development can prove extremely expensive in Britain. In reality a great deal of the increased value attracted to land by a new port proposal is created by the enterprise of the port authority. This is recognized wherever port authorities are granted compulsory powers. Below high-water mark, this recognition is not usually accorded, but in some continental countries land is transferred to ports at nominal charges. The problem is referred to in Chapter IX, but it is desirable that British ports should not be at a disadvantage compared with other European ports.

10. There is a need to reduce the number of authorities to whom applications are necessary for the various consents required for a new industrial development. In Britain it has been said that a particular industry made no less than 36 separate applications concerning various aspects of a new development, before full development was possible. At Rotterdam comparatively few applications are necessary to meet the corresponding requirements of Netherlands law.

11. All the most successful European ports apply a highly selective approach to the allocation of land in port areas. In 1971 the Deputy General Manager of Antwerp (M. Fernand Suykens) said: 'It is our intention only to admit those firms to the port which can guarantee intensive maritime traffic or which are technically tied to such firms'.†

* *A Comparison of the Costs of Continental and United Kingdom Ports* (Touche Ross & Co.), 1970. National Ports Council.

† *International Freighting*, 30 June, 1971, p. 14.

Chapter III

THE SEARCH FOR INDUSTRIAL PORT POTENTIAL

The suitability of any area for major port development must be the subject of examination in depth. Discussions at the College of Europe have considered the needs for cost benefit analysis and assessment of discounted cash flow. The importance of these studies cannot be underestimated, but it is also necessary to have regard to physical characteristics and the economic geography of the area studied.

It is also suggested that assessment should not be limited to the factors implied by physical, economic, or financial criteria. Social costs or savings also have a fundamental influence on decision making and have a special relevance to the declining areas of old-established industrial nations.

In Britain, regions like the Clyde and South Wales cannot be disinterested spectators of the trend towards maritime industrial development. In both cases the new trend is supplanting the type of growth, based on coal, which was the foundation of their earlier prosperity. Fortunately for both, and for the Mersey, they have the deep-water penetrations of the land mass created by major estuaries, and all three face westwards towards the deep-sea trading routes which carry the raw materials from new and distant sources.

For similar areas, the continental experience must prove attractive, since the capital intensive industry of maritime nature produces an agglomeration effect, drawing secondary industry based on prime materials as well as a wide variety of service industries.

The type of investigation which follows has, as its end, the assessment of potential under the following headings:—

1. Shipping access and relationships to major trade routes.
2. Extent of land availability for shore installations and major industry.
3. Markets and communications.
4. Labour availability and needs.
5. Native raw materials and energy sources.
6. Amenity, education, social needs, and infrastructure.
7. Practical demonstrations of potential based on past developments.

The full examination will add to these aspects an economic study of potential for growth in maritime industry, translated into terms of seaborne trade and prime industrial production, the growth factor being extended as a guide to future expansion of facilities. Cost benefit analysis should then show the advantage of planned provision of port and industrial concentrations with discounted cash flow analysis to demonstrate the likely income from an industrial port development in terms of return on capital invested. Political decision will obviously be needed to start a major development and this will be influenced, finally, by further imponderables, such as its effect on national and local economies, its role in solving other problems, e.g., areas of high unemployment, environmental effects, and so on.

Before providing a sample case study as a guideline for other investigations it is thought necessary to make some comments on the British situation in general. In particular the very substantial assets of the development areas and their tradition of heavy industry suggest that the causes of past growth, which are not dissimilar in principle to those of modern industrial ports, give them strong claims to a share in this new industrial pattern of growth.

Governments are notorious for looking no farther than the next election, but failure to carry out necessary development in the right place in the long-range sector of port planning could affect economics for a decade—and prejudice the chances of the same party in a future Parliament. As long ago as 1948 *The Economist* questioned the Development Areas proposals and suggested that forced revival might prove more costly than the development of regions having positive economic attractions.* The attractions of some declining areas for port-related industry would seem to suggest that in these regions development of the economic assets would play a vital part in reducing the cost of forced revival.

SHIPPING PROBLEMS

For bulk vessels the important factor is draft at low tide. If this is adequate, a port can provide facilities in the estuary, such as single buoy moorings or off-shore islands. It can also construct a wet dock facility accessible at high tide. If the latter, then the period of high water must be sufficiently long for the ship to leave its low water position and manoeuvre through the lock. The physical problems of handling a large ship, such as the time and quantity of water needed to level a lock, mean that the shortest distance between low-water anchorage and lock is desirable. The greater this distance, the deeper the lock must be, and, therefore, the higher the cost. A vessel of maximum size for a lock must be in position, ready to enter, at least 15 minutes before high tide. If the low water anchorage is 30 sea miles distant and the vessel's speed is 10 knots, it must be able to leave the anchorage 3 hours 15 minutes before high tide.

The dimensions of typical ships are of interest (*Table XIII*). There will, of course, be minor variations in draft for vessels of similar rating according to design.

The sizes quoted show that the position of the 10-fathom (60-ft.) contour at low tide is of critical importance for ships of 150–200,000 dwt., indicating the limit of safe moorings.

* FREEMAN, T. W. (1967), *Geography and Planning*, p. 144. London: Hutchinson.

The comments of the Managing Director of Scott-Lithgow, Mr. A. Ross Belch (*The Times, Business News,* 21 September, 1970), give an added interest to vessels around this size. In addressing a symposium on ship technology at Newcastle-on-Tyne he offered the opinion that the explosion in ship size had been too rapid. Practice had outstripped the theoretical and experimental investigations necessary to ensure trouble-free operation. Mr. Belchre commended

Table XIII.—DIMENSIONS OF BULK CARRIERS (1971)

Summer Deadweight Tons	Length ft.	in.	Beam ft.	in.	Draught ft.	in.
Oil Tankers						
52,260	750	0	102	9	40	0
70,700	800	0	110	2	43	8
71,270	878	0	112	9	44	11
81,440	852	0	117	0	46	9
117,980	870	0	138	0	50	5
109,500	870	0	138	0	49	0
207,750	1,076	0	155	0	62	4
255,000	1,150	0	170	0	66	0
312,000	1,140	0	178	0	79	0
326,000	1,140	0	—		81	0
500,000					85 to 90	0 0
Ore Carriers						
67,929	778	0	116	0	40	6
89,900	820	3	124	3	44	11
105,779	820	0	134	0	49	0
113,100	849	0	133	10	52	0
125,000	955	0	144	0	50	0
142,000	867	0	145	0	59	0
150,000	1,050	0	150	0	55	0
166,750	965	0	145	0	60	8

a pause for further research, with a consolidation around the 250,000 ton mark. These comments nearly coincide with the implications of a factor mentioned by Mr. R. O. Goss, Senior Economic Advisor, Board of Trade. In introducing a paper* given in Bruges, he drew attention to a graph showing the relationship between size of vessel and cost per ton of carriage. This showed a considerable saving in transport costs per ton, with increasing size, up to 270–300,000 dwt. At this point, the cost per ton showed a considerable increase. The basis of this increase is the need to introduce a second screw for vessels of greater size. Marine engine technology in 1970 faced this barrier, which would mean a considerable increase in construction and running costs once a weight of 300,000 dwt. is passed. No doubt the problem will be surmounted one day (in

* Goss, R. O. (1970), 'The Size of Ships', *Report of the Conference on the Future of European Ports*, Bruges. College of Europe.

the mid-1950s the limit was 120,000 dwt.), but this factor, combined with the advice of Mr. Belch, may lead to construction of a large number of vessels below this limit which will form part of the world's fleet for a considerable time. The restriction may be reinforced by a change in design criteria. The prospect of sea pollution from massive tonnages released by collision is likely to lead to greater subdivision of cargo space within a vessel. This could also affect the economics of ship size.

Of additional importance is the 20-fathom contour. Bulk vessels, of 10 fathoms or so in draught, reduce speed above the 20-fathom limit, usually to below 10 knots (11·5 m.p.h.). One reason for this is a factor sometimes called 'squat'. Moving vessels, with screw and marine propulsion unit at the stern, tend to settle in the water deeper in a proportion related to their speed. In effect, the vessel then draws more water than is suggested by its draft at moorings.

It follows from an examination of ships sizes and distribution that three marine low-water contours are of importance in assessing the shipping potential of an estuary or harbour. The 20-fathom contour indicates the speed restriction limits for the large bulk carriers. The 10-fathom contour indicates the limit of safe mooring for vessels around 200,000 dwt. The 5-fathom contour indicates the approximate limit for vessels up to 30,000 tons. Similar high-water contours indicate channels for such ships in the approaches to wet docks. Where reasonably sheltered conditions can be found, the low-water contours will also indicate the limit of sites for single-buoy moorings and offshore islands, where bulk liquid discharge can take place or transhipment can be carried out to discharge cargo or reduce draught.

THE LAND BRIDGE AND SAILING TIME

In their report on a land bridge for the Clyde and Forth Estuaries,* the Scottish Council draw attention to the position of the 20-fathom contour in the vicinity of the Golden Delta of Europe as well as London. The report suggests that this will lead to future port development along coasts where shipping is not so severely restricted by the position of the 20-fathom contour. This, perhaps, exaggerates the situation, but the existence of strictures on the sea approaches to London and the Delta increases the attraction of the West Coast of Britain for future development.

The phenomenon of North Sea sand waves, sometimes as high as 20 ft., must also be of concern to the leading Western European ports, causing unknown variations in depth which might become critical for outsize vessels. Rotterdam is already considering the dredging of an approach channel 11 miles in length to accommodate ships of 500,000 dwt. (for ships of 250,000 tons the channel is 8 miles long). Of even more concern is the announcement in 1970 that British and Dutch Navy Survey vessels were to carry out a fresh survey of the English

* *Oceanspan*: A Maritime based Development Strategy for a European Scotland (1970). Scottish Council (Development and Industry).

Channel to discover whether there is sufficient deep water for bulk oil carriers of 300,000 dwt. sailing for the Port of London. The need to carry out a new survey in such a well-surveyed channel must surely indicate the future difficulties to be faced as a result of increasing ship size. If no suitable channel had been discovered, the consequence would have been an additional voyage distance around Scotland of 840 miles to London or 720 miles to Rotterdam.

The possibility of a land bridge in the Severn has been discussed elsewhere.* Although the authors do not base any recommendations on it, they consider it worth keeping in mind. Their study was, of course, written before publicity concerning North Sea sand waves, which can only add to the logic behind the land bridge concept. This has been based on considerations of future difficulties, in ports using the English Channel as their main access, in relation to problems of congestion and insurance, as well as depth. The Channel, with a minimum width of 21 miles, is probably the most heavily used sea lane in the world. It is used by ships calling at all the major ports of North-West Europe and those of South-East England, and the main Channel routes are also affected by cross-channel traffic between Britain and Europe.

The Institute of Navigation Annual Report for 1968/69 draws attention to the present inability of deep-draughted ships to manoeuvre in the English Channel in accordance with the Collision Regulations owing to lack of sufficient deep water. Port authorities seek powers to control ships in their approach channels because of this fact in order to impose shore control for safety reasons. The Straits of Dover are also affected by fog. During the 28-year period 1923–1950, observations at Dover showed an annual average of 29·6 days of fog, of which 10·7 days were thick fog.† In contrast the figures for Cardiff are 17·3 and 3·9 days respectively. This is taken at 1,100 yards for fog and 220 yards for thick fog. The introduction of traffic lanes in April, 1967, (Fig. 15), reduced collisions, but with the growth of shipping there is no doubt that further traffic measures will be necessary.

Even periods of greater visibility can create hazards. The collision, on 12 January, 1971, between the *Texaco Caribbean* and the *Paracas* took place at 4 a.m. in misty conditions and visibility was estimated to have been 'no more than a mile' (*Guardian*, 12 January, 1971).

The introduction of inward bound and outward bound traffic lanes was recommended by the Intergovernmental Maritime Consultative Organisation. The scheme, which required inward bound traffic to follow the French coast, with outward bound shipping following the English coast, reduced collisions in the first year but is now being criticized. London-bound ships have to cross the outward bound lane east of the Sandettie Lightship. In addition, the collision rules often mean that a ship has to manoeuvre towards shallower water to

* HALLETT, G., and RANDALL, P. (1970), *Maritime Industry and Port Development in South Wales.* Cardiff: University College.
† *Atlas of Britain and Northern Ireland,* p. 33. Oxford: Clarendon Press.

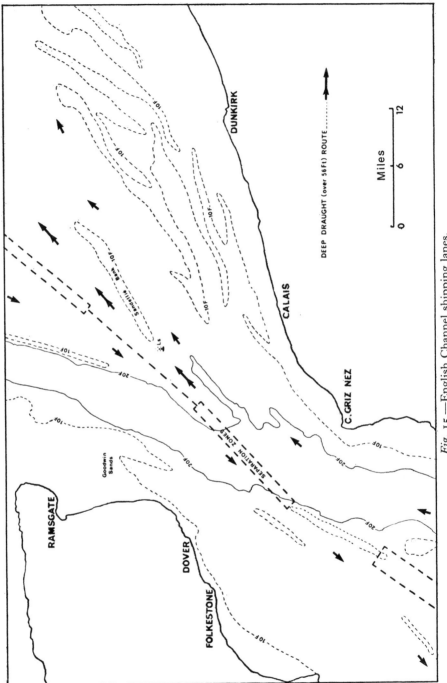

Fig. 15.—English Channel shipping lanes.

avoid cross-channel traffic. With increasing draught, this has raised more problems. Trinity House and the Honourable Company of Master Mariners propose that the routes should be reversed to avoid these difficulties. This will certainly reduce the number of London-bound vessels crossing at Sandettie Lightship, but there would still be danger between vessels outward bound from London and inwards traffic to Europe.

Numbers of other palliatives can be applied, such as shore control and boarding by pilots at greater distances, but it would still seem to leave the long-range problems arising from the tremendous increases in sea trade forecast by the end of the century.

The risks associated with restricted depth, congestion, and collision have their greatest effect on the largest ships. The study by Dr. Hallett and Peter Randall (op. cit., p. 19) puts the insurance rate on large bulk vessels as high as 40–45 per cent of running costs (i.e., including depreciation, wages, stores, lubrication oils, club calls, repairs, and survey). The Earl of Lauderdale, a parliamentary expert on port and shipping matters, put it as high as 50 per cent (*Hansard* (Lords) 4 November, 1969, col. 297) and the Scottish Council (*Oceanspan, Appendix C*, and *Fig.* 16 and *Table XIV*) shows percentages as high as 63 per cent. This figure was revised to 72 per cent for tankers of 500,000 dwt. in a further study which considered changes in the marine insurance situation in 1971 (*Oceanspan II, Appendix 8*, Table I).

These are serious considerations for future port planners.

Table XIV.—MARINE INSURANCE COSTS

Vessel tons dwt.	50,000 £	100,000 £	200,000 £	300,000 £	400,000 £	500,000 £
Marine insurance	55,000	110,000	200,000	310,000	450,000	600,000
Total running costs	200,000	300,000	440,000	580,000	750,000	950,000
Insurance as per-centage of total	27	37	45	53	60	63

(*Source: Oceanspan, Appendix C.*)

For West Coast ports there is already a time/distance advantage for deep sea shipping, the greatest proportion of which is concerned with bulk cargoes. This advantage is greatest on the south-west coast, reducing towards the north. The advantage increases greatly if future Channel shipping has to be re-routed around Scotland.

Over 90 per cent of ocean shipping trading with Britain and Northern Europe crosses a line from Cape Clear to Ushant.* A considerable percentage of this traffic is concerned with bulk raw materials carried in very large ships. Taking Swansea as a comparison, the following table compares time and distance advantage of a west coast port with Southampton, Tilbury, and Rotterdam.

* DREYER, Capt. J. R. F., R.N. (1969), correspondence with Capt. J. White, Dockmaster, Swansea.

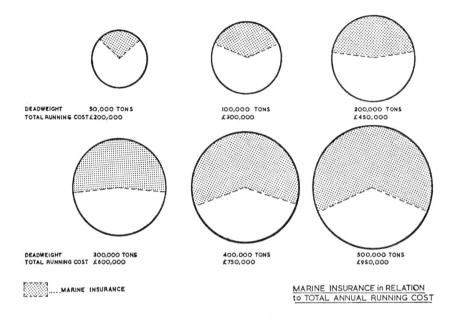

MARINE INSURANCE in RELATION
to TOTAL ANNUAL RUNNING COST

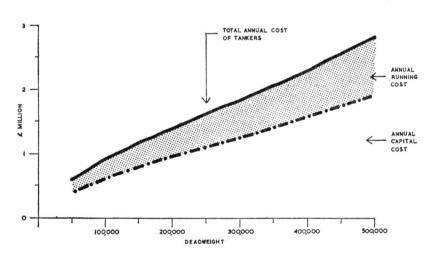

Fig. 16.—Marine insurance in relation to total annual running cost of tankers. (*Source*: Scottish Council (1970), *Oceanspan*.)

Table XV assumes a reduction in speed within the 20-fathom contour from 17 knots to 10 knots. The distance differences are based on the shortest route. Milford Haven shows even greater savings than Swansea, but most other Severn ports differ from these figures by only 2 or 3 hours.

It cannot be seriously suggested that Western British ports will take over the whole of European and east coast trade. The existing channels and ports will

Table XV.—Sailing Times

Port	Additional Distance	Additional Distance inside 20-fathom line	Increased Overall Passage Time
Southampton	45 n. miles	17 n. miles	6 hours
Tilbury	235 n. miles	110 n. miles	37 hours
Rotterdam	265 n. miles	138 n. miles	40 hours

The second column shows the additional distance from the Cape Clear/Ushant line to the port named compared with Swansea.

(*Source*: 'The Advantage of Trading through Swansea',
Talk by Captain J. R. F. Dreyer, R.N.)

continue to attract shipping and whatever spare capacity remains in the English Channel will affect growth. Rotterdam is forecasting a trade growth resulting in a total of 614 million tons by A.D. 1990 and over 800 million tons by A.D. 2000.*

Other Western European ports have forward projections showing considerable increases. The factors discussed will mean that the ports of Western Britain have an opportunity to intercept deep-sea trade and to create a land bridge to Europe. A British land bridge should involve industrial processing en route and this would combine the advantages of Britain for M.I.D.A.s with those for entrepôt trade. It is possible to visualize the development of the major inlets on the West of Britain, linked to those of the East in a complex of manufacture and transport. By geographic coincidence the major western estuaries already lie opposite the major eastern estuaries. The M.I.D.A.s Bridge, depicted in *Fig.* 14, will combine the savings in sea distance as shown below with the industrial tradition and infrastructure of Britain. So far as the Severn and Clyde

From	SEVERN miles	MERSEY miles	CLYDE miles
Cape Town	5,903	6,085	6,181
Panama	4,483	4,568	4,522
Port of Spain	3,700	3,830	3,927
St. Lawrence	2,726	2,811	2,729
Australia	10,879	11,021	11,127
Persian Gulf	6,400	6,510	6,618
Baltic	2,241	2,120	2,050

* F. R. Harris and Associated Industrial Consultants: *The Greater Delta Region, An Evaluation of Development and Administration*, December, 1968. ('The Blue Book'). See also *Plan 2000+: Development of the Northern Delta*, p. 32. Rotterdam City Council.

are concerned, thecoastal areas already have a strong prime industry content which will add to the attractions of these estuaries.

That this is not an idle claim is indicated by the fact that the Port Authority of Le Havre has come to similar conclusions,* and in planning future construction already allows for growth at Le Havre as a result of the trend.

* Discussions of University of Wales Study Group with the Port Direction, 20 July, 1970.

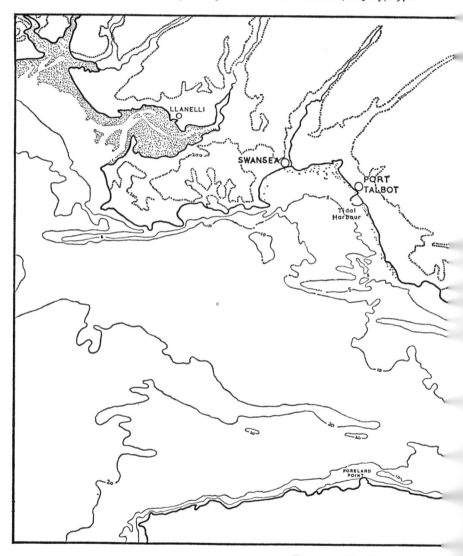

Fig. 17.—The Severn Estuar‑

Conversely East Coast ports lie opposite the coast of North-West Europe. With the great European population and market, and the removal of trade barriers as a result of Common Market membership, these ports will undoubtedly change in nature of trade to give a stronger bias towards inter market cargoes.

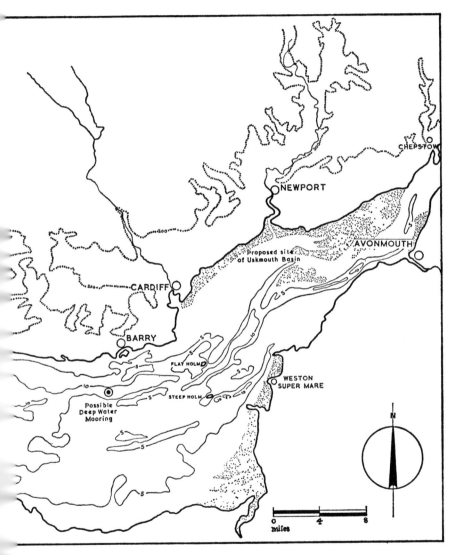

tours and land below 200 feet.

CASE STUDY:
Physical Characteristics and Economic Geography:
The Severn and South Wales

SHIPPING ACCESS

Upstream of Milford Haven the low-water marine contours in the Severn (*see Fig.* 17) show that the 20-fathom contour enters as far as the Gower Peninsula. Because of the nature of the adjacent coastline (Exmoor has cliffs and a rugged interior), the deep-water channel below 10-fathoms, for practical purposes, follows the Welsh coastline. Its deepest penetration lies along the South Wales coast as far as Lavernock Point. Beyond this point, pockets below 10 fathoms exist, separated from the outer channel by shallower water. The 5-fathom contour lies close to both sides of the estuary as far as Cardiff and Weston-super-Mare, with a sandbank off the latter. The channel below 5 fathoms (with a large pocket over 10 fathoms) then follows the centre of the estuary as far as Newport, where it forks. One fork leads to Newport Deeps and the other follows the Somerset coast almost to Avonmouth. One or two 10-fathom pockets lie off the Clevedon Hills (Bristol Deeps).

In the higher reaches of the tidal Severn, the main current follows the southern shore. This characteristic has led to the contrasting coastal conditions on either side. The coastal strip of South-East Wales is mainly alluvial in character and contains substantial areas of flat land. The southern shore, except at river confluences with the Severn, is rocky, with cliff formations at intervals. Cliff formations on the northern shore are not found, except briefly—at Goldcliff—between Penarth Head and Chepstow. There is also the line of the deep-water channel as far as Lavernock Point. This infers that, in geological times, the main flow of the Severn lay north of its present line in the areas where sandbanks occur and has moved southwards because of a meander, leaving alluvial deposits behind. By deduction, it would seem that the greater scope for large-scale port development in this reach lies on the north bank because of the softer bed for dredging channels. F. J. North confirms that irregularities in the marine contours indicate where river valleys lay when the land stood at a higher level.*

Milford Haven in South-West Wales is already the largest oil port in Britain (*see Fig.* 3). This port, which has recently been improved at a cost of £7 million to provide 68–70 ft. of water, is able to accept tankers up to 275,000 dwt. The new facilities, consisting of jetty berths for tankers, have led to the establishment of refineries, at present 3 in number, with Amoco obtaining the necessary consent for a new project on 19 January, 1971. In addition, the B.P. Swansea refinery, as a result of the intense competition in this industry and the post-Suez economics, has been forced to use larger vessels than those capable of entering Swansea Docks. It has constructed a jetty at Angle Bay, with a pipeline connexion to Llandarcy, a distance of about 60 miles.

---

* NORTH, F. G. (1964), *Evolution of the Bristol Channel*, 3rd ed., p. 97. National Museum of Wales.

The increasing difficulties in obtaining planning and other consents for refineries at Milford Haven, coupled with the shortage of suitable land, by no means exclude the possibility of further increases in throughput. Existing refineries have room for further production and also have reserve areas for increasing size, though some of these lie within the National Park. The berths themselves have spare capacity. The Gulf Oil Company's conception of Bantry Bay in Eire as a buffer storage between transfers from 300,000 dwt. vessels to the 100,000 dwt. size, thereby enabling a wider range of ports to be served, could also be applied at Milford. This would be less demanding in land than an extension of refineries there and would create no atmospheric pollution problems. The possibility of pipeline connexions to the large land areas farther east is one way in which Milford Haven can form part of a South Wales industrial port. In 1970 the Conservancy Board were examining ways of increasing capacity, including broad 400,000 dwt. tankers on the present draughts, and a 75-ft. channel costing £40 million to a common user terminal at Chapel Bay, with a capacity of 60 million tons per annum (*Table XVI*).*

Table XVI.—MILFORD HAVEN—STATISTICS

1958   Depth of water up to 60 ft.
1967   Decision to dredge.
        Phase I (£1 million) widening and straightening channel for vessels up to 58 ft. draught.
        Phase II (£6 million) deepening for vessels up to 64 ft. draught.

Current Investigations:
        Broad-beam vessels up to 400,000 dwt.
        Dredging to provide depth of 75 ft.—cost £40 million.

Existing refinery sites	3
Potential refinery sites	2

Trade		
	1960	2·8 million tons
	1962	11·5 million tons
	1964	17·7 million tons
	1966	28·9 million tons
	1968	30·0 million tons
	1970	40·0 million tons

Low-water anchorages also exist at Swansea Bay and Barry Roads. Here lie the deep-draughted vessels awaiting the tide for the existing ports up-channel. The distance of port facilities from these anchorages is of importance in assessing the economics of location, including costs of lock construction and utilization (*see* p. 60).

Ships up to 30,000 dwt. are accommodated at Swansea, Cardiff, and Newport. New Parliamentary powers (British Transport Docks Act, 1969) for Newport,

* WATTS, D. G. (1970), 'Milford Haven and its Oil Industry, 1958–69', *Geography*, vol. iv, pt. 1, January, pp. 64–72.

to improve the entrance channel, have already been obtained. This will enable the existing lock to accept vessels up to 35,000 dwt. Vessels up to 150,000 dwt. can be accepted at Port Talbot Tidal Harbour once further limited dredging has been carried out. The feasibility studies preceding the British Transport Docks Act, 1967, showed that Uskmouth Tidal Basin could be constructed to accept vessels of 100,000 dwt. on 100 per cent of tides and that the approach channel could be economically maintained. This implies that larger vessels could be accepted on a percentage of tides and, if entrance dimensions are adequate, even 200,000 dwt. ships could enter. This sort of proposal has been made at Hamburg,

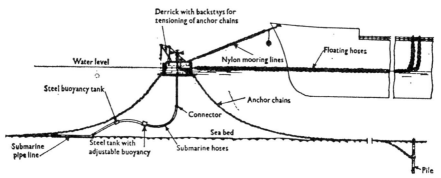

Fig. 18.—Single buoy mooring. (*Source*: J. M. Langeveld, 1969.)

where a lock to serve the port extension area will take ships up to 200,000 dwt. part loaded. The deepest draught planned is 15 metres and tentative dimensions are 480 m. × 57–65 m. wide.*

In addition to the studies for Uskmouth, the Bruce White Study for the port of Cardiff,† suggested that this port could be adapted to take vessels up to 100,000 dwt. inside the existing Queen Alexandra Dock.

Of prime importance for maritime development in the Severn is the recent study of possibilities for offshore moorings in Barry Roads.‡ This has shown up three possible sites for vessels up to 300,000 dwt. and two inshore sites for vessels of 50,000 dwt. Vessels of the latter class could be provided with facilities inside the breakwaters. All these sites are within reasonable pumping distance of the shore. The study has been carried out with knowledge of similar conditions in the Bay of Fundy, Canada, where a single-buoy mooring is being built

* Sobisch, H. (1970), *Report of the Conference on the Future of European Ports*, Bruges. College of Europe.
† Sir Bruce White, Wolfe Barry and Partners (1965), *Report on the Proposed Development of the Port of Cardiff*. Cardiff Corporation.
‡ Radway, E. R. (1970), *Barry Docks Approaches: An Appreciation of Various Schemes for handling 35,000–200,000 dwt. ton Tankers*. British Transport Docks Board (South Wales).

(*Fig.* 18). Linked with the suggestion referred to for broad 400,000 dwt. tankers at Milford, there would appear to be considerable significance in this discovery.

Further studies carried out by the British Transport Docks Board have shown the possibility of anchorages for vessels of 1,000,000 dwt. off South-West Wales.

The mooring sites at Barry are capable of serving any selected M.I.D.A.s in South-East Wales. The distance from the best 200,000 dwt. mooring to land available for buffer storage at Barry is $3\frac{1}{2}$ miles; to Wentloog level, Cardiff, $13\frac{1}{2}$ miles; and $21\frac{1}{2}$ miles to Caldicot level, near Newport.

All these areas are within known economic pumping distance of the offshore mooring. Llandarcy is 60 miles from its jetty at Angle Bay. Antwerp receives crude oil from Rotterdam, 40 miles away, whilst Netherlands policy has sited an oil refinery (Mobil) at Amsterdam, based on crude imports at Rotterdam, 35 miles away. Crude oil is also pumped from Rotterdam to refineries at Duisburg and at Frankfurt, 280 miles away. The latter installations, however, are concerned with high-demand refined products such as petrol and diesel fuel. Continental experience suggests that the amount of industrial spin-off in the way of variety of refined products and petrochemicals reduces in proportion to the distance crude oil has to be pumped. The Antwerp and Amsterdam refineries, based on Rotterdam imports of crude oil, are generally thought to be at the limit of economic pumping distance if a full range of refining and petrochemical activities are to be carried on. Oil companies have represented in the Low Countries that the economic distance is even less—around 30 kilometres (19 miles). The Llandarcy practice does not give a true guide since this was conditioned by the existence of a refinery based on a facility suitable for pre-war crude oil carriers. With refinery capital already committed, the increase in vessel size to reduce shipping costs forced the decision to construct a terminal at Angle Bay.

LAND AVAILABILITY

Land is a prime requirement for port development and increases in importance where there is to be associated maritime industry. One forecast for Rotterdam* shows an additional need for 19,080 hectares (47,700 acres) by the year 1990. Another, by extrapolation, shows a total need for 41,257 hectares by A.D. 2000 (*Table XVII*).†

The fact that suitable land is physically available in South Wales has created favourable comment.‡ South-East Wales has been placed in the first three of potential sites in Britain by a physical study carried out by Sir William Halcrow and Partners.

* *Plan 2000+* : *Development of the Northern Delta* ('The Yellow Book'). Rotterdam City Council.
† Consultation Organization for Seaport Development in South-West Netherlands (1967), *Exploration of Some Aspects of Development Possibilities for Seaports in the Delta Region*.
‡ House of Commons Official Report (*Hansard*, 'Written Answers', vol. 787, No. 151), 17 July, 1969, p. 165.

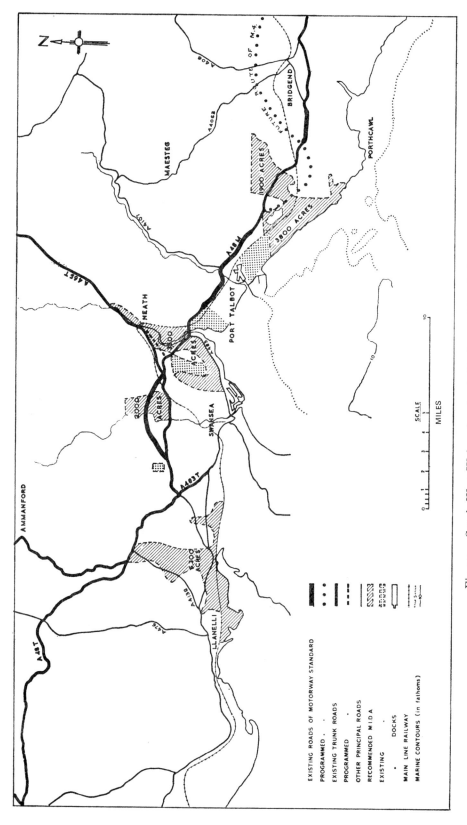

Fig. 19.—South-West Wales. Land suitable for maritime industry.

Table XVII.—Rotterdam—Land Requirements to 2000 A.D.

Area (net) of allocated terrain in port areas January, 1950–65 in HA and extrapolation to year 2000.

	1950	*1955*	*1960*	*1965*	Growth per year (per cent)	*1970*	*1980*	*2000*
Light industry, trade, and shipping	62	89	108	141	6	189	338	1,085
Piece goods	60	66	76	127	6	170	305	978
Bulk goods	23	48	165	268	10	432	1,094	7,524
Basic industries	425	503	997	1,551	9	2,386	5,650	31,670
Total	570	706	1,346	2,087		3,177	7,387	41,257

(*Source*: Mayor of Rotterdam's Port Budget Statement, November, 1966.)

Maritime industry locations require large areas of relatively flat land to accommodate the industrial units which will be attracted. In order to gain the maximum economic advantage from nearness to a port, it is desirable that all the prime industry should be located close to the port facilities. This implies large sites of several thousand acres. The National Ports Council has suggested 5,000 acres as a minimum,* but this is probably too small. Antwerp has a port area of 25,000 acres and Le Havre (excluding the Seine Valley) about 20,000 acres.

The geography and present industrial development of South Wales suggest two areas apart from Milford Haven in which maritime developments are possible—Greater Swansea and Cardiff/Newport. The Milford area has been referred to on p. 70.

Both have existing port facilities and existing heavy industry; both are centres for their respective sub-regions and are separated by the agricultural and amenity belt of the Vale of Glamorgan. Each is capable of separation from other future growth areas by existing countryside such as the Wye Valley and Eastern Monmouthshire, Vale of Glamorgan, and Carmarthen.

South-West Wales (*Fig.* 19)

Greater Swansea runs from Llanelli to Port Talbot. Flat land is still available for development in coastal areas, whilst over 3,000 acres are devoted to maritime industry such as oil refining, petrochemicals, non-ferrous metals, and steel. In the Swansea/Port Talbot area as a whole, a further 6,700 acres of land below the 50-ft. contour can be identified along the coast. This total might be increased by land reclamation adjoining Crymlyn Burrows, at an economic cost, using natural accretion after the construction of half-tide walls.

Studies of a similar project at Spurn Head in the Humber some years ago suggested a cost of approximately £600 per acre. A site of over 1,500 acres at

* National Ports Council (1969), *Port Progress Report*, p. 57.

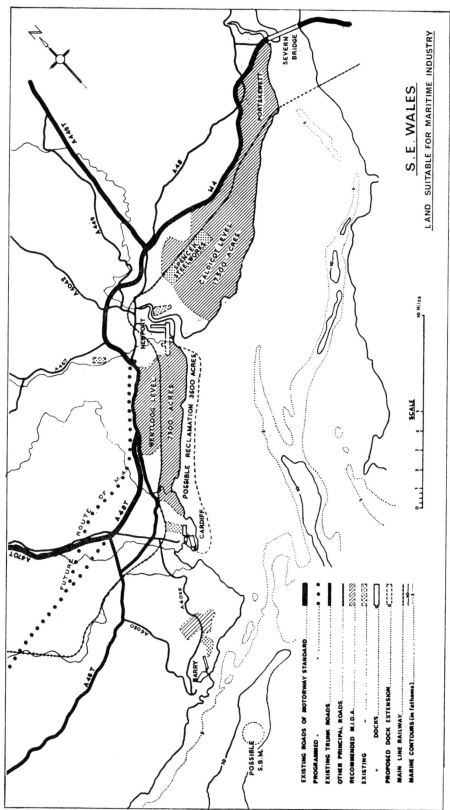

Fig. 20.—South-East Wales. Land suitable for maritime industry.

Penybryn, east of Port Talbot, is also suitable for maritime development connected with the new tidal harbour. Large areas of backing-up land exist in or near Llanelli and the Llwchwr estuary exceeding 5,000 acres. Sites for secondary industry also exist in quantity with about 2,000 acres in or near Swansea alone, including individual sites of up to 300 acres.

South-East Wales (Fig. 20)

The physical land assets of this sub-region run from Barry to Chepstow. The port of Barry covers 755 acres of land and 278 acres of water. To the east of the port lies an area of flat land, 900 acres in extent, physically suitable for port-related development.

Between Cardiff and Chepstow lie two areas of flat land of considerable size. That between Cardiff and Newport is known as Wentloog Level. Below the 50-ft. contour, lies an area of 7,300 acres, mainly agricultural, and used to a considerable extent as accommodation land for the adjacent population. Reclamation is considered possible for a further 3,500 acres.

East of Newport is Caldicot Level. Since the construction of the Spencer Steelworks at Llanwern, this is sometimes called Llanwern Flats. Between Newport and Chepstow, 17,100 acres lie below the 50-ft. contour.

A scheme was put forward several years ago for an international airport in the Severn estuary. This shows that possibilities also exist of reclaiming the extensive sandbanks in the estuary off Caldicot Level, known as the Welsh Grounds.* The effect of this scheme on the remainder of the estuary needs to be investigated further, but the possibilities of reclamation are important in reducing the effect of any scheme on inland areas. The Medway scheme has proposed reclamation of 8,000 acres.†

As in South-West Wales, backing-up areas for secondary industry exist in the old industrial zones. Both Glamorgan and Monmouthshire County Councils are active in promoting industry and a large number of sites are available. The provision of industrial sites in eastern Monmouthshire is rendered difficult for reasons of amenity, but an area at Cinderford in the Forest of Dean has been suggested for growth, whilst the Severn Bridge permits further development in South Gloucestershire and around Bristol.

Reference must be made to the cost of land, particularly in South-West Wales. In 1970 in South-West Wales it was possible to obtain industrial land near the large towns ranging from £2,500–£6,000 per acre, and values of £600 per acre and less have been recorded at Milford Haven. Values rise towards the east but still do not approach values in congested industrial areas of England.

---

* Notes on W. S. Atkins & Partners' proposals for an international airport, deep-water port, and reservoirs on reclaimed land in the Severn Estuary. Cardiff: W. S. Atkins & Partners.

† *Dock and Harbour Authority*, July, 1967, p. 73.

Road-served industrial land in the Midlands costs from £12,000 per acre upwards and still higher figures are recorded in the London area. Even in some development areas in North-West England, values range from £8,000–£16,000 per acre.

MARKETS AND COMMUNICATIONS

The largest market in Britain is South-East England, whilst one of the largest remaining industrial areas is the Midlands. The depth of the Severn Estuary, reaching in navigable terms as far as East Wales, places both of these markets within easy distance of a Severn growth zone.

In the past South Wales was not well served with road communications. Its period of greatest growth occurred during the railway age and the extensive rail network, with the Severn Tunnel, led to one of the highest rail traffic densities in Britain. This main line network still remains and is now a major link for high-speed, bulk traffic services, including containers. Freightliner depots have been set up at Cardiff and Swansea, serving existing ports and all parts of Britain. Unfortunately, the decline in attraction of railway carriage from 1920 onwards was not counteracted by new road construction and the main road link was a narrow two-lane road from Newport to Gloucester; others, no less confined, ran towards the Midlands and the North. The commencement of motorway construction has now radically altered the picture.

Midlands Link

Motorway M.5 from Birmingham to Bristol was originally constructed as far as Tewkesbury. Because of the demand by heavy road traffic from South Wales for a Midlands route, a link—the M.50—was then constructed as far as Ross. This link, with a spur towards Monmouth, was opened in 1961. A roadway of near motorway standard connected it with another motorway, M.4, at Coldra Junction, near Newport in 1972.

London Link

The prime road access to South Wales was made possible by the construction of the Severn Bridge, opened by Her Majesty the Queen in 1966. This major project, sought for over a century, at last made possible in roadway terms what had been a fact in railway terms since the Severn Tunnel was opened in 1886.

The bridge was part of the M.4 motorway and, after engineering problems had been overcome, construction from Newport eastwards was completed by the end of 1971. Construction of M.5 from Tewkesbury has now been completed and links with M.4 just south-east of the Severn Bridge.

Roads—External Effects

Motorway construction and high-standard dual carriageway roads have, therefore, brought the benefits of high-speed road transport to the eastern borders of South Wales. Whilst distances have been somewhat reduced—the M.4 route to London represents 140 miles from Newport in contrast to the old distance of 150 miles—the important factor is time/distance. Modern legislation has placed important restrictions on working hours for long-distance drivers and has increased standards of maintenance for vehicles. The higher standard of motorway construction increases the radius of action. Improved performance results from the high surface standard, the absence of sharp changes of gradient or direction, and the absence of junctions and heavy road congestion. The result should be a smoother driving load for engines and reduced use of gears, brakes, and steering mechanisms. Tyre wear increases with speed, but such maintenance is quick and low in labour costs.

Efficient use of manpower requires that economic journeys should make the fullest use of driving periods. These can either result in round trips by a single driver, or one-way trips with a rest before return. Motorways increase the radius of action by both methods, thus increasing the size of market that can be served. A further variation is the 'exchange trailer' method. This means that a driver can do a one-shift return journey, whilst his load does a one-way trip.

Road improvements up to 1970 have meant that Canadian timber has been supplied to Scotland from Newport, fruit to Covent Garden from Cardiff, and a major distribution of bananas from Barry is possible. Traffic flows are affected by efficiency of port operations but, without adequate roads, would not have been possible. Hauliers regard the radius of operation by motorways to be 150–200 miles for shift return trips, according to non-motorway content of trips, as compared to 110–125 miles for older roads, or 400 and 250 miles respectively for one-way journeys. Average speeds for heavy goods vehicles are 50–55 m.p.h. on motorways, 30 m.p.h. on A and B roads, reducing to 18 m.p.h. or less in towns.

The effect has been to bring the greater part of the Midlands and a large part of the London area within shift return trip distance of the Severn Estuary. Journeys are based on trailer exchange for delivery purposes.

One disadvantage likely to show in the future, is the restriction of M.50 and M.4 in South Wales to four lanes. This causes delay with increasing heavy vehicle use, and the need for a further lane in each direction can be foreseen.

Roads—Strategic Effects

By 1972 motorway construction will have provided high-speed access over a huge rectangle with London, Newcastle-on-Tyne, Carlisle, and South-East Wales at the four corners (*Fig.* 21). This will put the Severn within one-shift's driving distance of Glasgow. In 1970 long-distance night transport can reach Glasgow in one shift, with good traffic conditions. Regular one-shift journeys can be made from the Severn to Dumfries, Newcastle, Sunderland, and Dover; to Dover it is possible to make four round trips per week. Return journeys on an exchange trailer basis are made to Knutsford, Derby, Stoke-on-Trent, and London, the latter being night journey time.

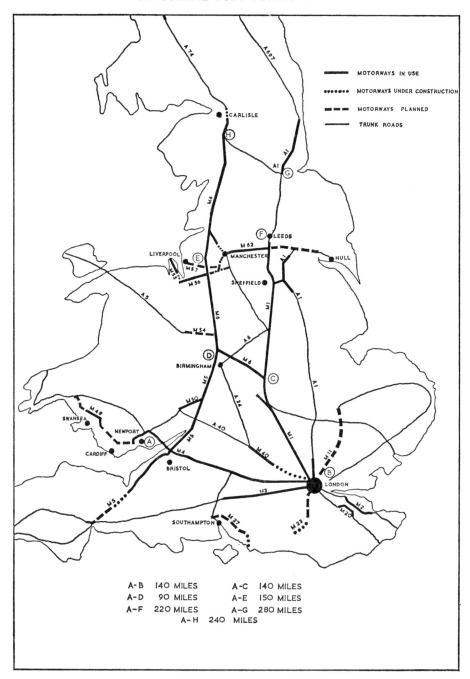

Fig. 21.—The motorway network, Great Britain.

British Road Services are planning a new Motorway Express Service based on the new motorway pattern. This pattern is shown in *Fig.* 21, which illustrates four quadrangles enclosing important sectors of Britain. The Severn lies at the south-western corner of this network and such a position should be extremely important, corresponding to that of London at the south-eastern corner.

Road transport planning is conditioned by the initial loading, market availability, return loads, and the ability to achieve the optimum driving distance per vehicle. A satisfactory location under these heads has an initiating effect on further development. The quadrangle pattern of motorways is of particular importance in achieving the optimum driving distance, both for vehicle and driver. This can either be based on the larger quadrangles (say ABFE) with driver exchange or on the smallest quadrangle (ABCD). A route to Birmingham could mean a driver from Newport completing one and a half trips a day based on laybys for trailer exchange. This planning is possible with motorways because of the ability to predict average speeds.

J. E. Sussams,* has shown a table indicating strategic positions of factory sites from a distribution viewpoint (*Table XVIII*).

Table XVIII.—DISTRIBUTION OF CONSUMER PRODUCTS FROM FACTORIES

No. of Factories

Factory Locations:	*1*	*2*	*3*	*4*	*5*	*6*	*7*
			Percentage of Production				
Birmingham	100					16	16
London		50	50	33	33	33	29
Manchester		50	33	33	33	22	22
Glasgow			17	17	11	11	11
Cardiff/Bristol				17	17	12	11
Newcastle					6	6	6
Southampton							5

(*Source: Operational Research Quarterly*)

Whilst this deals with factory distribution, the principle applies equally to distribution centres for imports or reception centres for exports.

It will be noted that, in England and Wales, only London and Manchester appear on the table more frequently than Cardiff/Bristol. Furthermore, the position of the Severn in relation to Birmingham means that this centre can be served from the estuary as easily as from any other port in Britain. In fact, if this table is taken in conjunction with a Dutch estimate that 20 km. of approach channel equals 100–120 km. of total sailing distance, a Severn location, at least to Barry, improves in relation to alternative schemes.†

* SUSSAMS, J. E. (1968), 'Some Problems associated with the Distribution of Consumer Products', *Operational Research Quarterly*, **19**, No. 2, June, pp. 162–3.
† Rotterdam Municipal Estimates 1970, Appendix 5.

The establishment of road haulage centres will be likely to follow the pattern shown in the table. In this, the Severn has an added attraction in the quantity of prime industrial products manufactured there.

The impact of such a road network has hardly begun to show; nor is it probable that the effects have been fully evaluated in terms of the increased attraction of the area to industrial development. An evaluation may indicate a repeat of the growth characteristics of the nineteenth century. What had been done by the main line railway network for South Wales then, could at last be done by the twentieth century motorway network.

Internal Road Networks

In the development of communications, physical geography plays a large part in shaping a network, whether by road or rail. After allowing for the greater flexibility of construction principles in road making, the framework shown by railways in South Wales is repeated in the complete picture of roadways. The coastal plain is of varying widths, but once inland, the topography shows river valleys with southern exits, rising to the heights of the Brecon Beacons. This geography has militated against east–west lines except on the coast. Considerable expense was involved in utilizing some gaps to drive railways across valleys and involved major enginering works, such as the Crumlin Viaduct. Generally, major roadworks ignored difficult routes and only relatively minor routes existed.

In evolving a roadway strategy for South Wales, the Welsh Office and Department of the Environment have produced the simple framework illustrated in *Fig. 22*. This encloses the major part of the industrial population by two east–west routes, starting from Swansea, one inland and one along the coast. Apart from existing A class roads in a north–south direction and programmed improvements, a major road link between the east–west roads is proposed from Cardiff to Merthyr to augment the high-standard road link already referred to, from Coldra Junction to Raglan and Ross.

The very serious disadvantage of the Upper Valleys in recent times has been their distance from the coastal route A.48. In order to remove this disadvantage and utilize the high social investment in the Upper Valleys, a major engineering scheme was conceived which has become the Heads of the Valleys Road.

Construction started in 1961, overcoming considerable difficulties, and when the link from Abergavenny to Raglan is completed, there will be a direct fast route from Swansea to the Midlands. Using this road, the distance from Swansea to Birmingham is 120 miles. Reasons of terrain and construction costs have made this road a three-lane link in parts, and undoubtedly this increases hazards and reduces potential load. However, in the circumstances in which it was conceived and built, it represents an important contribution to future growth.

The coastal route will consist of an extension of M.4 from Newport westwards. Part of this route—probably the most difficult—has already been constructed at Port Talbot. In March, 1971, the Secretary of State for Wales announced that the motorway to Swansea would be constructed within five years.

Now that there is a comprehensive network planned and a foreseeable date for completion, the road communications from South Wales to major market areas will give the region the road network it needs to compete for maritime development. In fact, the completion dates for main routes do not go beyond possible completion dates for port facilities, even if an early decision on port development is made.

Furthermore, the position of the Severn in relation to a M.I.D.A. Bridge (*see Fig.* 14) gives locational value to South Wales in relation to markets.

The southernmost Bridge—from Severn to Thames—crosses the most densely populated and the most heavily industrialized parts of Britain. It has the shortest sea communications, both deep sea and short sea, with alternative routes into North-West Europe via Southampton, Humber, and perhaps the Channel Tunnel. The past growth, particularly in the South-East, and the present congestion in the Channel, add to the economic attraction of this Bridge.

LABOUR AVAILABILITY AND NEEDS (*Fig.* 23)

Forecast increases in population, of nine million or more by A.D. 2000, prompted the estuarial studies commenced by the former Department of Economic Affairs, which were intended to discover locations for major new population areas (*see* p. 22). Undoubtedly, any major new development, such as that for maritime industry, would provide employment capable of absorbing a proportion of this population increase and the long-term labour problem would probably be solved by the attractions prime industry would have for labour-intensive industry and resulting population movement.

Until these attractions could make themselves evident, existing growth areas might well find it impossible to provide the labour reserves for satisfactory establishment. A labour reserve has come into existence as a result of the structural change in South Wales industry. A commentary on this change* has suggested that 40,000–45,000 jobs will have disappeared through redundancy between 1965 and 1971 and that a further 20,000 new jobs will be needed to employ the increase in size of the working population. Manners considers that a further 35,000–40,000 jobs will be required by 1981. These figures imply a need for a total job creation of 100,000 by 1981, thus adding social reasons to the economic attractions of labour availability.

The unemployment figure in August, 1972, for Wales, was 51,809 and the rate for wholly unemployed was 5·3 per cent compared with 3·9 per cent in Great Britain (Dept. of Employment, August, 1972). The male ratio is higher

* MANNERS, GERALD (1966), *Some Planning Needs and Opportunities in South Wales.* Swansea: Manners.

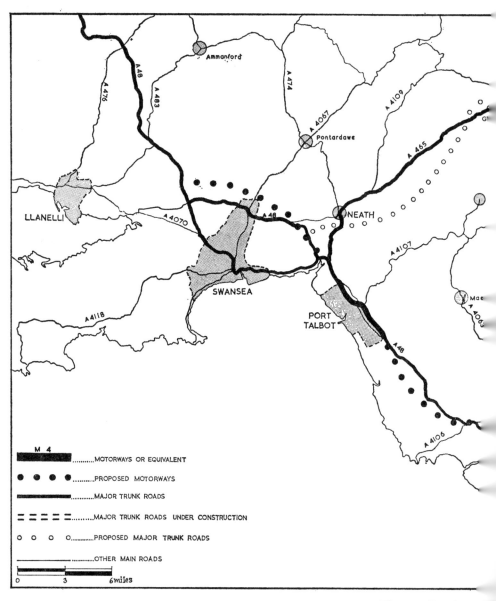

Fig. 22.—Road cor

84

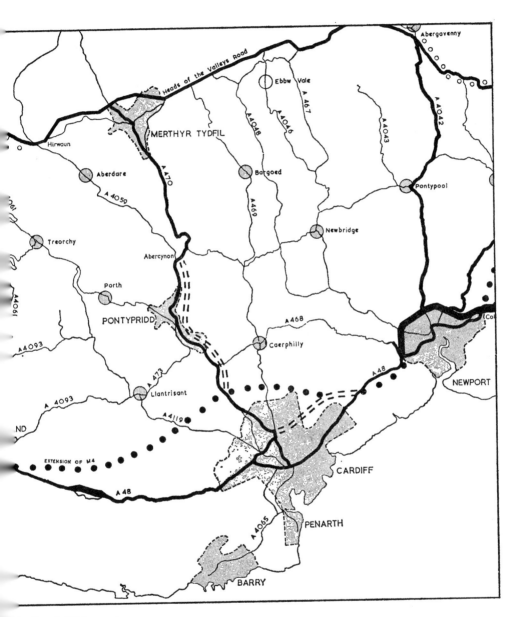

in South Wales, 1970.

(6·4 per cent Wales, 5·1 per cent Great Britain). In South Wales lives 80 per cent of the population of Wales and so do 38,414 of these unemployed. *Fig.* 23 shows the distribution of labour reserves.

Reference is made in *Table I* to the amount of maritime industry already in South Wales. In a longer time scale, South Wales has been involved in heavy industry since the beginning of the Industrial Revolution. Malkin★ also noted

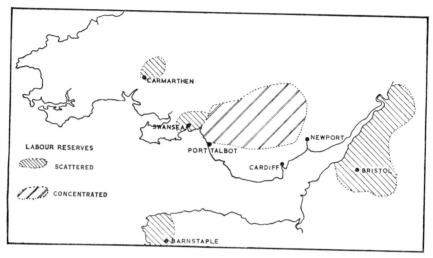

TOTAL UNEMPLOYED

Date	South Wales	Bristol
12 December, 1967	30,227	6,280
12 December, 1968	27,938	5,799
12 December, 1969	27,173	6,406
12 December, 1970	25,111	6,875
August, 1972	38,414	6,212†

†Bristol group total, 10,151.

Fig. 23.—Distribution of labour reserves in Bristol and South Wales.

in 1809 the cheerfulness and desire and love of learning of the people. These characteristics were noted by the new industries brought to the Depressed Areas of South Wales, both before and after the war. Professor Alfred Zimmern, in the Great Depression, noted the same assets of character.

Much of the labour reserves are unskilled or have the wrong skills, but maritime industry is introducing a range of new skills. In these circumstances the qualities noted by Malkin and Zimmern could have a special value. It is important that labour is not only available for new developments, but is also capable of being trained in new skills.

★ MALKIN, BENJAMIN (1809), *The Scenery, Antiquities and Biography of South Wales.*

RAW MATERIALS AND ENERGY SOURCES

Water Reserves

Next to the raw materials of industry, such as oil or ore, water is the most important commodity required.

Not only is it required for human consumption in the working population—and demand per capita rises with living standards—but it is a vital raw material in manufacture, both for processes and for cooling. So important is this commodity that it frequently controls the choice of location. Alternatively, the cost of conservation and supply can have an important effect on industrial economics. The hill system of South Wales is an ally of industry in this respect. The physical effect of hills on clouds—and the highest in South Wales (Pen-y-fan) is over 2,900 ft.—brings to the area a high rainfall. The rainfall average shown on *Fig.* 24 reaches figures of 90 inches a year for appreciable areas and, indeed, 100-inch averages are recorded. Both the physical nature of the valleys and the rivers could assist conservation. In passing, it will be noted that some coastal areas have much lower levels and, therefore, prove more attractive for living and amenity.

Over the whole of Wales, an average annual rainfall of 50 inches, less losses of 19 inches, would give a long-term run-off of 31 inches, equal to 3,800 gallons/head of population.* The industrial valleys, with a population of 1·9 million, have 1,160 gallons/head per day potentially available. The Welsh Advisory Water Committee estimate a total domestic and industrial demand by A.D. 2000 of 310 m.g.d. for South-West Wales and 329 m.g.d. for South-East Wales. Existing demand in the valley areas is 60–70 gallons/head per day, including the waste resulting from subsidence, old mains, etc. By A.D. 2000 this figure may have reached 100 gallons/head per day or more, after allowing for curtailment of waste (*Fig.* 25).

Reference is made on p. 97 to the water needs of the steel industry. Secondary industry, such as trading estates, has an average requirement of 1 m.g.d. per 100 acres. The 1960 industrial use for South Wales was estimated as 84 m.g.d. metered and 87 m.g.d. unmetered,† but these are conjectural figures and there is a great deal of re-use. Steelworks cooling water loses 10 per cent or more of its volume by evaporation before return.

Cooling water need not be of the same standard of purity as other supplies and so, perhaps, use could be made of disused colliery workings for storage. Old colliery workings may also themselves be sources of supply, as is the Severn Tunnel. In the longest term, many barrage schemes have been proposed for the estuary. These schemes, if at all viable, are a long way off, but they would enable

*OFFORD. R. S. (1970), 'Water Supply, Distribution, and Resources, *Proceedings of a Conference on Civil Engineering Problems of the South Wales Valleys*', Cardiff, 1969, p. 115. London: Institution of Civil Engineers.
† Estimate of Welsh Advisory Water Committee.

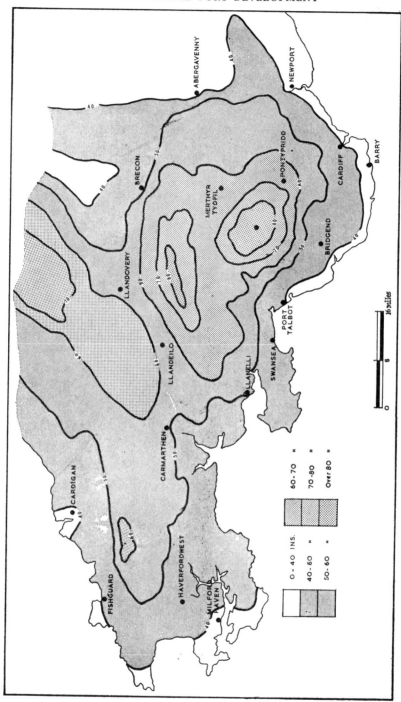

Fig. 24.—Annual rainfall in South Wales.

0 - 40 INS.
40 - 60 "
50 - 60 "

60-70 "
70-80 "
Over 80 "

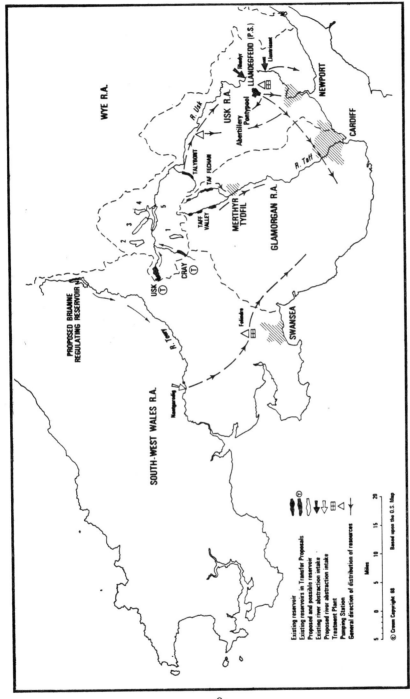

Fig. 25.—Water supply in South Wales—the strategic plan. (*Source:* R. S. Offord (1969), Institution of Civil Engineers.)

the water quality upstream to be changed from salt to fresh, therefore becoming a source of industrial supply.

Power and Energy

The introduction of oil-based industries involves the establishment of an energy source and refineries already exist in South Wales. There is, in addition, the native fuel consisting of coal, with large reserves of steam coal or anthracite, both having important industrial uses. The major demand is for electricity and, here, South Wales has a surplus of generating capacity. New power stations completing at Milford Haven and Aberthaw raise the South Wales generating capacity to 5·8 megawatts compared with a 1968 demand of 1·9 megawatts.

It is essential to investigate type and extent of energy needs in depth for any new development and to ascertain the new investment needed.

Mineral Resources

South Wales is so well known for its coalfield, and rainfall that the existence of other resources has tended to be overlooked, yet early development was attracted by metal ores. Many of the minerals found have considerable industrial importance and have played their part in industrial site selection. The existence of raw material reserves forms an attraction to prime industry which enhances the suitability of a region for growth. The steel industry, in particular, uses many minerals, apart from iron ore.

Limestone and Dolomites

Carboniferous limestones are found in a ridge around the margin of the coalfield and liassic limestone as outcrops along the coast and in the Vale of Glamorgan. Carboniferous limestone is used for the production of lime, for roadstone and for ballast. High-purity limestones on the northern edge of the coalfield would be suitable for cement manufacture.*

On the south-eastern margin of the coalfield, the beds have a high magnesium content and have been quarried as dolomite. The output is governed by amenity considerations rather than any limiting geological factor. The area of outcrops, both carboniferous and liassic, is measured in square miles rather than acres.

Sand and Gravel

The area is rich in these deposits, of importance for construction. They lie in river deposits at the lower ends of the main valleys and are virtually untapped. The floor of the estuary is also a major source of the material and at present almost the whole existing demand is met by offshore dredging.

Clay and Shale

As with the minerals mentioned above, these materials, of importance for bricks, earthenware, and pottery, exist in total deposits measuring many square

* Discussion and correspondence with J. G. L. Anderson, Professor of Geology, University College, Cardiff.

miles. They are found in the clays and shales of the coal measures and the clays of the Old and New Red Sandstone systems. Some river-glacial clays exist in river valleys and have been used for quality pottery.

Fireclay is found in association with the coal measures, but is usually extracted by mining. The potential reserves are enormous and the material is of importance for manufacturing refractory bricks.

Metal Ores

Haematite (iron ore) is now only being worked at Llanharry, but there are a number of other ironstone pockets near the carboniferous limestone outcrop. The ore is of high quality but total amounts are comparatively small.

Other ores exist in thin veins, usually in the limestone outcrops. In the past, lead, zinc, and barytes have been worked on a small scale but deposits are small.

Oil and Gas

Licences are currently being granted for exploration of the seabed off South-West and West Wales. Apart from stating that exploratory surveys have shown justification for further investigation, it would be rash to attempt a forecast. The existing steelworks are gas producers in their coke ovens and supply this gas to the Gas Board.

There are localities in South Wales, particularly between Cardiff and Usk, where underground geological structures exist which might well be suitable for underground gas storage.

AMENITY, SOCIAL NEEDS, AND INFRASTRUCTURE

Amenity

Rising living standards and reduced working hours increase the demand for amenities. Car ownership creates an influx, in leisure hours, to areas often remote from working areas.

South Wales is fortunate in this respect. *Planning Bulletin No. 8* of the Ministry of Housing and Local Government deals with the proximity of unspoiled areas to population centres. Map No. 1 of this Bulletin shows that South Wales is one of the best placed regions in England and Wales in this connexion (*see Fig.* 26).

Adequate amenity is not only of importance in general terms but forms a major attraction to managerial staff. The standards regarded as essential to modern existence, the need for stresses caused by urban life to be countered by improved recreational facilities, give it a greater priority than in the past. It will not suffice to ensure that a variety of choice is available; the density of use must not, itself, create problems. One of the worries resulting from speculation on growth in Gloucester/Cheltenham, for example, arises from the fact that the surrounding countryside is already heavily used by the large population of the English Midlands as a safety valve. Type and extent of amenity are equally important and

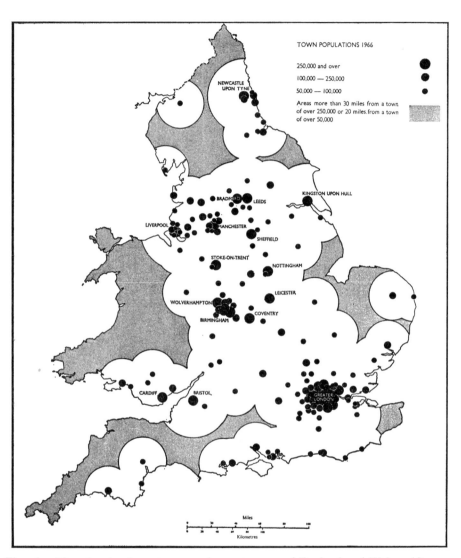

Fig. 26.—Map showing large towns and remote areas of England and Wales. (*Source*: Department of the Environment.)

both must be judged with knowledge of the population to be served. Once an amenity survey is complete it would be wise to plot densities of existing population and use, and to superimpose on this, projected increases.

In South Wales lies some of the most beautiful countryside in Great Britain. Even where scars have been left by old industry, there is an active programme of treatment and The Derelict Land Unit of the Welsh Office has been created to deal with the problem. Where treatment has not been carried out, it is possible to find large areas where unspoiled views are found. The convex shape of the South Wales hills almost always conceals industrial decay, where this still remains, and provides walks and scenery of great amenity value along the crests.

Among the major attractions of South Wales are the Pembrokeshire and Brecon Beacons National Parks; the Gower Coast; the beautiful coastline between Greater Swansea and Greater Cardiff and the Vale of Glamorgan; Wentwood and the Black Mountains in Monmouthshire; the Usk and Wye Valleys. Other smaller areas of natural beauty, too numerous to mention, reach into the heart of the industrial areas.

Activities can be followed in sailing (sea, lake, or reservoir), riding and pony trekking; canoeing on rivers, canal boating; hill walking or mountaineering and pot-holing in numerous areas. Antiquarian and artistic opportunities are plentiful, whilst even the industrial areas are full of interest for industrial archaeology.

Education

The comments of Malkin and Zimmern not only have relevance to the problem of job training, but also to the whole aspect of education. In an increasingly scientific age the standards for employment are increasing and will increase further. To follow this trend educational facilities must be provided.

The interest in education noted by these two commentators has created a structure which can serve the future. Traditionally, education was seen as a way, and sometimes the only way, out of the rut of heavy industrial employment, particularly mining. Now that the physical tasks of labour are being taken up by machines, the tradition has created an educational base for the new worker.

The University of Wales has two University Colleges in South Wales, at Cardiff and Swansea, as well as the Institute of Science and Technology and Medical School at Cardiff. In the second echelon are numerous Colleges of Advanced Technology, such as Glamorgan Polytechnic of Further Education and Adult Education. Both groups have built up a considerable expertise in relevant specialist studies, including, for example, the first Department of Maritime Studies in England and Wales.

Education is prominent in the priorities and the proportion of pupils receiving a grammar school type of education is at a high level by national standards.

Here, again, a population increase means further investment in educational facilities and the need must be quantified.

Social Needs

Enough has been said about old declining industries and employment problems to show the special social need arising from changing industrial patterns. Considerable attention to possible solutions in declining areas of Britain has been given by Development Area policies. These have involved grants for new factories and machinery, advance factories constructed for new industry, regional employment premiums, and many other inducements.

Unfortunately the grant system has had the disadvantage of blindness of choice. It has not distinguished between industry which would have settled for normal economic reasons and that which would not. Before Intermediate Area grants became available, there was a strong tendency for industry to move short distances over boundaries into grant-aided areas despite the fact that unemployment rates might be similar.

As a result of the grant system, some of the industry attracted has had a 'colonial' nature, as branch factories of other complexes, extremely susceptible to closure or run-down during economic difficulties. Not all have been an unqualified success. Rationalization in large national firms has often led to development area plants being the first to close.

Finally, the large sums devoted to the grant programme have necessarily affected the investment available for improving infrastructure: communications, schools, residential areas, amenities, and so on. Starvation of physical investment inevitably defers the day when economic attractiveness removes the need for grant support.

This, then, is an added argument for maritime development; for the improvement of port and communications infrastructure, as well as other aspects of community needs. It is suggested that this policy can only, ultimately, lead to a saving, by changing the economic environment which has created situations calling for heavy financial support. Investment should not have the transient nature of much of a general grant programme since the physical assets will remain for future exploitation. 'It is the creation of physical assets which has the major role in leading towards the solution of the problems of South Wales and its Valleys'* as well as other development areas. Reference has been made, in Chapter II, to the connexion between the investment policy at Dunkirk and the problems of the old declining industry at Lille.

Infrastructure

An important feature of the redevelopment of an older industrial area lies in the amount of existing infrastructure which is capable of use, saving new investment. Reference is made earlier to the opinion of the Ministre d'Equipage et Logement in France that it is better to develop around an existing growth than in virgin areas (p. 44).

* *Proceedings of a Conference on Civil Engineering Problems of the South Wales Valleys,* 1969, Cardiff, p. 55. London: Institution of Civil Engineers.

The available infrastructure in South Wales consists of city facilities at Cardiff and Swansea, the former also having Capital status; roads, housing, commerce, education, amenity and an administrative framework already geared to an area of maritime characteristics. W. S. Atkins & Partners have estimated that the existing asset value of the valleys in housing and services alone is £908 million.*

Perhaps most important is the nature of any existing port structure. In the chapter on Land Problems reference is made under 'Planning' to the need for an economic layout. Expenditure on ports can be reduced by use of existing port facilities, where suitable. Le Havre, Dunkirk, Antwerp, and Rotterdam, all have industry which is based on an older port. With the high proportion of vessels below 30,000 dwt. likely to remain in existence, the presence of ports of this capacity is of advantage together with existing investment in prime industry. The completion of civil engineering studies and the existence of Parliamentary powers, both important time savers, can almost be included in any description of existing infrastructure. All of these assets exist in South Wales.

THE PRACTICAL TEST

An examination on the lines described should give a reliable guide to the potential of an area for industrial port development. It is suggested that the conclusions would be reinforced by a study of existing maritime industry and the reasons for choice of location. It has been possible to examine the reasons for location of major units of the steel industry in South Wales and these are of interest because they concern decisions taken for investment in modern plant.

Margam and Ebbw Vale

The conception of Margam originated before the last war when the steel industry was experiencing economic difficulties. In Europe, the Bessemer furnace, based on local ores, produced a low-cost steel. The introduction of a steel tariff made a new British plant possible and investigations were started. The first British integrated strip mill had been opened at Ebbw Vale in 1938. This was the result of an original proposal to build a strip mill at Redburn based on home ore. Fortunately, it was realized in time that the fine quality steel for strip mill production required ore which was low in sulphur and phosphorus content. Because such ores were imported, a coastal site became essential.

The works was finally located at Ebbw Vale because Messrs. Richard Thomas and Baldwin were able to buy an existing works with two blast furnaces and mining rights at a low price. The coal reserves consisted of the best coking coal in Monmouthshire. Because of these advantages, Ebbw Vale, although 18 miles inland, was regarded as a coastal site.

In the planning for Margam, a market investigation was carried out. This provided the justification for a large strip mill based on standardized widths and

* *Op. cit.*, p. 44.

qualities. The need for imported ore again dictated a coastal site. Among the sites investigated were Newport, Swansea (two), Cardiff, Southampton, and Thames.

Eventually, the investigation showed Margam to be the best site. It was 5 miles long, uninterrupted by buildings and mainly consisted of low-value agricultural land. Sand dunes protected the site from the sea and the average piling depth was 25 ft. The area possessed adequate coal, limestone, and water reserves.

Port Talbot docks, with a limit of 10,000 dwt., was not a hindrance at that time since 68 per cent of the ore came from Sweden and the remainder from Sierra Leone and North Africa. Over such distances (as indicated by *Fig.* 2), the ship costs varied only slightly from those of larger vessels. A special fleet of ships was ultimately built or adapted to take the fullest advantage of lock size. By coincidence this fleet was able to serve the works past the date when the new trends based on more distant ores became apparent. Other important factors were that the use of sand from the dunes, and local limestone, saved many millions of pounds in construction, and also there was the strong industrial tradition of the area, including that of shiftworking.

Work was delayed by the war, but planning continued so that a company could be formed in 1947 and work started later that year. As a result, Margam was the first major steelworks completed in Europe after the war.

Llanwern

The Spencer Steelworks site was the result of a similar investigation.* Consulting engineers were engaged to examine various sites. Dr. Hallett identifies the factors for comparison as follows:—

1. The economics of assembling raw materials on the site.
2. The costs of distributing finished products.
3. The ease of providing main services in the way of an adequate water-supply and satisfactory effluent disposal arrangements.
4. Port facilities.
5. Inland transport links.
6. The availability of labour.
7. The availability of housing for imported labour.
8. Availability of coke and limestone supplies.

The consultants examined ten sites—including Kidwelly, the South-East, Immingham, and Grangemouth—and finally decided that from almost every aspect the best available site was Newport.

Given a coastal site, the former Secretary of the Margam company, Mr. David Young, has given in order of significance, the raw materials required in steel manufacture: (1) Water; (2) Ore; (3) Coal and Limestone.

* HALLETT, G., and RANDALL, P. (1970), *Maritime Industry and Port Development in South Wales*, p. 79 et seq. Cardiff: University College.

At Llanwern, in a pollution sense, the site is well selected. The prevailing winds are from the south-west and the site lies to the east of Newport, with open country to the north-east. Nevertheless effluent treatment must be improved, and this aspect is dealt with elsewhere, in drawing certain lessons from the Continent.

Water is required in large quantities for cooling purposes. Works elsewhere without cooling towers, take quantities up to 5 million gallons per hour for, say, 3 million tons of steel per annum. Although cooling water is usually returned to source, the temperatures in the process mean a loss of 10–15 per cent, which is a very large loss when related to such total requirements. The Spencer Works lies close to the hill system of high rainfall (see Fig. 24) and, moreover, is close to the River Usk, which is fed from this system. An extra source is the Severn railway tunnel pumping station at Caldicot, whilst a new reservoir near Pontypool is also available. The works take 10–15 million gallons per day.

Coal and limestone is readily available in Monmouthshire. Good coking coal is mined on the eastern edge of the coalfield, whilst large numbers of limestone quarries are to be found. The coking-coal reserves purchased when Ebbw Vale was developed, and the existence of these works 18 miles away, formed another attraction. Ebbw Vale works have an excess of sheet-rolling capacity, and the valley location prevents new blast furnace development, for reasons of space. Previously, slabs had been brought from Scunthorpe in Lincolnshire. The construction of Llanwern has made for more efficient works integration.

Ore, of low sulphur and phosphorus content, is imported and the site is 2 miles from Newport Docks, which has a capacity of up to 35,000 dwt. At the time research was first being carried out, it was thought that this size of ship was most economic in cost of carriage for ore, but subsequent developments by Japanese and U.S. steelworks showed this to be too small. Nevertheless, the Severn Estuary is sufficiently deep in this reach to provide for vessels up to 100,000 dwt. Two jetty schemes have been investigated and, latterly, Parliamentary powers have been obtained (British Transport Docks Act, 1967) for an impounded basin of 100,000 dwt. capacity at Uskmouth. The decision to build has not been taken but the establishment of maritime industry in the area would be encouraged by this investment. For the present the intention is to use Port Talbot Harbour for Llanwern ore. Britain's long-term interests demand that a Newport ore terminal should be built, not only to give Llanwern its designed role as a coastal steelworks but also to provide a rational development for maritime industry.

In 1971 it was decided to provide an extra blast furnace at Llanwern, after long and careful consideration, and the increased capacity brings nearer the need for a bulk berth near the works.

CONCLUSIONS

This outline case study shows potential for industrial port development in South Wales. It might perhaps be extended to include studies of the potential of the estuary for barrage and major airport development but their inclusion in this work might overload what is intended to be an example of a case study. It should be stated, finally, that the past tradition is emphasized by the fact that, in 1967, with under 5 per cent of the population of Britain, Wales produced 11 per cent of its coal, 26 per cent of fabricated aluminium, 27 per cent of oil products, 32 per cent of steel, over 60 per cent of sheet steel, and 100 per cent of tinplate. Since 1950, over £1,000 million has been invested in maritime industry in South Wales without the encouragement of a maritime policy.

The methodology should be of value in analysing any area. It is, in fact, an extension of the physical study already carried out on behalf of the Ministry of Transport and National Ports Council (see Chapter I). It has additional usefulness in throwing up weaknesses and deficiencies, which could then be further investigated to see if these could be overcome.

A study will almost inevitably uncover additional data of value to the assessment of potential. The general analysis of Halcrow and the cost benefit analysis suggested by the College of Europe did not mention the question of amenity, or mineral resources. Steel manufacture needs both water and limestone and these are shown to be present by the South Wales study. Amenity is a necessary attraction for managerial classes.

Studies for industrial port development will undoubtedly deal with the question of pollution in depth, especially after the publicity given to this feature in recent years.

The case study for South Wales is influenced by the nature of British industrial needs. In other countries the emphasis may be on export of raw materials and import of manufactured goods. The method could be adapted to these ends.

It might be of advantage in developing nations, with natural resources, to explore the possibility of introducing some prime manufacture to reduce ores to a product which will occupy less shipping space. Exports of steel and aluminium ingots, refined copper, or zinc concentrates will not only reduce shipping costs, but introduce industry to a country which may need development.

If energy, in the form of oil or coal, must be imported, then perhaps the right location for that industry would be in the port. If both ore and energy materials are found inland, a location near the source of the bulkiest material may be correct. Conditions throughout the world will vary so much that no precise rules can be laid down. What is important, is to keep an open mind in the study and to investigate and analyse all data which could have any bearing on the potential for industrial port development.

Part II

TECHNICAL ASPECTS OF INDUSTRIAL PORT DEVELOPMENT

CHAPTER IV

OWNERSHIP AND LAND USE CONTROL

THE location of maritime industrial development will depend upon the considerations already outlined in Part I and it would appear that urgent attention ought to be directed by the British Government to the problems of this form of development in the United Kingdom.

In deciding where maritime industrial development should take place, it is necessary that the problems of location and development should be tackled objectively. The expertise for so doing is largely available within the Port Authorities. When questions of time and place have been answered, the major problems will be associated with finance, planning, construction, and land. This chapter deals with some of the land use problems which will arise.

OWNERSHIP POLICY

Two questions of principle arise in a maritime industrial development area: (1) Should the ownership of the industrial area and the port area be vested in the same authority? (2) Should industrial port development be carried out under freehold or leasehold ownership? These questions increase in importance as the port increases in size and as industrial units become larger. The greater the area that can be changed from port-related uses, and the more complex the port activities become, the greater will be the damage to the port's efficiency or prosperity as a result of 'alienation of use'. The principle is also of importance to small transit ports, particularly where land is in short supply as a result of physical geography or urban growth.

Both questions can be answered in an empirical sense by drawing on continental experience. Antwerp and Rotterdam are both municipally-owned ports and the port and industrial areas are under municipal ownership. In the case of the Ports Autonomes of France, all are independent authorities, but are subject to financial and administrative oversight by the State. Each Port Authority is, as a matter of policy, also the owner of an industrial zone of sufficient size to ensure the port's viability. Each of these continental authorities controls its industrial area by means of a leasehold or contract system.

An analysis of the problem in Britain requires consideration of the principles of land use and of the respective characteristics of leasehold and freehold development.

LAND USE POLICY

The categories of land for port and industry may be classified by use. Apart from water areas for shipping, the principal classes fall into six main groups (*Table XIX*).

Table XIX.—Land Use Categories in Port Zones

1. Operating Areas:
   Quays and jetties

   Marshalling areas $\Big\}$ rail / road

   Handling appliances
   Transit sheds

2. Cargo Storage:
   Liquid   —   tanks
   Dry
       Covered   —   shed
       Uncovered $\Big\{$ hopper / open storage

3. Portside Industry:
   Conveyor served
   Pipeline served
   Road or rail served
   Export oriented (packers and assemblers)

4. Port Service Industry:
   To ships   Transport
   To port operator $\Big\}$ Maintenance / Services
   To port users   Dry docks

5. Commercial:
   Supplies
   Warehousing and long-term storage
   Bond
   Agency
   Insurance

6. Land for Port-related Industry:
   a. Prime Manufacture, e.g.,
       Oil and petrochemicals
       Steel and non-ferrous metals
       Chemicals
       Grain
       Timber engineering or saw milling
   b. Service Industry and Selected Secondary Industry, e.g.,
       Machinery and plant
       Transport
       Car manufacture

Categories 1–5 are those normally found in port areas in Britain. With some exceptions, as at Immingham and Barry, major units of category 6 are usually found outside port boundaries.

The National Ports Council has drawn attention to the fact that very few suitable areas for maritime industrial development remain in this country and that the competition for land near deep water and major population areas is intense. It described such land as a 'scarce national resource'.* In the light of such an authoritative and responsible comment, it is not only right that studies should be undertaken to determine the desirability of establishing industrial ports but, also, if one is created, to secure that the land remains dedicated to such use. Such a dedication is not only essential to ensure continuation of the benefits of economies of scale but is also conservationist because of the way in which it will limit industrial sprawl.

The major risk which comes from a policy of separate ownership and freehold industrial sites is one of alienation of use. The effect of alienation is to deprive future maritime industries of locations close to the port and to drive their development farther out. This will add to the cost of transport of the bulk raw material and, therefore, reduce the economic advantage of location. It will also create a spread of prime industrial activity, causing further environmental problems.

Planning control over land use, as currently practised, may only have a limited effect, since Planning Authorities are bound to be under great pressure to release land for a variety of needs. In these circumstances, they may well find that it is difficult to reserve the large areas likely to be required for future industrial port development unless they can be given a policy directive from central government.

The industrial planning categories at present are broadly:—

1. Light industry
2. Heavy industry
3. Industry likely to be injurious to health and amenities.

Although some authorities have an informal category for industry of national importance, none of the formal categories is directed towards the preservation of land with a maritime bias in appropriate areas. There seems to be an urgent need, therefore, for the creation of an extra planning category for land having maritime characteristics.

Even if a satisfactory designation can be achieved to protect land reserves, the needs of an industrial port go beyond the limited effects of planning designations. Ports are extremely expensive to build and it is essential that land forming the immediate port hinterland should not only be used for related purposes but that very close ties should be created between port and industrial area for the sea transport base. Too frequently in recent times have industrial plants been established close to ports for the sole purpose of using port facilities, only to change the transport mode because of substandard carriage rates quoted with the deliberate intention of establishing a new transport pattern, which may be less economic in the long run, and destroying an old one.

This should not be interpreted as meaning that out-of-date and inefficient facilities should be kept in being or that land bridge traffic should be hindered,

* N.P.C. Annual Report and Accounts, 1966, para. 52–54.

but the heavy investment of the nation in a new port should not be undermined by unfair commercial practices. Perhaps the relative efficiency of sea and land transport could be made the subject of arbitration in contracts, but the pattern of transport flows should not be upset on relatively frivolous or artificial grounds.

In this respect planning control should be regarded as supplementary to landlord control and as having an environmental as opposed to an economic importance.

These problems of land use control must be considered in some detail.

LAND USE CONTROL

Freehold Development

The problems of land use control are increased if port and industrial zones are in separate ownership and further increased if industrial development is carried out on a freehold basis, creating multiple ownership.

In the case of freehold development, control could be imposed by restrictive covenants provided that all land is initially in one ownership. Positive covenants (e.g., 'to use the port') have disadvantages. At common law, under certain conditions, the rule is that the benefit, but not the burden of a covenant, can run with land. This means that, although the successors of the vendor would continue to be entitled to the benefit of a positive covenant, successors of the purchaser would not be bound by the burden. The burden would bind only the initial purchaser and his estate.*

It is common for the initial purchaser A, on a subsequent sale, to seek a covenant of indemnity against future breaches of covenant from his successor B, and so on. The first vendor's remedy, where action is possible, is to sue A, who will, in turn, recover from B. This is clearly an unsatisfactory method, which can easily be upset by death or disappearance of one of the parties, or by neglect to secure an indemnity at some point in the chain.

The negative or restrictive covenant ('not to use the land for any purpose other than . . .') provides better control. In certain conditions, the Law of Equity permits the burden of restrictive covenants to run with the land on re-sale.

The equitable remedy recognizes that the value of a covenant lies in securing its continuance rather than in damages. In the case of *Tulk* v. *Moxhay* (1848) 2 Ph. 774, a restrictive covenant was held to be enforceable against a subsequent purchaser who bought with notice of the covenant. An important point to remember is that such covenants should be for the benefit of the land belonging to the covenantee. This suggests that port and industrial zone should be in the same ownership at the initial stage.

In order for the rule to work, the covenant must be negative; it must be for the benefit of land retained by the covenantee; it must have been intended to

* *Hall* v. *National Provincial Bank*, 1939. L.J.N.C.C.R. 185.

run with the covenantor's land; and it runs only in equity. The last point means that a purchaser without notice is not bound and that only equitable remedies are available (in this case an injunction).

This, in itself, provides a considerably involved method of control, but the law also provides a way of removing a restrictive covenant. Section 84 of the Law of Property Act, 1925, as amended by the Lands Tribunal Act, 1949 (Section 3), enables an application to be made to the courts for modification or discharge of a restrictive covenant, with or without the payment of compensation. One of three grounds must be shown to exist:—

1. That by reason of changes in the character of the property or the neighbourhood the restriction is obsolete.
2. That the persons entitled to the benefit of the restrictions have agreed either expressly, or by implication, by their acts and omissions, to the discharge or modification of the covenant.
3. The discharge or modification of the covenant will not injure the persons entitled to the benefit of the covenant.

Once again, opposition to an application based on the third ground is possible only if port and industrial zone were originally in the same ownership.

The second ground implies a similar principle since a port authority, by its commercial nature, is less likely to condone breaches by acts and omissions than an industrial estate which derives its revenues solely from industrial development.

LEASEHOLD DEVELOPMENT

The argument thus far has favoured unitary ownership at the outset. It is now argued that proper control is best enforced by leasehold development and that this, too, implies single ownership of port and industrial zone.

The advantage of leasehold development lies in the continuation of overall ownership and control throughout the life of an industrial port and in the direct covenants possible between landlord and tenant. With single control, the whole form of lease can be directed at the relationship between port and industry with reasonable prospects of enforcement.

The length of lease to be granted should be assessed on the life of the industrial asset in economic terms; the likely trend towards change; and the desire of the lessee for reasonable depreciation life for his asset. Continental practice is generally towards leases in multiples of 25 years and the British in multiples of 7 years. Of the two, the British practice is the more flexible. The land use and port relationship must be specified in the lease and the extent of this relationship will be greater for land close to quays and berths.

As well as terms linking the development with the port, such leases should require a cleared site on termination; the nineteenth and twentieth century desire for valuable reversions has yielded some doubtful bargains to port landlords (e.g., surplus concrete grain silos and obsolete multi-storey warehouses). The pace of change in design and technology is now so swift that the structures likely to remain at the end of any properly paced lease are unlikely to have much continuing value. In any event, trade fixtures are removable by lessees at law under age-old doctrine.*

Should there be justification for the renewal of an expired lease the situation is governed by Part II of the Landlord and Tenant Act, 1954. Section 30 of this Act sets out the conditions under which the landlord can oppose an application for renewal. These conditions do not have a specific alienement with the special considerations of a M.I.D.A. authority and so the maritime content of a lease arrangement could conceivably be lost if a port does not own its industrial zone, and make proper provisions in the initial lease. Since it is not possible to covenant out of the 1954 Act, the relationship must be retained by the covenants of the lease itself, in particular the user clause. Breaches of these can be contested at any time during the lease as well as under Section 30 (1) (c) of the Landlord and Tenant Act, 1954 at termination.

The user clause should be clear in its terms in order to avoid ambiguity and any remote possibility of change arising under Section 19 of the Landlord and Tenant Act, 1927. Even a minor departure from absoluteness, requiring a lessee to obtain the landlord's consent to change of user, can prevent a landlord from obtaining financial advantage other than the actual damage to or diminution in value of his neighbouring premises. (This again tends to support unitary ownership, although the extent to which such a claim can extend to loss of trade in port has not been tested in court.) The simplest way is, of course, to incorporate a strict use clause. In the event of breach of this clause, the remedy is by injunction or damages. Unitary ownership offers the best sanction against change from a port bias since, in the absence of an injunction, a port owner is able to justify a heavier claim for compensation than an industrial landlord whose loss could well be nominal. Covenants concerning traffic guarantees and the scale and type of investment can also be included as added guarantees.

It should be emphasized that although references have been made to injunctions and damages, the real purpose of this discussion is to discover a way of preventing the need arising. The essential purpose is to choose the best form of control to secure the continuation of an industrial port as an economic entity and to preserve the port/industry relationship. Ownership and methods of land allocation and grant form the core of this problem.

* *Year Books* 20 and 21, Henry VII, pp. 13 and 26; and Poole's case, 1703 (I.Salk.368).

CONCLUSIONS

The recommended method of control (which is similar to that of Rotterdam) may be summarized:—

1. OWNERSHIP

The port and industrial zone should be under the same ownership and should be developed by the leasehold system. This will not only ensure proper control and prevent alienation of land use, it will prove the most satisfactory way of providing that the necessary common policy for port and industrial zones is applied. With increasing demand for coastal location, it is also vital that early decisions are taken to reserve and acquire land and to prevent wrong industrial or other development taking place in positions that could distort the shape of a regional plan for the rest of the century. It is also essential to avoid the expense caused by the need for resettlement of conflicting developments wherever possible.

2. LAND USE CONTROL

Although strict user clauses are sometimes unpopular, it is vital that the correlation between the grant of a lease and the trade of a port should be made clear at the outset. The most common new user clauses are those which describe the industrial activity and include the words 'to be imported (or exported) through the port of . . .' in relation to the trade element.

Strict user clauses should be linked with a commercial (and therefore substantial) rent to strengthen the contractual pressure for correct use. Lessees should also be required under a lease to invest substantial capital in sites themselves. The financial obligations thus imposed induce responsible attitudes in lessees, encourage careful preliminary assessment of prospects before contract, and, in the event of change, make lessees themselves seek suitable alternative lessees, particularly if the landlord insists on his legal rights.

The existence of control, in the event of lack of success by lessees in seeking alternative users, is also an encouragement to lessees to surrender leases. This is in the industrial port's interest since it enables suitable redevelopment to take place. The landlord should, however, be prepared to be lenient in his financial terms for surrender, thus recognizing adverse economic circumstances, should these be the cause, as opposed to company rationalization.

If alternative uses are available which are also related to port use, the existence of strict user control enables the landlord to modify other clauses of the lease as a condition of consent. In a change, for example, from dry cargo storage to petroleum products, clauses concerning safety can be introduced into the lease. If there is no user control, the lease cannot be amended and only general rules apply. Alternatively, as a condition of relaxing absolute user control, financial penalties could be imposed which would be at least as effective as a traffic guarantee in monetary terms.

The pressures for surrender, lacking suitable alternative uses, are less where penalty payments (usually minor) can cause a weakening of the user clause.

The landlord should be prepared to accept occasional cases where an installation is completely closed down for a period, whilst a new user is sought.

In some cases, lessees use the threat of development elsewhere to weaken user clauses. Such cases need policy decisions by management, but with the possibility of common policy in industrial ports, for reasons of logic and common cause, this situation should become less frequent, particularly where major dock facilities are involved.

3. Traffic Guarantees

Some ports regularly include guarantee clauses in leases based on either minimum tonnages or minimum payments. Lessees do not like guarantee clauses since the enforcement of a minimum penalty payment usually coincides with a period of general trading difficulty. The value of using guarantee clauses as a general practice is debatable. Because of the fears of lessees, acceptable minima often fall very much short of average throughput. For example, an actual oil distribution proposal with proposed throughput of 100,000 tons, rising to 250,000 tons, had a minimum guarantee in respect of dues of £15,000—only a fraction of the normal revenue. Lessees are usually unlikely to agree high fallback figures, and inflexible attitudes can drive trade to other ports. In addition, the inclusion of a minimum guarantee gives a lessee an argument for weakening the user clause, on the grounds that maximum flexibility in use is necessary to cover the minimum guarantee. This can affect a port authority's attempts to secure a rational zoning of quay and berth specialization and hence create a difficult situation in meeting cargo handling equipment needs.

The inclusion of traffic guarantees, suitable in some cases, must not be allowed to weaken the lease, particularly the user clause, or to drive away attractive proposals where specific trade levels cannot be guaranteed. It is easier to negotiate a satisfactory guarantee where the port is also called upon to invest a substantial sum in order to make a new development possible. It can then be more easily argued that a guarantee is necessary as security for the port authority's investment. Traffic guarantees should be based on tonnage, with provision for penalties at current dock rates.

Experience of fallback guarantees in some ports infers that such a guarantee does not add greatly to the pressures on lessees, provided that they have a sufficient capital investment and pay commercial rents. In all cases, there should be proper assessment of traffic potential by commercial management before leases are recommended.

4. Additional Clauses in Port Leases

This chapter has dealt with the problem of proper control of land use and ways in which parts of the contract or lease can help in achieving this aim.

The port lease is, of course, an extremely complex document and must cover a wide range of matters connected with industrial or operational use as well as more conventional landlord and tenant matters. Regard must be had to the effects of uses on adjoining premises and on general port activity. For example, the external lighting common in chemical industries must not interfere with navigation lights. Fire risks must be kept to a minimum and measures taken to prevent spread of any blaze. Increasing attention must be given in the new form of port to anti-pollution and amenity measures in leases, as well as to commercial objectives in securing optimum use of port facilities.

Because port operation is highly competitive, port authorities jealously guard the form their contracts take, except to developers, but enough is known of them to say that the leases and contracts of most successful port authorities are similar in form.

CHAPTER V

LAND REQUIREMENTS FOR MARITIME INDUSTRIAL DEVELOPMENT

GENERAL CONSIDERATIONS, RESERVATIONS AND ACQUISITION

THE classification of areas required for the combined industrial port may be further summarized from the list on p. 102.

1. Port-related industry.
2. Port operational areas, including cargo storage.
3. Portside industry.
4. Port service industry and commercial areas.
5. Port water areas.
6. Sea approaches and facilities, including offshore islands, moorings, etc.

In considering a location for maritime development it must be emphasized that land, in association with shipping access, is the dominating factor, subject to market availability. If change from a restricted site to an unrestricted site means, for example, a 25 per cent increase in civil engineering costs but 100 per cent or greater increase in land availability, then the larger site must be the long-term choice provided that the market will sustain the increase in development potential.

Should economic conditions defer the extended development for too long a period, then the discounted cash flow calculation might move in favour of the smaller scheme.

If the smaller site means an early curb on port trade, or if there is no increase in construction costs, the choice of a larger site is even more obvious.

The National Ports Council has already given an indication of land requirements for a M.I.D.A. in specifying a minimum area of 5,000 acres as one of the criteria. Other authorities regard this minimum, which, for example, equals the area of two major steelworks, as too low.

The Halcrow Report, for which the criteria were laid down, had, as its purpose, the task of discovering in purely physical terms whether there were sites in Britain capable of maritime industrial development. The fact that this study discovered that only three sites substantially satisfied all the physical criteria, and that the National Ports Council describes such a site as a scarce national resource, suggests that the whole of the suitable areas should be preserved and prevented from falling into alien uses.

This implies the town planning control already referred to and which may well have to be imposed on planning authorities by central government in the national interest because of the pressures on land for development. Considerable troubles have been experienced by ports in Britain in seeking to reserve land at their boundaries for future development. Part of the difficulty follows from the frequent inability of ports to acquire land by agreement or to obtain sanction for compulsory purchase until land is required for an approved scheme. Cases have occurred, in South Wales, of extreme pressures to release M.I.D.A. quality land for housing speculation and, in one case, a blank refusal was given to a request by a port authority to purchase land by agreement for similar speculative reasons.

The area required for an industrial port and its reserve depends upon the amount of maritime industry which can be attracted to it and the long-term growth prospects. Areas of continental schemes have been quoted and much research has already been devoted to assessment problems there.*

In assessing areas for industrial port development it is clear, from experience of forecast and result, that the best that can be hoped for is an approximation in the short term and a wider range of possibility in the long term. In 1970 port land demands at Rotterdam were increasing at the rate of 10 per cent per annum.† If this rate of increase is compared with the 'Orange Book' forecast to the effect that Rotterdam will grow along the new Waterway from 25,000 acres to about 75,000 acres by A.D. 2000, it seems that the rising curve of demand must flatten out. Whilst Rotterdam's Harris Report substantially agrees with this figure, the 'Blue Book' also forecasts a gross increase in port and industrial area of 40,000 hectares (100,000 acres) in the entire Delta by the year A.D. 2000. In fact, one of the restricting factors at Rotterdam is the physical one of making sufficient suitable land available for extension in time for succeeding phases of development.

Whether or not accurate results can be expected, it is essential to try to gauge the likely demand for land by port and industry and the better the techniques which can be devised, the more satisfactory will be the results. The first estimate must be based on an economic forecast before deciding the policy on acquisition and reservation for maritime industry. The next task will be to coordinate the economic and land forecasts with physical features and the desirable planning requirements.

The economic forecast will also provide a basis for the planning authority to investigate areas likely to be required for secondary and service industry, housing, and other infrastructure. The extent of this investigation will depend on the

---

* E.g., Report of Consultation Organisation for Seaport Development in South-West Netherlands ('The Green Book'), *Plan 2000+* ('The Yellow Book'), Harris Report ('The Blue Book'), and 'The Orange Book' for Rotterdam Port Authority.

† Conversation with Dr. Postuma, Managing Director, Rotterdam Port Authority.

nature of any existing infrastructure and the amount of additional infrastructure required, and the location of the port in relation to main markets.

The land forecast will enable a land purchase programme to be prepared. Ideally, land should be acquired for development on a programme basis, that for the first stage being limited to the amount required over the period of establishment, with a phased purchase programme for future extension. If the forecast development for the first ten years should be 5,000 acres at £1,000 per acre, the capital required for land purchase is £5,000,000. Interest on sums of this magnitude, to which must be added the cost of roads, services, and drainage, is quite an important consideration in the expenses of a Port Authority.

Whilst the lack of grants might act as a spur to greater efficiency in port undertakings, it is certainly a strong reason why land purchase programmes should be properly assessed and requirements too far ahead should be catered for by planning designation (*see also* pps. 103, 111). If, on the other hand, large areas can be purchased cheaply, as where extensive reclamation is possible or where interim income can be obtained from short-term lettings, the purchase programme should be flexible enough to permit this to be done. These views have authoritative support. The Harris Report ('Blue Book') for Rotterdam recommends that land should be allocated very selectively and planning should be always looking ten years ahead.

ASSESSMENT—THE ECONOMIC STUDY

The analysis of land requirements demands, as a base, a general economic study of the development potential, with emphasis on those industries most likely to achieve substantial economies by reason of a port location and including forecasts of the probable future growth rate of those industries. Such studies should not ignore agglomeration effects, entrepôt trade, or trade not destined for the immediate hinterland, since the greatest benefit will be gained if there is sufficient land for maximum utilization of port facilities.

The class of industry involved can be readily ascertained by examination of continental ports and this account includes lists of maritime industries at Rotterdam, Antwerp, and Le Havre. Various types of industries likely to benefit from transport economies are given in *Table XX* and the most important, in continental experience, are those concerned with bulk ore, crude oil and derivatives of oil, and chemicals.

A sample case study would be beyond the scope of this chapter but a preliminary study of potential in South Wales has been carried out, although this does not deal with agglomeration effects to any extent.* Other studies on a national scale were to have been initiated.†

* HALLETT, G., and RANDALL, P. (1970), *Maritime Industry and Port Development in South Wales*. Cardiff: University College.
† *Hansard*, 17 July, 1969, col. 166.

The potential for growth is affected by the size and type
is both variable and conditional.

It will be variable—of a different size for different c
variation will apply both to direct shipments through the
and other products of the M.I.D.A. industry. This v
principally upon the bulk/value ratio and its effect on tran
The higher the value in relation to bulk for imports or prin
less the effect of distance in percentage terms on the pr
commodity. This factor will give a flexibility to the industriaᵢ ᴐuucture, enabling
distant markets to be served with suitable prime products, the latter being
produced or imported at the port and the user having a location close to the
market. It can also be exploited to fulfil a social need, in placing secondary
industries of low bulk/high value manufacture in problem areas.

Table XX.—Maritime Industry: Some Typical Examples

Port Commodity	Principal Industries	Associated Industry
Dry Bulk		
Ores	Steel, aluminium, zinc, nickel	Sheet rolling, wire manufacture, metal boxes, tin
Slabs and ingots	Steel, aluminium, copper	stamping, casting, moulding and pressing (e.g., car bodies)
Grain and cereals	Milling and processing	Distribution ⎤
Animal foodstuffs	Milling and processing	Distribution ⎬ packaging
Fertilizers	Manufacture	Distribution ⎦
Chemicals and chemical ores	Processing	Paint manufacture
Timber and wood pulp	Sawmilling, paper manufacture	Construction furniture, printing, packaging
Liquid Bulk		
Crude oil	Refining	Petrochemicals
Feedstock	Petrochemicals	Plastics, pharmaceuticals, fibres
Problem Cargoes		
Liquid natural gas	Bottling, distribution	
Liquid sulphur	Chemicals	

The hinterland is also conditional, in relation to other ports, upon the port's
(and port-related industry's) locational advantage, the efficiency and cost of port
operations, and other factors such as land communications. Comparative progress in such fields as road improvement programmes, labour relations, and ship
and traffic congestion may well lead to fluctuations in the size of this conditional
hinterland from time to time, but since there can be no direction of shipping to a
particular port this must be catered for. It is felt that at a national level sufficient
control should be kept to prevent too much duplication of high-cost facilities,
although some overlapping is inevitable.

From such a study calculations should be possible of the likely total United
Kingdom demand and of the proportion likely to be attracted by a particular

At this point it should be possible to form an estimation of land requirements. The Scottish Study, *Oceanspan II*, has examined the possible future growth of a number of maritime industries.

ASSESSMENT—COMPARISON WITH OTHER PORTS

The simplest basis of estimation can be gained from a comparison of the discovered potential for a new industrial port with a port area of similar size elsewhere, where maritime industry policies have already been applied. Care must be taken to apply corrections to take into account differences.

As an example, the total trade of the South Wales seaboard (including Milford Haven) in 1968 was 48,700,000 tons, of which 32,000,000 tons was oil and 7,000,000 tons was iron ore.*

The trade of Antwerp in 1968 was 72,000,000 tons, of which 28,000,000 tons was oil and about 12,000,000 tons was ore.†

As a hypothesis, if an economic forecast were to show that South Wales' trade in 1980 will equal that of Antwerp in 1968, the superficial conclusion is that the total land requirements of South Wales for port and industry in 1980 will be similar to those of Antwerp in 1968—approximately 26,000 acres. At this stage, comparisons of the respective hinterlands should be made and corrections applied in respect of differences between the two areas. Corrections must be made for such factors as:—

1. The relative types and sizes of hinterland and locational advantages.
2. Existing dock areas with maritime industry potential in South Wales, or Antwerp.
3. Existing maritime industry located outside port areas in South Wales which is inside the port area of Antwerp.
4. Existing maritime industry which is inside port areas of South Wales and outside port areas of Antwerp.
5. The proportion of Antwerp's port area allocated to trades unlikely to be attracted to South Wales, e.g., entrepôt trade such as barge traffic to the Rhine.
6. The proportion of South Wales ports land allocated to trade unlikely to be attracted to Antwerp.
7. The changing position at Antwerp dictated by the lack of berths for ships of 200,000 dead weight tons.
8. The relative efficiency of communications.
9. The changes in port operation and land use since development of the port studied.

To these calculations must be added future reserve areas.

* NATIONAL PORTS COUNCIL (1969), *Digest of Port Statistics*.
† Published statistics of the Port of Antwerp.

DETAILED INDUSTRIAL ASSESSMENT BY LAND USE ANALYSIS

It would seem that the most relevant detailed method of assessing land requirements should consist of examining relatively stable ratios in existing modern ports and modern industry. The proper subject of examination would be one or more of the principal factors concerned in the occupation of space.

In industry, physical examination seems to suggest that plant design or production figures decide the area required. Ratios obtained from either of these would only be likely to change as the nature and design of plant changes. The effect of such a change on production ratios would show up in a continuing research programme. In most maritime industry (e.g., steel) the ultimate production is directly related to raw material input.

Similarly, in port operational zones, the principal factors are plant and the bulk and stacking characteristics of cargo.

In both port and industry, buffer storage forms an important part of land occupation. This proportion must always be identified in individual analyses but, for the purpose of overall estimates, it has been included in the general analysis. Development of the method will produce greater sophistication by subdividing broad classifications, investigating variations in industrial processes, and extending the scope of inquiry.

MARITIME INDUSTRY

The recommended method for estimating industrial areas consists of using the economic forecast to provide production figures or raw material requirements of maritime industry. From these it is possible to calculate the required areas by land use analysis of existing production units. It is important not to confuse production figures with volume of port trade. The latter will be reduced by the quantity of land-borne materials involved.

One present disadvantage of this method lies in the difficulty of obtaining data. Perhaps this might be rectified if such a method became more widespread, but criticisms have been made of the secrecy with which some industries treat information.* It is essential, in the interests of future research, that attitudes should be modified. Responsible research can always conceal sources if this is necessary and, in a complicated world, the ability to refine methods and extend research by discussion and use of improved data is vital.

Land use analysis of major maritime industries produces guidelines given below:—

BULK LIQUID AND CHEMICAL BASED INDUSTRY

1. *Oil*

Llandarcy oil refinery, at Swansea, occupies an area of approximately 1,000 acres, exclusive of the port facility and has a production capacity of 8 million

* HALLETT, G. and RANDALL, P. (1970), *Maritime Industry and Port Development in South Wales*, p. 6. Cardiff: University College.

tons per annum,* or 125 acres per million tons. The Texaco refinery at Milford Haven has an existing site of 450 acres for a throughput of 6 million tons and 475 acres in reserve, a present use of 75 acres per million tons. Gulf oil refinery at Milford Haven occupies 300 acres for 3 million tons throughput or 100 acres per million tons and a further 160 acres for petrochemicals and reserve.

An average ratio for refinery development in South-West Wales, therefore, would be 100 acres per million tons of production or 10,000 tons per acre.

The oil refining industry at Antwerp (see Appendix III) occupied a total acreage of 1,200 acres on 1 January, 1969, with total annual production of 24,650,000 tons and individual averages ranging from 7,000–32,000 tons per acre.† This gives an average throughput of 2,054,000 tons per 100 acres (20,540 tons per acre) or twice the average throughput per acre of South Wales refineries, and an improvement of one-third on the most concentrated—Texaco. At Le Havre the oil refining throughput/acreage ratio seems to be approximately the same as at Milford Haven, but the relationship is not clearly shown in published statistics.‡

Other more isolated refinery sites show rather less intensive use. Antar Refinery at Nantes occupies 200 hectares for a production of 4·6 million tons or 43·5 hectares (109 acres) per million tons. The Shell refinery at Bordeaux occupies 210 hectares for a throughput of 4 million tons or 52·5 hectares (131 acres) per million tons.

2. *Petrochemicals*

Petrochemical manufacture at Milford Haven is limited. In order to assess land requirements in a better market location, areas for this use must be assessed elsewhere.

At Baglan Bay, near Swansea, a petrochemical complex is being constructed in association with the Llandarcy refinery on a site of about 466 acres. There are no official figures for production but general statements seem to suggest a production total of about 1 million tons or 2,145 tons per acre.

The petrochemical industry at Antwerp produced 1,061,000 tons on 468 acres in 1968, an average of 2,918 tons per acre.

The only British petrochemical plant which supplied information for analysis also showed an average of 2,200 tons per acre, but this will be increased substantially when a new large cracker, which is planned, is installed. The figure of 2,200 tons per acre represents net production and is exclusive of fuel, gas, and cracked spirit returned to refinery which could increase the production total by up to one-third.

---

* *Western Mail*, 29 June, 1970.
† Published statistics of the Port of Antwerp.
‡ Refinery acreage 421 HA.; throughput 12·8 million tons crude oil.

Further guidance can be obtained from a comparison of the allocation of land between uses at various refining and petrochemical complexes; at Llandarcy, petrochemicals will occupy an area 47 per cent of the size of the refinery site; at the Gulf refinery in Milford Haven 53 per cent; Antwerp 39 per cent, and Le Havre 33 per cent. (The last figure may be incorrect since the refinery area of Compagnie Française de Raffinage is believed to contain a certain amount of petrochemical development. If so, a higher percentage will apply). As a test, therefore, the economic projection and land forecast should show a land area for petrochemical use between 30 per cent and 55 per cent of the refinery area.

3. *Chemicals*

Basic chemical manufacture at Antwerp occupied 1,371 acres (net) for a production of 2,363,000 tons, or 1,720 tons per acre.

To illustrate the possible range of tonnages, a British chemical plant (silicones) shows an output of only 200 tons per acre. The reserve area at this plant represents an increase of 66 per cent on the present industrial area. Conversely, Petrochim at Antwerp, on a site of 76 acres, has a production of 11,900 tons per acre or a ratio as high as the South-West Wales average for oil refining.

4. *Variations in Density of Production*

The analysis should provide a useful basis for estimating since it is derived from actual maritime industry growth areas and shows the average land requirements of a wide variety of industries under the general headings of oil refining, petrochemicals, and chemicals.

The contrasting figures of land requirements for refining at Milford Haven/ Swansea and Antwerp with a continental throughput average which is double that of Milford seem to illustrate the differing conditions in the two countries. The Low Countries, with their high population density and closely situated towns, are bound, as in their agriculture, to make the most intensive use of land. The result of this is seen in the concentration of industry, the large proportion of flat dwellers, and the short distances between settlements. In contrast, Milford Haven, lying partly in a National Park, is lightly populated and, although large sites are scarce, has a number of suitable areas of adequate size. It is also at an earlier stage of development than some European ports. Because of National Park considerations, the refineries at Milford, as well as Llandarcy refinery, show evidence of greater attention to location and appearance than some continental schemes.

The lower density of production has three advantages:—
1. Pollution effects are reduced considerably.
2. Opportunity is given for landscaping, tree screening, and amelioration or conservation treatment.
3. There is an eventual possibility of increasing density of use if growing land shortage becomes a critical problem. By this time anti-pollution

techniques should have improved to an acceptable efficiency for the greater density.

ORE-BASED INDUSTRY

1. *Steel*

An examination of British steelworks sites where areas and import figures for iron ore can be obtained has indicated the following situation:—

Developed Area	Reserve	Import Tonnage
Major Works:		
2,680 acres	1,120 acres	3·0 million tons
1,537 acres	1,005 acres	2·7 mililon tons
Smaller Works:		
1,240 acres	—	1·0 million tons
345 acres	—	900,000 tons
(240 without processing)		

The Hamburger Stahlwerke has a site of 46 hectares (115 acres). It is planned as an 'electrosteel and rolling mill' with an annual *production* of 400,000 tons of steel and rolled products.* The plant description and acreage suggests that only a proportion of the steel will be rolled in this works. One ton of steel requires approximately 1·5 tons of ore in manufacture or a similar quantity of pellets.

Only the first two of the samples represent fully integrated strip mills and the raw material/land ratios are 890 and 570 acres per million tons of ore. These are in respect of works of about 3 million tons steelmaking capacity at full production, but the average is based on present ore intake.

The lower-tonnage works yield figures of 1,240 and 380 acres per million tons of ore. The Hamburg figure represents 300 acres per million tons of production or 200 acres per million tons of ore.

All the British examples are based on confidential information and may not be identified. They do have individual physical and other characteristics which partly explain the variation of ratios. These characteristics include site shape, contours, industrial requirements, such as manufacture of ingots or slabs for other works, reservoir provision, more extensive sidings on rail-served sites, areas for deposit and treatment of scoria. One site manufactures special steel. The examples show the sort of variation which may be encountered. This might be explained by further analysis extending to age, design, and layout of plant as well as economic and other influences which may have led to the establishment of production limits. This new analysis would require more information than the steel industry is able to divulge at the present time.

The ideal site is rectangular and integrated strip mills occupy a rectangle up to 2–3 miles in length. Present planning for new strip development envisages

*SOBISCH, H. (1970), *Report of the Conference on the Future of European Ports*, Bruges. College of Europe.

works up to 10 million tons annual production. Special types of steel will probably continue to need much smaller works.

Reservoir areas can be substantially reduced by the provision of cooling towers at a cost (1970) of about £1 million each and site areas may be adjusted on this score.

After adjustment the analysis indicates a need for an average 600 acres per million tons of raw material in the case of strip mills, reducing to 400 acres per million tons for an ideal site for works of this size. With increasing works pro-production this ratio should fall.

Smaller types of steelworks could require 350 acres per million tons, but these examples vary widely in relation to the amount of steelmaking for milling elsewhere.

Finally, the purely steelmaking parts of works seem to require approximately 50 acres per million tons of ore in the larger steelworks but this area does not vary in direct ratio to tonnage and the smallest size works actually occupies about 100 acres for 1 million tons of ore intake.

2. *Aluminium*

Difficulty has been experienced in obtaining British data on alumina plants, but from the limited amount of information available the requirement seems to be 65 acres per 100,000 tons of alumina (raw material) or 50,000 tons of aluminium (production).

The British example is a smelter. In Hamburg, Reynolds Aluminium Company is erecting a combined smelting, rolling, and processing works. The entire leased area is 180 hectares, with a present planned production of 100,000 tons of aluminium per annum* or three and a half times the land requirement for a smelter only.

MOTOR INDUSTRY

Associated with the steel industry will be industries using steel sheet in the manufacturing process. The attraction of strip mills for this class of industry in Britain is blurred at the present time by the practice of selling sheet steel on a delivered price basis. It should be said that this policy does not necessarily have the force of a physical or economic law and that the policy is open to change. The resulting attraction for steel users towards a maritime location needs careful consideration, but some of these, such as the motor-car industry, also have export potential and could be suitably located near the port area.

Published statistics relating area to manufacture are limited but analysis of three plants at Antwerp shows ratios of 638 cars per acre (assembly), 1,000 cars plus 1,670 radiators per acre, and 1,070 tractors per acre respectively. The tractor factory site is exclusive of the tractor storage area, which requires a further 100 acres (*see* Appendix III). Storage for cars and parts occupies 41 acres.

* SOBISCH, H. (1970), op. cit.

LAND AND LABOUR RATIOS

It is not suggested that land requirements for port-related industry can only be assessed by land use analysis based on raw material input or production as outlined above. It is thought, however, that relating area either to raw material input or production provides the most practical and reliable index (*see* p. 115). Certainly, so far as the port is concerned, the expected trade will be an adjusted figure, the amount of adjustment depending on whether raw material input or production figures are used. One set of figures obtained shows in petrochemicals, for example, that a production of 1 million tons also yields approximately 300,000 tons of port export traffic, but even in the same industry this ratio will vary according to circumstances.

A paper by the Director of the Harbour Board of Malmo, delivered at the 22nd International Navigation Congress, Paris, 1969, gave an indication of one Swedish approach to the land assessment problem.* This paper suggests that the most satisfactory way of calculating land requirements might be by relating the land and building areas of the varying industries to the predicted number of employees. It precedes this suggestion by remarking that an estimate must first be made of the advantages and disadvantages of any site, from which a prediction is made of the type of industry likely to be attracted and the likely employment.

This method may be of value in a stable situation, although it is less direct in its approach than the method of relating area to production or raw materials requirements. A redundancy situation at Margam steelworks illustrates one possible defect which will be found frequently unless factors can be identified at the time of analysis. Unfortunately, both industry and the industrial port exist in a changing situation and the pace of change is increasing.

In industry the emphasis is on reduction of labour costs, and there is a strong trend towards automation. This means that as new plants are designed the labour requirement for a given production is likely to reduce. In addition, similar changes have been shown, in port operating, to be related to an increased land requirement. Whilst this is a special feature also linked to a quicker ship turnround, it is possible that similar effects may be found in industry.

In the industrial port the great increase and annual growth in relatively new industries like petrochemicals mean that new types of plant are continuously coming on stream, for which no past labour evidence is available. In these cases an average relationship between area and throughput over a wide range of similar industry seems to offer a better solution. Appendix III shows wide variations in employment levels between different petrochemical and other plants, but average production levels for the industry have already been given which should provide a more reliable guide. Furthermore, a production area

* WALDEMARSON, A. (1969), 'Technical and economic problems connected with the planning, securing and reservation of land for long term port development'. P.I.A.N.C. 22nd International Navigation Congress, Paris.

ratio is more capable of coping with a situation where annual growth in demand can be projected. In short, land requirement for plant seems a better base than a land/employee relationship.

Notwithstanding this argument, the Swedish point of view does provide some useful and interesting comparisons which can be of value in the more detailed work of planning a new area.

Table XXI relates surface area to employment and sales value of products in Swedish kroner in a number of industries. It should be possible to relate these to an analysis like those given in Appendix III once a labour comparison has been made between Swedish and other continental industry.

Table XXI.—SWEDEN: GROUND AND PREMISES AREAS PER EMPLOYEE AND PREMISES SURFACE PER 100,000 SW. CR. SALES VALUE DISTRIBUTED AMONG THE TRADES OF INDUSTRIAL STATISTICS.

	Ground Surface per Employee (sq. m.)	Premises Surface per Employee (sq. m.)	Premises Surface per 100,000 Sw. cr.
Metals and engineering industry	167	31	86
Soil and stone industry	648	79	162
Forest industry	304	52	134
Pulp and paper industry	431	61	118
Food industry	125	42	65
Textile and clothing industry	43	13	39
Leather, hair, and rubber industry	132	23	65
Chemical and chemico-technical industry	379	62	109
All trades	170	32	80

(*Source*: P.I.A.N.C. 22nd International Navigation Congress, Paris, 1969.)

Table XXII classifies the relationship according to the type of region. From this, the limited information available demonstrates a smaller land requirement per employee in the most prosperous regions. This would seem to indicate a greater amount of labour-intensive secondary industry and supports the view that growth attracted by a prime industrial base has an ultimate social significance in relation to employment levels.

Another useful table (*Table XXIII*) produces an analysis of the ratio between site width and depth for sites of varying size, to produce the best site shape for industrial use. None of these examples is for large industrial units where internal road systems make site proportion less important.

Finally, Waldemarson has analysed the percentages of area dedicated to different uses in a Swedish port showing the increasing percentage of area devoted to industrial use (*Table XXIV*).

Table XXII.—Sweden: Area per Employee distributed among Trades and Regions with Different Rates of Extension of the Industrial Statistics

	Steeply Increasing Regions	Normally Increasing Regions	Decreasing Regions	All Regions
Metals and engineering industry	20	31	23	28
Soil and stone industry	—	79	—	79
Forest industry	—	52	126	62
Pulp and paper industry	—	61	—	61
Graphic industry	29	—	—	29
Food industry	—	42	28	39
Textile and clothing industry	11	13	15	13
Leather, hair, and rubber industry	—	23	—	23
Chemical and chemico-technical industry	49	62	—	58
All trades	22	32	35	30

(*Source*: P.I.A.N.C. 22nd International Navigation Congress, Paris, 1969.)

Table XXIII.—Sweden: Site Proportions and Areas

Site Depth	Site Width (m.)		Site Size (sq. m.)	
	Min.	Max.	Min.	Max.
40	20	40	800	1,600
50	33	100	1,650	5,000
60	40	120	2,400	7,200
70	47	140	3,300	9,800
80	53	160	4,250	12,800
90	60	180	5,400	16,200
100	66	200	6,600	20,000
110	74	220	8,500	24,200
120	80	240	9,600	28,800

(*Source*: P.I.A.N.C. 22nd International Navigation Congress, Paris, 1969.)

Table XXIV.—Sweden: Port Land Utilization

Industrial Harbours

	1946		1965	
	Hectares	Percentage	Hectares	Percentage
Harbour industry	125	61	35	77
Streets, parks	45	22	6	13
Port tracks and stockpiles	15	7	2	4
Railway tracks	10	5	1	2
Harbour purposes	10	5	—	4
Land area in total	205	100	46	100

(*Source*: P.I.A.N.C. 22nd International Navigation Congress, Paris, 1969.)

ASSESSMENT FOR SUBSIDIARY AND SERVICE INDUSTRY

The methods and areas described relate to land required for major maritime industries. Other industries will be contenders for sites and similar techniques can be applied to these industries if the economic forecast shows a demand. The area required for service industry can be estimated only from experience. It will depend upon the type of industry in the industrial port and many other factors, especially the availability of land outside the industrial port within reasonable distance.

A great deal of maritime industry is capital intensive and needs complete plant replacement from time to time. The position, in relation to markets, determines the number of journeys and vehicles required for delivery and so the area required for handling, servicing, and garaging. Plant machinery and vehicle parts need overhaul and replacement. The Dutch expect employment in maritime industry to be matched by the numbers employed in service industry.* Since employment density is higher in service industry, the land demands per employee are less. For maritime industry, average employment densities vary from 4 per acre† to 6 or more per acre.‡ Service industry employment may vary from 15 to 50 per acre.

An approximate result can be obtained by using the following formula:—

Area of Service Industry=
$$\frac{\text{Area of Maritime Industry} \times \text{Employment Density Maritime Industry}}{\text{Employment Density Service Industry}}$$

The result must be corrected to take account of any variations in the factors mentioned above.

ASSESSMENT OF LAND REQUIREMENTS FOR MAJOR INDUSTRY

The figures gained from the detailed analysis of a maritime industry forecast will provide a guide to the land needs of the industrial zone, but it would be dangerous to rely on this alone as an upper limit for requirements.

Rotterdam's average annual increase in area of 10 per cent would lead to a doubling of requirements every $7\frac{1}{2}$ years. Antwerp has been shown to have had a large increase in land demands over 10 years and in September, 1969, had 17 industrial applicants for which no land could be made available before further port development took place. Undoubtedly this difficulty may owe something to the port layout and could be different with an improved plan, but plans are frequently dictated by geography, and sometimes by politics.

The lesson is again emphasized by these experiences that suitable land, as a scarce resource, should be husbanded, although land acquisition is cheap in

* *Plan 2000+*, p. 10.
† Antwerp: Discussion with Port Authority.
‡ *Plan 2000+*, p. 11.

relation to civil engineering costs. It is reasonable to plan on an acquisition at least double the amount needed for the initial industrial forecast on the basis that a 10 per cent growth rate may be repeated. This will achieve two aims: first, it will provide sufficient reserve to avoid pressure on the authority to extend purchases whilst in the surge of work connected with development of the project. Secondly, it will enable purchases to be negotiated away from an atmosphere of crisis. This will ensure more reasonable settlements and consequently a lower capital debt for the authority.

Limited purchase ahead of requirements is not necessarily capable of being criticized on financial grounds, provided that the port can carry interest charges until development takes place. The investment in port facilities will be reflected in an increase in value of the authority's holding and the effect can be illustrated from a practical example.

At Barry Docks land was purchased for No. 3 Dock extension in 1902 at what would be regarded as a nominal cost per acre today. In 1950 about 30 acres were sold for £700 per acre. This amount, invested at 7 per cent (average) compound interest, would have accumulated in 20 years to £2,709 per acre. In 1970 similar land was attracting rentals of £850 per acre, or a capital value of £9,000 per acre.

From the analysis, a typical formula for assessing land needs for maritime industry might therefore be:—

$$\left(\frac{a \times 100}{1,000,000} + \frac{b}{2,200} + \frac{c}{1,700} + \frac{d \times 600}{1,000,000} \right) \times \frac{e+f}{f} \text{ in acres}$$

where:—

a = Crude oil requirement (millions of tons)
b = Petrochemical production (in tons)
c = Chemical production (in tons)
d = Iron ore requirement (in millions of tons)
e = Employment density per acre (maritime industry)
f = Employment density per acre (service industry).

If the initial economic forecast is used for the calculation, the result is then increased to provide for expansion in the first decade or so.

ASSESSMENT FOR ASSOCIATED DEVELOPMENT

Land Requirements and Employment Densities

One aspect of maritime industry which is of importance in planning and assessing land requirements is connected with employment densities, and here the Swedish analysis can be of value. Knowledge of these is required for planning homes, schools, services, and other aspects of the local infrastructure. In the industrial area the figures are used in calculating traffic load at peak hours, and the allocation for car parking spaces and off-site services such as garages, shops, and cafes.

A further relevance springs from the interest, particularly of Development Areas, in the attraction of industries with high-density employment. In the main, of course, this must be gained from secondary industry, but the service industry attracted by port-related industry has a high employment density, as do some elements of the port-related industry itself.

Figures of employment density have been given in the land use analysis for Antwerp. Whilst difficulty has been experienced in obtaining a wide range of information elsewhere on land and production ratios, rather more has been available for employment (*Table XXV*).

Table XXV.—MARITIME INDUSTRY—EMPLOYMENT DENSITIES

Industry	Land Let (hectares)	Land Occupied (hectares)	Employees	Employees per Hectare	Net Densities (where known)
Rotterdam, Botlek (1964)					
Refinery	386	169	724	4·3	
Petrochemicals	196	39	747	19·1	
Port storage	83	70	304	4·3	
Ship building and repairing	112	60	2,041	34·0	
Europort forecast, 1980					
Refinery		255		4·0	
Chemicals		444		10·0	

(*Source*: Town Planning Service, Rotterdam.)

Industry	Land Let (hectares)	Land Occupied (hectares)	Employees	Employees per Hectare	Net Densities (where known)
Rotterdam, 1966					
Carbon black		8	135	17·0	
'Zoutchemie'		11	160	14·5	
Titanium oxide (paints)		8	200	25·0	
Automobile assembly		2·7	335	124·0	
Storage of liquids		43·8	161	13·7	
Animal and vegetable oils		11·9	216	18·2	
Molasses, wines, etc.		23·9	130	5·5	

(*Source*: *Fonctions portuaires et Devéloppement urbain dans quelques Grands Ports européens* (November, 1966), Seretes, Paris.)

Industry	Land Let (hectares)	Land Occupied (hectares)	Employees	Employees per Hectare	Net Densities (where known)
Antwerp, 1965/66, gross densities					
Refineries	351		2,310	6·6	
Petrochemicals:					
Petrochims	30·4		310	10	11·7
Amoco	9·82		49	5	11
Cobenam	10·1		288	28·5	
Plysar	30		240	8	24
	80·32	80·32	887	11	
Ship repairs		64	4,000	62·5	
Timber		6·87	341	49	
Cars:					
General Motors	25		3,251	130	
Ford	13·6	38·6	2,000	147	

(*Source*: Study Centre for the Expansion of Antwerp, May, 1966.)

Table XXV.—Maritime Industry—Employment Densities—*continued*

Industry	Land Let (hectares)	Land Occupied (hectares)	Employees	Employees per Hectare	Net Densities (where known)
Ghent (Right bank), Future forecast					
Steel	650		3,800	6	
Cars (Volvo)	28		1,000	36	
Ship repairs	29		220	7·6	
Construction materials	46		2,050	44·5	
Chemicals and petrochemicals	143		325	2·3	
Power station	100		300	3·0	
Ghent (Left bank)					
Chemicals and petrochemicals	218·7		2,250	10	
Wood	6		50	8·3	
Paper	30		720	24	
Metals	110		420	3·8	
Construction materials	10·9		90	8	
Paper and cardboard	5·91	5·91	477	81	81
Cement works	1·4		42	30	

(*Source*: Port of Ghent.)

Genoa					
Steel	150·75		7,713		
Ship repairs	22·5		3,818		
Ironworks	37		4,000		

(*Source*: Port of Genoa.)

Finally, in addition to the employment data, it will be of interest to note statistics for continental residential areas and combined projects associated with port development given in *Table XXVI*.

Table XXVI.—Maritime Industry Residential Neighbourhoods

Settlement without Industry

Pendrecht, Rotterdam

Area	133 HA
Residential area	99 HA
Population	22,000
Dwellings	6,300 (60 per HA)
	24 per cent single units
	68 per cent blocks of flats
	8 per cent double level flats
Shops	150 units in neighbourhoods
	128 units in centre
Schools	27 of all types
Churches	4
Sport	6 playing fields for schools
Parks	1 principal (60 HA) (13·5 sq. m. per person: 47·5 sq. m. per dwelling)

Settlement with Industry

Genoa, Outer Appenine Project Alessandria

Of 120,000 employees (corresponding to total population of 260,000) one-third live in Genoa. New zones have been planned for others.

Projected population for project: 20,000

	HA	per cent
Service centre	150	3
Management centres (including Local Government)	105	2·1
Bus stations, etc.	85	1·7
Commercial centre	40	0·8
Sports	35	0·7
	415	8·30
Open space	655	13·10
Residential zone	70	1·40
Industrial zone	3,860	77·20 (divided into 11 sub-zones)
	5,000	

(*Source: Fonctions portuaires et Devéloppement urbain dans quelques Grands Ports européens* (November, 1966), Seretes, Paris.)

CHAPTER VI

LAND REQUIREMENTS FOR PORT OPERATIONS

GENERAL CONSIDERATIONS

The variety of activities carried on in the operational areas of an industrial or transit port are so wide that it would be impractical to deal with the problem of assessing total requirements on the basis of individual uses, but the technique for dealing with these is of value in considering planning and location of the various activities. The activities include cargo handling and storage of the wide variety of trades handled in a port, requiring provision of handling appliances ranging from quayside cranes and portainers to conveyors, pipelines, and grain elevators; provision of transit sheds, hoppers, tank farms, and open areas or hardstanding; depots for distribution with road and rail transport facilities; service areas for the port operator, shipping (including dry drocks), transport, port users, and shippers; and sites for preliminary and reduce-bulk industrial processes such as grain milling.

The methodology which follows has been evolved from a basis used some years ago to persuade port traders to abandon traditional methods of handling imported commodities in favour of new handling and storage procedures. One considerable obstacle was their fear of the need for very large storage areas and, therefore, excessive land costs. The analysis produced was one of the convincing factors in acceptance of new procedures.

Before dealing with the problem as a whole in Chapter VII, it is of interest to consider the relationship of throughput to area for specific activities.

QUAYSIDES AND TRANSIT AREAS

In considering land requirements for this use, it is essential to bear in mind that a quay is capable of accommodating a series of ships in rapid succession; that the traffic variation can be considerable except for specialized berths, such as container berths and timber berths; that the land requirements will vary according to discharge rates, and stacking and handling characteristics of various types of cargo; and that the working zone required for handling appliances, marshalling, and movement will depend upon the nature of the appliances and the cargo. Standardization of crane track widths within a port, or even in a group of ports, is common, but there are sometimes mixed gauges. Great increases in lifting capacity usually require increased span of track for stability.

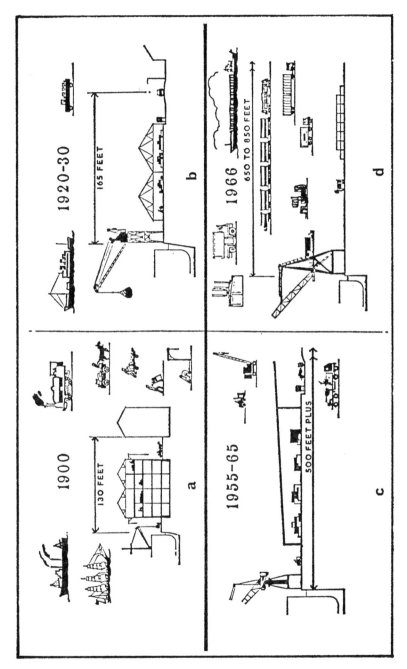

Fig. 27.—Cross-sections of berths in London, 1900–1966. (*Source*: 22nd International Navigation Congress, Paris, 1969.)

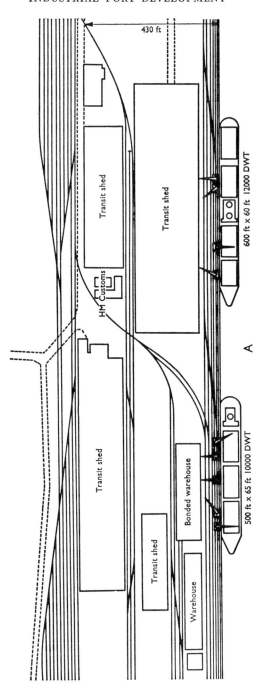

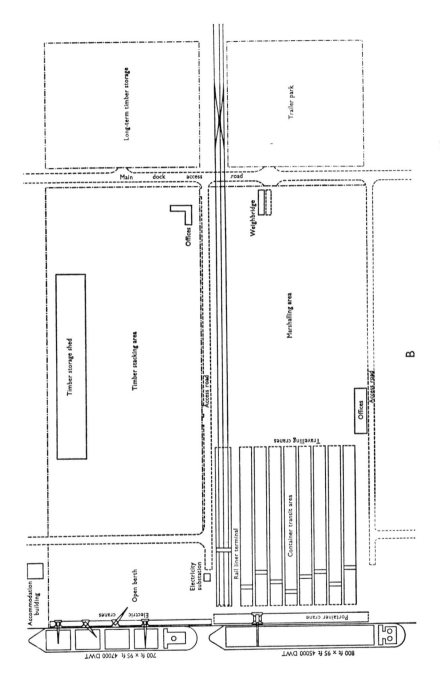

Fig. 28.—A, Modern timber and container berths; B, Typical old-style berth. (*Source:* T. S. Roberts and R. E. Takel, 1970.)

The Minister of Transport has made comments on the annual capacity of a berth for trade.* It is pointed out that a traditional general cargo berth can handle 100,000 tons of traffic a year, whilst a container berth has a potential of up to 1 million tons. These figures were used to illustrate the fact that the greater the cargo capacity of berths the less the number of berths required. Equally, it should be pointed out that the increase in throughput causes escalation in land requirements. With high throughput, more and more cargo must go to ground alongside the quay because of the emphasis on speeding up ship turnround. This means speedy removal of cargo from the vicinity of the ship and cargo storage areas close at hand.

As long ago as 1965 the New York Port Authority was thinking in terms of 17 acres of land a berth for a certain new development in the congested conditions of the banks of the River Hudson. If that reasoning was sound, it is reasonable to consider that, where land is more freely available, this ratio should be increased to between 20 and 30 acres per berth, and 20 acres, fronting a berth of 600 ft., will occupy a depth of about 1,400 ft. Compare this with the depth of the timber terminal at Newport Docks (approximately 2,500 ft.) and practical proof of the deduction is seen, at least in the timber trade. Bremen in 1967 showed a land provision in new port sectors of 110 hectares gross for each 1,500 metres of quay, exclusive of industrial areas, roughly 34 acres for each 600 ft. of quay and requiring an average depth of 2,300 ft.† Antwerp appears to be planning a minimum of about 20 acres per berth and Rotterdam 25–30 acres.

LAND USE ANALYSIS AND DETAILED ASSESSMENT

Working Areas

With the changes in handling techniques there has been a gradual increase in depth of land on berths as shown in *Fig.* 27. This diagram illustrates the increases in depth of quaysides as well as transit stocking areas or transit sheds.

The dimensions of the working area must be calculated for individual berths on the basis of the maximum demand likely. Quayside aprons with good throughput potential are in use in South Wales and vary from widths of 75 ft. to 350 ft., the narrower widths being associated with transit sheds for traffic requiring cover. In other cases the advantage accruing from greater freedom of movement on the quayside must be weighed against the costs involved in a longer movement from quay to storage area.

The wider zones are usually associated with bulkier specialized dry cargoes such as timber, where space is necessary for dumping by shipboard or quayside appliances and for carriage and sorting by forklift or other means. Provision must also be made for access by road or rail vehicles to ship side.

* *Reasons for the Minister's Decision not to authorise the Construction of a New Dock at Portbury, Bristol* (1966). London: H.M.S.O.
† Lutz, R., and Thode, G. (1969), Report of P.I.A.N.C., 22nd International Navigation Congress, Paris, p. 6.

TRANSIT STORAGE AREAS

These probably represent the crucial area of any port, since the ability of the port to operate efficiently and economically depends upon their adequacy for the total quantity of cargo passing over the quays (*Fig.* 28).

Open or shed areas alongside the operational zone involve consideration of the factors outlined earlier, but it is important to observe that increase in ship size will also have a fundamental effect on the acreage required. A change to ships of increased length, also means an increase in beam and depth. If all dimensions, including hold dimensions, are doubled, this means an increase in cubic capacity of a vessel to eight times the former total, although the quay frontage has only doubled. If the height factor for stacking cannot be increased, the areas required will be increased eightfold, with a quadrupling of depth.* Thus the relative ship capacity will be a cube of the dimension ratios. The land area required will be directly related to a cube of the dimension ratios and the depth of the site to a square of the depth and beam ratios.

This rate of increase in ship capacity, in fact, might be an answer to the proposition that with increasing ship size, locks have become obsolete. Locks have been built in the past in competition with ports that needed no lock and they do enable port developments to take advantage of locations of economic importance.

Even if costs of lock construction should increase at a much higher rate with increase in depth, the fact that ship capacity also increases at a rate related to the cube of the dimension ratios could justify investment in lock construction.

The only qualification, as in past dock developments, relates to the physical and economic limit to the number of ship arrivals of the increased sizes; in other words, if the number of vessels remains the same but the cargo capacity has increased at a similar rate to the increase in lock costs, a lock remains an economic proposition. It means, of course, a highly selective approach to lock construction.

Example

Lock A 900 ft. × 100 ft. × 40 ft. = 3,600,000 cu. ft.
Largest ship capacity 30,000 tons.

Lock B 1,450 ft. × 175 ft. × 70 ft. = 17,762,500 cu. ft.
Largest ship capacity, say, 250,000 tons.

i.e., Cubic capacity of lock pit increases 4·934 times; Cargo capacity of largest ship increases 8 times.

(The new lock for 250,000 dwt. vessels at Le Havre is 1,312 ft. × 220 ft.).

Fig. 29 illustrates the effect of ship size on land areas for cargo storage. For the sake of simplicity, the conception of holds and hatches is omitted, but in practice the cubic measurements x y z will be replaced by actual cargo measurements. All storage is assumed to be at one level and to one height. In the

* THORBURN, T. (1970), 'The Function of Maritime Ports: The Changes of Structure foreseeable', Conference on the Future of European Ports, Bruges. College of Europe.

133

examples which follow, the concept of cargo dimensions in cubic feet or metres can be abandoned, provided that the stacking factor (F) is calculated on the same unit of measurement as that chosen for cargo. The stacking factor represents the unit of ground area occupied by the chosen unit of cargo measurement.

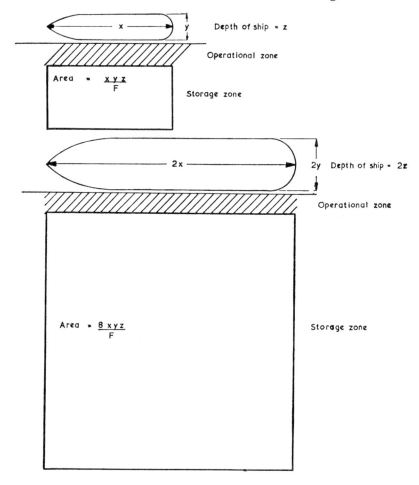

F = Stacking factor or area required per unit measure of cargo

Fig. 29.—Relationship of dimensions of vessel to land requirements.

The theoretical proposition illustrated (*Fig.* 29) assumes that all cargo will be stacked to ground. In practice there will almost certainly be carriage from port area from the outset. The possibility of increase in ship size could also have effects on the layout and equipment of operational zones to achieve greater throughput and greater density of storage and the prospect of changes must be taken into account in estimation of requirements and planning at the outset. Failure to do so will lead to operational and planning problems in the future and in extreme cases would lead to strangulation of the port.

Two further examples of methodology for area assessment should be given.

The first example concerns the calculation of the area required for unloading dry bulk cargo where the interval between dry bulk ships is sufficient to allow removal of all cargo before the next ship arrival. The total area required is that needed for the peak load residue of each ship, normally the area occupied at the moment that discharge ceases. Thus the minimum transit storage area will be the net area for one ship load after deducting the deliveries from ship side and storage area during the unloading process, and can be calculated by formula:—

Example 1

Let R = Average rate of discharge in units of cargo per day.
  r = Average rate of delivery from port in units of cargo per day.
  F = Stacking factor in units of cargo per unit of area.
  t = Unloading period in days.

Then:

$$\text{Area required} = \frac{(R - r)\,t}{F} \quad \text{or, alternatively,}$$

$$\frac{\text{Total cargo in unit measurement minus } tr}{F}$$

The first formula is preferable, being related to the mechanics of the discharging process. It can be adapted to deal with a mixed or part cargo, as well as being capable of revealing the state of affairs at any moment in ship discharge.

In the second example, account is taken of a series of ship arrivals at intervals. It must be assumed that cargo is cleared at the end of each year, otherwise a creeping paralysis would affect the port! The formula is particularly suitable for assessing requirements for seasonal cargoes, such as fruit and timber, where there is an intensive season followed by a pause.

Example 2

Let R = Average rate of discharge in units of cargo per day.
  r = Average rate of delivery in units of cargo per day.
  F = Stacking factor in units of cargo per unit of area.
  t = Average time of discharge per ship in days.
  x = Average interval between ships in days.
  n = Number of ships per annum.

The residue of area occupied at the second ship's arrival will be:—

$$\frac{(R - r)t - xr}{F}$$

and the full storage requirements for the year or season will be calculated:—

$$\text{Area} = \frac{(R - r)\,t + (n - 1)\ [\,(R - r)\,t - xr\,]}{F}$$

The formulae can also be used in a number of other ways; as a test of available area to ascertain the extent to which speed of handling must be increased to prevent congestion; to discover the most suitable commodity for a given area; and to check the percentage use of leased wharves. They deal with the area required for a particular traffic flow and will only give the total transit land area required per berth if the traffic flow is sufficient for full berth utilization. In other cases a separate calculation is necessary for each category of traffic which will pass over a particular berth, and in these cases special attention will have to be paid to site layout in order to preserve maximum accessibility for each of the traffic flows between ship and the respective storage areas.

Neither of the formulae in themselves take account of practical problems which could arise. These would include the need for segregation of different types of cargo from the same vessel/or storing to bills of lading, the inadequacy of the operational zone area for handling new types of cargo, labour difficulties, breakdown of appliances, and shortage of transport. Delayed shipping arrivals and bunching also lead to complications. It should also be stressed that where there is a variation in cargo characteristics, such as the combination of loose timber and packaged timber (which have different stacking factors) in one ship-load, allowance must be made for the bulkier commodity. The formulae must be applied with experience of port operations and some, at least, of these problems could be dealt with by adjustment of the stacking factor. In the worst cases, where vessels are of greatly different sizes and intervals between vessels vary widely, the formula will take its most complicated form with a separate expression for each ship arrival.

For cargo liners loading exports after discharge, an additional area is required for cargo accumulation up to the area for a complete ship load, less the percentage of load which can be delivered direct to ship during the period of ship loading. If ship arrivals are close, this must also include extra space for cargo for subsequent sailings which can be calculated by a similar process. With some part cargoes, such as steel 'bottom' cargo, space is only necessary for a low proportion—say, one-third—of the load, the remainder being loaded direct from vehicle whilst the ship is in port.

Where specialist export berths are provided or volume of exports is high, a formula basis of calculation of area may be required. This is similar to that for imports, being a mathematical expression of the operational process.

Using the following symbols:

Average cargo capacity of vessels = C
Rate of loading per day = R
Rate of delivery to dockside per day = r
No. of days loading = t = $\dfrac{C}{R}$
Stacking factor = F
Average interval in days = i
No. of vessels = n

For a single vessel the area required would be found from the formula:—

$$A = \frac{C - tr}{F}$$

For two vessels the area would be:—

$$A = \frac{C - tr}{F} + \frac{C - (t + i)\, r}{F}$$

The area for a season of similar vessels would be found from the formula:—

$$A = \frac{C - tr}{F} + \frac{(n - 1)\, [C - (t + i)\, r]}{F}$$

Similar adjustments must be made, to meet variations, to those which apply to import areas.

With import areas, maximum land occupation occurs at the end of the importing season, but with exports the maximum area is required at the beginning.

In the case of a year-round service, the area allocated must ensure the most efficient use of land. This means that deliveries to or from dockside must be phased to match exactly the loading or unloading rate for vessels after taking into account the interval between sailings or arrivals.

Stacking Factors: Typical Data

1. *Timber*

The stacking factor and the unit chosen can, of course, vary widely. Loose timber is stacked on the quayside in piles 18 ft. high and one standard without 'stepping' occupies a pile measuring 21 ft. 6 in. × 3 ft. 6 in. × 4 ft., or 4½ standards per pile. With 'stepped' piles and allowance for spacing between piles, a figure of 700 standards per acre is reached.

The stacking factor to give an answer in standards per acre is, therefore, 700. In yards which still do not use mechanical aids, higher figures will be possible, but, for practical purposes, these examples will have relevance only for yards outside ports. When sorted and stacked out, the effect may be to reduce the density. Depending on sizes, this can mean a figure as low as 270 standards per acre. This figure is unimportant for calculation of transit areas and only has relevance for more permanent occupation as a timber storage yard.

Packaged timber can give a higher density of stacking where the packages consist of timber of constant lengths.

On well-consolidated and surfaced sites, the piles of packaged timber are 18 ft. high and vary in dimensions according to origin. On sites up to 10 acres, roads and gangways occupy 15 per cent of site area, between 10 and 15 acres, 20 per cent, and 15–20 acres, 25 per cent.

Stacking densities for packaged timber are as follows:—

Source	Size of Packages	Density per Acre
Canadian timber	4 ft. 0 in. × 2 ft. 3 in. × various lengths between 6 ft. and 40 ft.	1,000 standards
Canadian spruce	2 ft. 6 in.–3 ft. 6 in. wide × 2 ft. 0 in.– 2 ft. 6 in. high × various lengths	800 standards
Swedish timber	3 ft. 6 in. × 2 ft. 6 in. × length	} 800–900 standards
Finnish timber	3 ft. 6 in. × 3 ft. 0 in. × length	
Russian timber	3 ft. 2 in. × 2 ft. 6 in. × assorted lengths. (These packages are 'stepped', i.e., timber is not in standard lengths).	700 standards

Unpackaged timber may be unloaded at the rate of 40 standards per gang per shift, with 2–4 gangs working on a ship at the same time. British Columbia packaged timber, in larger ships enabling 4–7 gangs to work, can be unloaded at the rate of 150–200 standards per gang/shift. This rate is achieved with purpose-built ships and high capacity 10–12 ton deck cranes. With conventional ships' gear the rate falls to 80–120 standards per gang/shift. One standard weighs between 2·5 and 3 tons according to type of timber.

Examples of the open quay method of timber handling show depths of up to 2,000 ft. or even more from quay face and give a guide to the depth of land required between quay and maritime industry.

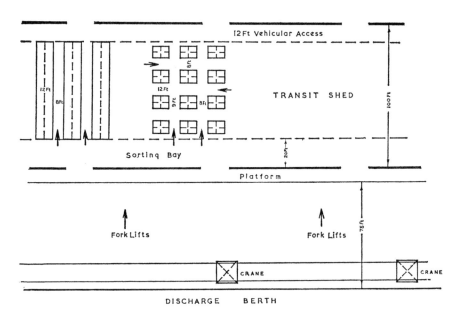

Fig. 30.—Cargo stacking layout for fruit discharge.

138

2. Fruit (Fig. 30)

Citrus fruit is discharged into shed, in a typical port, by quayside cranes up to $7\frac{1}{2}$-ton capacity. The cargo is measured in packages and a typical ship would carry 365,000 packages in up to five holds, each with three decks plus lockers. Discharge would be by 4–5 gangs per vessel, unloading at the rate of 10–12,000 packages per gang/shift. Packages are unloaded on pallets and space in shed is necessary for sorting to marks. Delivery to road transport through shed may be at the rate of 40–45,000 packages per 12-hour day.

Sorted fruit is stacked on pallets measuring 6 ft. × 4 ft. 6 in. and stored two pallets high, each pile containing 56–64 packages. If all packages are of one mark, stacking will be in a continuous row of two pallets' width from sorting area to back of shed, with 8 ft. lanes for forklift trucks. If there are numerous marks, stacking will consist of columns containing four pallet piles with cross-lanes of 8 ft. In both cases, a cross-lane of 12 ft. width is necessary at the back of shed for larger vehicles and appliances. For the purposes of calculation it should be assumed that sorting takes place at 90 per cent of the discharge rate. Fruit which is palletized at its place of origin can be discharged in two-thirds of the time for packaged fruit, whilst containerized fruit has a much faster rate and may not even require covered accommodation.

In a sample site with Northern and Southern Hemisphere fruit imports, an operational zone and transit shed totalling 3·5 acres deals with 87,000 tons of fruit per annum—an average annual rate of 25,000 tons per acre.

3. Containers

The container is an aluminium box on a steel framework, designed to lock with others in stacking and thus reduce movement on voyage. It is also provided with catches for lifting appliances.

The container was introduced on a wide scale between the wars as a means of carrying 'door-to-door' railway freight, providing relative security from pilfering and damage during transit. The serious rise in costs in post-war shipping led to attempts to improve the performance of vessels by reducing time spent in ports. The present-day container was introduced at first in the United States as a means of providing a standard and large unit of packing and loading cargo, particularly general cargo. The effect has been to create a new form of special-ized cargo.

The size of containers is based on a sectional module 8 ft. square, with lengths up to 40 ft. A larger sectional area (8 ft. 6 in. square) was introduced principally for road haulage use but this raises problems for rail carriage, particularly with bridge and tunnel clearances. A 40-ft. long container will require approxi-mately 120 sq. yd. of land including access lanes. Placed to ground, to single height, 1,000 containers will occupy up to 10 hectares or 25 acres.

The layout of a container storage area will resemble that for packaged timber except in scale. The dimensions of access ways will depend on whether straddle carriers are used (as at Antwerp and Southampton), sideloaders (as at Newport), or Goliath cranes (as at Freightliner terminals). In the design of these access ways, regard must be had to problems of visibility for drivers of the carriers and turning requirements. If straddle carriers are used for movement, containers can only be stacked in single rows. With sideloaders, double rows can be used. Sideloaders are at least 12 ft. 6 in. wide and can require lanes up to 40 ft. wide if right-angle turns are necessary. Sideloaders have more operations to perform in the lifting process (e.g., jacking). Straddle carriers require a slightly narrower access way and are inherently stable. Goliath cranes can have a reach up to 100 ft. Although access way dimensions could be as high as sideloaders and straddle carriers, containers handled by Goliath cranes can be stacked in large blocks. The cost of these cranes tends to exclude them from dock operations, particularly where a new trade is being built up. The other mobile lifting appliances can be purchased at considerably lower cost and supplemented by additional appliances as trade grows.

Containers can be loaded aboard ship by means of derricks which are slow, inflexible, and relatively cheap, or by 'portainer' cranes which are speedy, flexible, and expensive (£200,000 or more each). The span of track for a portainer is usually about 50 ft. and the space between stacking area and portainer must be large enough for manoeuvring and turning mobile carriers with or without containers up to 40 ft. in length.

Rotterdam prefers its containers on trailers loaded one high but one restricted site has an area of 18 hectares (45 acres) to serve three berths. The containers there have to be stacked three high.

Portainers at Rotterdam are of 51 tons capacity and, when used with a spreader weighing 8 tons for the largest containers, have a lifting capacity of 43 tons.

Sites in Holland are prepared with soil/cement foundations, 40 cm. thick, and a concrete brick surface. Asphalt is considered unsuitable for the heavy loads. At present rates, unloading 1,000 containers and loading a similar number takes $2\frac{1}{2}$ days, working 24 hours per day, an average of approximately 20 containers per hour. Berths are normally provided with two portainers. If only one is provided, the cargo handling is combined with a roll on/roll off facility.

4. Ores

Iron ore forms a major part of the import trade of many British ports and could form an important trade for a new industrial port. Suggestions are made later on suitable locations for such industries in relation to the quayside. The raw material, however, is relatively expensive to carry (normally by conveyor) and it is possible that the ore stockyard will be located in the area between quay and steelworks. This will reduce handling costs between ship and works, enabling stocking, sorting, mixing, and (if necessary) sintering on a straight-line layout rather than inserting the extra length of handling involved if ore is to be carried direct into works area from ship.

The normal method of handling is by grab unloader to conveyor. Only when works are located in unsatisfactory positions in relation to ports does vehicular handling of imported ore become necessary. The two unloaders at Port Talbot Tidal Harbour each have a capacity of 1,800 tons per hour, or 3,600 tons/hour in total* and the conveyor 6,000 tons/hour.† The Tidal Harbour jetty has been designed to accommodate auxiliary equipment if self-discharging ships should be used in the future.

Imported iron ore comes from many parts of the world. As well as the traditional European sources, such as Sweden and Spain, ore fields have been expanded since 1950 in North Africa, Canada (Labrador), Venezuela, and Australia. One of the effects of this spread to more distant sources has been to emphasize the cost advantages of large ships. From the point of view of land requirements, it is necessary to take into account the different ores and grades of ores to be imported. In discussing the advantages of South Wales for maritime or port-related industry, and the basis of choice for the post-war steelworks, mention has been made of relative properties of iron ore from different sources. Ore varies both in the nature of constituents other than iron (gauge) and in the percentage of its iron content. Because of the importance of producing suitable grade steel for a particular purpose, control is necessary over the blending of ores for blast furnaces in order to provide the exact proportions of other constituents of the blast furnace load, the most important being limestone and coke. Other processes could also require the addition of scrap steel and trace elements like manganese or nickel for particular purposes.

It is, therefore, necessary to segregate ores according to properties. This means that each shipload may have to be kept separate and each stockpile area must be of sufficient size to accommodate at least a full shipload from that particular source. At Port Talbot each stockpile has been made 50 per cent larger than the capacity of the largest ship used‡ in order to accommodate a subsequent shipload of similar ore before the first arrival has been fully used up in the blending.

Iron ore is a very heavy material and stocking height depends on ground conditions and load-bearing capacity. It is said that large tonnages of iron ore were lost at Llanwern Steelworks by settlement, due to ground conditions. At Port Talbot ground conditions would have permitted stocking to a height of 12–15 ft. without consolidation, but after vibroflotation treatment of the (mainly sand) surface soils, stocking to 30 ft. is possible. Assuming the same angle of repose for each stockpile, it follows that a doubling in height means a doubling in base and, therefore, a quadrupling of the quantity per unit of lineal measure in any stockpile, but only a doubling of capacity per unit of square surface

* Dale, R. N., and Mason, D. F. (1970), 'Ore Handling Equipment at Port Talbot Tidal Harbour', Proceedings of the Institution of Civil Engineers, Paper 7288, para. 1.
† Ibid., para. 30.
‡ Ibid., para. 39.

measure (*see Fig.* 31). The calculation of area will, therefore, depend upon economic appraisal of the merits of ground consolidation, which will also involve the cost of increasing the 'reach' of boom stackers.

SECTIONAL AREA OF ORE PILES

(a) *Low height stocking:*   (b) *High stocking:*

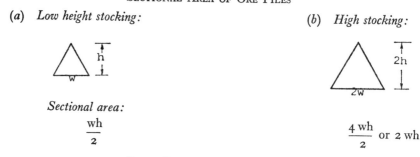

Sectional area:

$$\frac{wh}{2}$$

$$\frac{4\,wh}{2} \text{ or } 2\,wh$$

CUBIC CAPACITY OF ORE PILES

Volume of stocks of equal length:

(c)   (d)

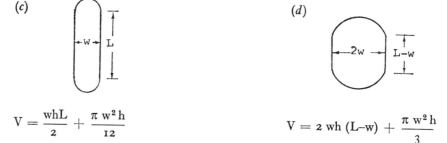

$$V = \frac{whL}{2} + \frac{\pi\,w^2\,h}{12}$$

$$V = 2\,wh\,(L{-}w) + \frac{\pi\,w^2\,h}{3}$$

Fig. 31.—Ridge stockpiling of iron ore.

Increased density of stocking can be achieved by 'flat top' as opposed to ridged piles (*see Fig.* 32).

This again doubles the capacity, per unit of area, of individual stockpiles for the area occupied by full height stocking. In the case of 30 ft. or any other stocking (see example (b) *Fig.* 31) the width of pile is increased by the proportion stocked to the full height ('y'). (*see Fig.* 32).

If the total length of pile is 'L', the length of pile of standard cross-section is L—(2w+y).

The volume of the length of pile of standard cross-section will then be:—

$$h\,\frac{(2w + 2y)}{2}\,(L - (2w + y))$$

$$= h\,(w + y)\,(L - 2w - y)$$

The volume of the frustum will be obtained by the formula:—

$$V = \frac{h}{3} (A + \sqrt{AB} + B)$$

where A and B are the areas of the horizontal parallel faces. The total volume of pile will simply be sectional area by length plus frustum.

In a theoretically endless stockpile the overall increase in density will depend on the width of stocking to full height. If this width (y) is equal to the width at the base of a ridged stockpile of the same height, then the pile will occupy twice the area and hold three times the volume. The extent to which the intensity of land utilization should be increased will depend on the cost effect of machinery such as boom stackers for access to wider piles, in relation to land availability.

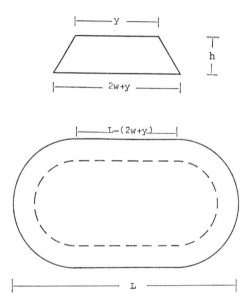

Fig. 32.—Flat top stockpiling of iron ore.

The tonnage capacity of the stock will depend on the weight of the particular ore sample, but since ore ships have a known volumetric capacity, the volume of a cargo should be easily ascertained. In calculating average stockpile areas, it is, of course, easier to work from volumes rather than weights.

From analysis of the ore stockyard plan proposed for the Port Talbot Tidal Harbour (*Fig.* 33), it would appear that the average capacity with a 30 ft. stocking height and access for conveyors and boom stackers will be 39,000 tons per acre.*

* DALE, R. N., and MASON, D. F. (1970), *Ibid.*, Fig. 5.

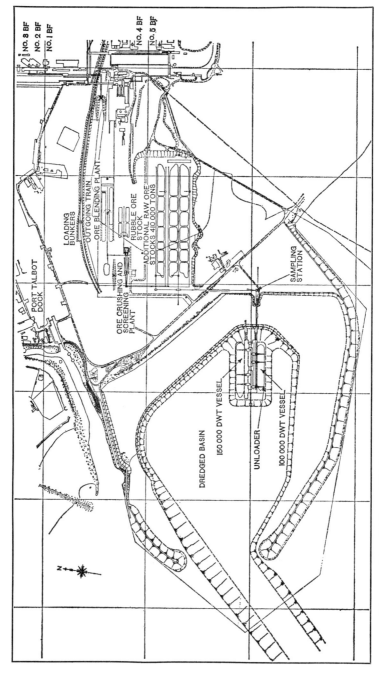

Fig. 33.—Port Talbot: Tidal harbour and ore handling. (*Source:* R. N. Dale and D. F. Mason, 1970.)

The annual throughput of the stockyard should be approximately 3½–4 million tons for a 21-acre site or 166,000–190,000 tons per acre. The area could be increased by 10·5 acres to handle additional ore, perhaps to a total of 7 million tons, giving an average throughput of 220,000 tons per acre. This increase would be achieved by a much faster rate of turnover on the additional area, which would be used as a transit site.

These areas are exclusive of land for blending, crushing, screening, and sintering.

It should be noted that the areas and throughputs given are for part only of the total area shown in *Fig.* 33.

The ore stockyard represents only part of the handling before ore enters the blast furnaces, and the Port Talbot site also includes provision for further expansion. It may be that the area has been increased because of the possibility of steelworks developments up to 10 million tons capacity. The total area for stockyard, reserve, handling, train loading, and ore preparation shown on the illustration is 160 acres and it is capable of expansion in a south-east direction by a further 100 acres, if necessary. Should this additional area not be wanted for steelworks development, it could be used for other dock traffic.

INTERNAL COMMUNICATIONS

Allied to the operational and cargo storage zones are the communication links. These may be likened to arteries which divide and subdivide and finally become the capillaries. The complex starts as capillaries at quays and storage areas, and combine and recombine to become motorways and trunk railways. The capillaries will have been taken into account in the operational zone and the storage area, in the form of access ways to quayside and cargo stacks, and are allowed for in the stacking factor for storage areas.

Behind this area of high activity should come the main port communications, and for land movements these will not be confined to main road and rail links. They will include lorry parks or rail sidings for waiting commercial vehicles, car parks for employees, pipeline routes for gas or liquid products, and conveyor belts for ores. However trivial their individual land demands may seem, the combined effect is considerable.

If an existing operational zone plus transit shed is 500 ft. deep, the addition of a parallel strip of 50 ft. for road and footpaths increases the area by 10 per cent; a 25 ft. reservation for pipelines by 5 per cent, and each railway track at an average of about 10 ft., including spacing on one side, by 2 per cent. Thus a normal roadway plus pipeline strip plus only two rail tracks would require a reservation 100 ft. wide or an increase of 20 per cent on operational area. If a 50 ft. wide strip is added between quay and rear access at each end of a 600 ft. shed, the communication allowance is increased by a further 16 per cent, making a total of 36 per cent (*Fig.* 34). It should be stressed that this is an extreme example with intensive use of land. With slower off-site delivery and deeper sites, the

145

percentage should fall. The percentages exclude circulation space on quay and within the storage area.

Lorry parks require a minimum of 450 sq. ft. (including turning space) per vehicle, whilst sidings for 1,000 wagons of short wheelbase occupy 6½ acres. These allowances must be adjusted upwards to allow for increased vehicle size, awkward shaped sites, or small dispersed locations.

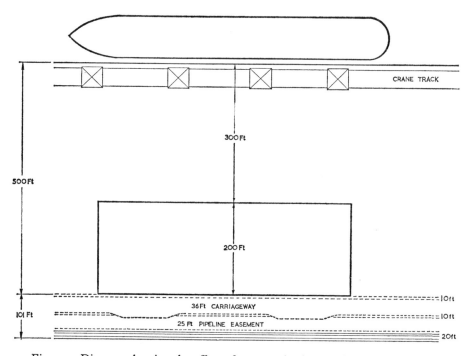

Fig. 34.—Diagram showing the effect of communications on land requirements.

Car parking for employees should be arranged within industrial sites, but if other parking is required, it should be on a basis of 200 sq. ft. per car to allow for circulation and access to vehicle.

Sizes of car parks are directly related to numbers of employees and those having business in the port with ships, port authorities, and traders. In view of the increasing use of vehicles, it is recommended that areas calculated for present use should be increased by at least 50 per cent to allow for future increase in demand. As a rough guide, at least 1½ car spaces are provided for each 1,000 sq. ft. of factory plus office up to 10,000 sq. ft. gross covered area, and 1 space per 1,000 sq. ft. thereafter. As an alternative, car parks could be provided at the perimeter of the port with an internal transport service, if the numbers of users justify the running costs.

The size of lorry parks is dictated by the maximum estimated demand for cargo handling and the use requiring the heaviest flow of road vehicles. The calculation is based on the number of vehicles required to be in position awaiting call to ship side or transit shed at any one time. A number of small regularly spaced vehicle parks is preferred to one single park for reasons of traffic flow and cargo handling economy.

A pipeline and cable reservation of 25 ft. width has been mentioned in the example (p. 145), but in fact, in a high capacity port, the need is much greater. In Rotterdam a reservation of 25 m. (82 ft.) was made at Botlek and has proved to be too narrow. In Europort the pipeline strip is 50 m. wide. This provision, away from the quay (since some refineries are placed on the water's edge there), is made to allow for the exchange of products between different plants as well as transfer between ship and industry. Rotterdam's preference is now for 'above ground' pipelines.

PORTSIDE INDUSTRY*

Industry which may be allowed to establish itself within the operating areas of the port, is necessarily limited. In the industrial port an industrial zone of considerable size must be created at the operational limit and all major industry must be located there. The only exceptions are those industries which need to employ processes for reducing bulk at the earliest possible stage between ship and manufacture and these processes are normally carried out in the operational zone.

This type of industry occupies relatively small areas for uses such as grain milling for flour, animal foodstuffs, or special cereal. Maize for breakfast food is imported from South America and a quayside mill to handle 150,000 tons of maize per year would occupy a site of 5 acres, giving a throughput ratio of 30,000 tons per acre. Flour milling from wheat in two typical plants requires sites of 3·5 acres for 60,000 tons of import and 3·12 acres for 65,000 tons, with averages of 17,150 and 20,800 tons per acre respectively. In one plant some home grain is also used and this probably increases the ratio to 30,000 tons per acre.

Other specified equipment can be installed for particular imports where the manufacture takes place elsewhere. Bones for gelatin or glue can be provided with hopper storage and, although sites are small, the average throughput is as high as 120,000 tons per acre, including road vehicle loading areas. Oil storage tank farms for distribution often include provision for blending and an overall average of about 20,000 tons an acre is shown by analysis, although individual sites may exceed this by 25–50 per cent. The lower the provision made for such blending operations, the higher is the tonnage ratio.

PORT SERVICE INDUSTRY

Land should also be allocated for those industries providing services to port users. These include ship repairers, scalers and painters, specialists in electrical,

* See Tables XXVII–XXIX.

mechanical, and refrigerating plant; tug owners, export packers, and transport companies. The land requirements for these uses vary so widely between ports that general guidelines are not practicable. The needs will depend directly on the nature of port traffic.

Commercial sites should also be provided in the form of offices for shipping agents and warehouses for highly specialized traffic including cold stores. These again vary according to the nature of trade.

In the South Wales ports land for port service industry and associated commercial uses forms approximately 2 per cent of the area of land let.

The port operator will require areas for the business of administering the port, with offices, workshops, engineering yards, road and rail services areas, dredging plant, and equipment. Areas will vary according to the proportion of work retained by the Authority. In operational zones analysed, these areas occupy approximately 0·6 per cent of total area (including water area).

WATER AREAS AND SEA APPROACHES

The methods so far discussed for assessment of areas have all been for land activities.

Water area is excluded from these calculations and is dependent on civil engineering and shipping requirements. The factors to be considered are the physical ones of site characteristics, ship size, and volume of traffic.

APPROACH CHANNELS AND TURNING AREAS

The depth and width of approach channels will be based on the dimensions of the largest ship to require access and involve considerations of weather exposure, angles of channel, currents, etc. If vessels are to pass in this channel the width should be increased to allow for a safe distance between vessels.

Turning space for vessels must be provided and, if there is a considerable tidal range, this should be inside the impounded area. The size of turning space will depend, again, on weather and tidal conditions, and the diameter may be up to twice the length of the longest ship.

IMPOUNDED DOCKS

The dimensions of dock water area to be provided will depend on the number of berths, the size of vessels, and the expected volume of traffic. As well as any necessary turning space, the dock should provide berths for wet repair facilities, buoy moorings for shipping awaiting berths or tides, and sufficient space for in-dock manoeuvres other than turning.

If the port approaches are subject to bad weather then, ideally, the port should cater for bunching by allowing for sheltered anchorage either inside or outside the dock.

No general rule can be propounded for assessment of water areas, and acquisition levels for this aspect must be assessed on an *ad hoc* basis, particularly from an engineering, berth, and ship control viewpoint.

CHAPTER VII

GENERAL ANALYSIS OF THE OPERATIONAL ZONE

GENERAL CONSIDERATIONS

Apart from shipping trends and the tendency to develop major port-related industry, the change in cargo handling techniques and, indeed, in the principal functions of ports, has caused otherwise useable docks to become obsolescent and even obsolete. London has been forced to develop Tilbury and close Surrey Docks; Mersey has its Seaforth development; Hull is closing its Town Docks whilst King George Dock, Saltend, and Immingham are all undergoing development. Bristol has put up a tremendous battle to secure either its Portbury or West Dock development and will close City Docks.

All of these new proposals have been affected by land starvation in the existing ports, especially in their operational zones. It could well be that some of these new developments will in turn suffer the same defects. This possibility is discussed in the planning commentary, but it should not be dismissed as a criticism, since there are features inherent in design or location in some which point towards future difficulties in trade and industrial expansion.

Enough has been said of the basis of calculation for cargo handling areas and other parts of the operational zone to show the difficulty of a detailed approach as a method of calculating the total operational requirement for an industrial port. The economic forecast can give only broad guidance on the tonnage of traffic to be handled. Whilst forecasts for imports of crude oil, ore, and other raw materials might be reasonably specific, it would be impossible to forecast all traffics by commodity.

The examples given in Chapter VI enable calculations to be made of the capacity of a given site or, alternatively, the size of site required for a given throughput. In practice, however, throughput may well be below full capacity, particularly in the opening stages of a new industrial port. Specific examples from analysis of existing developments in ports sometimes give a variation in tonnage/area ratios for the same type of cargo. It is wise to approach the overall problem with expansion in mind and as expansion may be needed in an area next to the quays after port-related industry has dictated the rear boundary of the cargo handling zone, it is of vital importance to set this boundary in the best position at the outset.

The practical approach is to consider the problem from the point of view of a general analysis of throughput of ports, related to the area devoted to the operational zones. This method of calculation would include those areas used

*Table XXVII.—*Site Area/Tonnage Analysis

Commodity	Type of Use	Site Category *	Annual Throughput (tons/acre)
Timber	Transit	B	5,000
Timber	Transit	D	4,500
Timber	Transit and storage	D	3,900
Timber	Transit and storage	D	15,000 (1970)
Lineboard, plywood, and packaged timber	Transit and storage	B	24,000 †
Timber	Sawmill and processing	B	2,000
	Sawmill and processing	B	3,000
	Sawmill and processing	C	1,500
Grain	Silos and milling	B	17,600
	Silos and milling	B	20,000
Potatoes	Warehousing	A	4,500
	Warehousing	A	9,000
Fruit	Transit warehouse	B	25,000
	Unloading, transit, and processing	C	29,000
Iron ore	Unloading and conveyor	C	190,000
	Unloading and conveyor	C	550,000
	Storage (actual capacity)	D	39,000
	Storage (annual throughput)	D	140,000
Oil and liquids	Agency storage	B	12,900
	Agency storage	D	2,600
	Storage and distribution	D	21,400
	Storage and distribution	C	20,600
	Storage and distribution	D	25,000
	Storage and distribution	D	18,200
	Loading, unloading, pumping, and buffer storage (refined exports)	D	127,000 ‡
Petrochemicals	Storage and export	D	25,000
Sand and gravel	Import wharf and storage	B	70,000
	Import wharf and storage	B	127,000
	Import wharf and storage	A	330,000 §
	Import wharf and storage	B	120,000
Containers		A	100,000
Crushed bones	Hopper storage	A	123,500
Latex	Storage	A	6,400

Total area: 255 acres. Average site area 8 acres

Total tonnage: 11,990,000.

Average: 47,000 tons/acre.

* Site category: A, Under 1 acre; B, 1–5 acres; C, 5–10 acres; D, Over 10 acres.

† High throughput based on established market and guaranteed customers.

‡ In association with refinery.

§ Small congested site with vehicle overflow onto dock roads.

for portside industry, where similar problems of variety militate against a detailed approach.

SPECIALIZED BERTH ANALYSIS

Table XXVII shows actual examples of developments relating net area and annual trade. Names of ports and firms have been omitted to preserve confidences. The table is based on 1969 figures except in one case.

The table shows consistencies between like uses in many cases, with occasional wide variations. These point out the need for a more intimate knowledge of the economic background in particular examples. A low throughput often indicates a development which is in temporary trade difficulties, whilst a high one could indicate excessive exploitation of a site, perhaps due to lack of planning for trade expansion. The whole of the 1969 timber figures are low and are due to the lack of attraction of a British market for British Columbian timber following devaluation of sterling in 1967. This was followed by attractive trading conditions in Australia and Japan. The picture is changing once more and timber throughput should reach much higher figures. One 1970 result is shown to illustrate a general wharf, timber and timber products, level of 15,000 tons per acre. The annual throughput for this berth represented a turnover of six times the site capacity. There is, therefore, a possibility of even higher figures.

The value of figures showing variations is that they also demonstrate the variable nature of trade due, not only to world conditions, but also to the trading abilities of individual firms. Development agreements such as leases cannot legislate for efficiency in traders and developers. They can only encourage efficiency by making a commercial bargain which provides the spur to efficiency and full use. For these reasons, it is always wise to calculate overall requirements on the basis of average figures rather than on peak figures in order to provide the spare capacity which boom conditions will utilize. If this factor is taken into account at the outset, then the land costs will be low in relation to the advantage gained.

The practice is necessary for port management reasons. Berth construction is expensive. If land allocation is made and any development costed on peak throughput figures, it will mean that every year throughput is below peak level the berth is not viable. A higher land allocation increases the port's prospects, though it may not all be used for the purposes on which the calculation was originally based. The surplus area can be utilized for developing other port-related uses and thus provide operator's insurance in lean years.

This situation is well illustrated by the difference between timber import figures in 1969 and 1970. Timber wharves were, in fact, sometimes used for other purposes such as car export and assembly of export cargo.

Tables XXVIII and *XXIX* show a further analysis of port-related development proposals, with related tonnages, not all of which became established.

The average figure for individual developments is reduced, as a rule, as the manufacturing content in the examples analysed increases. The later examples have a lower average site area but a higher area/tonnage ratio.

Tables XXVII–XXIX show the marked difference between the averages for operational/storage zones and port-related or portside industrial developments in terms of trade/land ratio. Taken together, they are valuable in assessment of specific requirements.

Table XXVIII.—AREA/TONNAGE ANALYSIS
PROPOSALS 1954–1964

Industry	Commodity	Site Category	Tonnages/Acre Throughput
Abrasives	Aluminium oxide	D	1,200
Car export	Vehicles	D	10,000
Import depot	Aluminium	A	60,000
Import depot	Black sand and sulphur	D	650
Engineering	Machine assembly	D	60
Sawmilling	Timber	C	8,000
Sweet manufacture (depot)	Gum and other raw materials	B	600
Fertilizers	Raw materials	D	4,000
Paper manufacture	Pulp	D	6,000
Total			326 acres 1,470,000 tons

Average 36 acres per site and =4,500 tons per acre

Table XXIX.—AREA/TONNAGE ANALYSIS
PROPOSALS 1964–1970

Industry	Commodity	Site Category	Tonnages/Acre Throughput
Zinc smelter	Lead/zinc/ore	D	7,000
Breakfast foods	Cereals	B	30,000
		(Dockside mills)	
		D	4,300
		(Processing mill)	
Aluminium smelter	Bauxite	D	3,000
Paper manufacture	Woodpulp and paper exports	D	2,000
Chemicals	Liquid feedstock	D	1,000
Copper smelter	Copper concentrate	D	1,000
Sugar refining	Raw sugar (transit)	B	160,000
Total			270 acres 1,518,000 tons

Average 33·75 acres per site and = 6,000 tons per acre.

COMPARISON WITH EXISTING MODERN PORTS

Assessment of land requirements for a future port operational area should not be carried out by a series of individual calculations. Apart from the uncertainty on details following a general economic analysis, the complexity, and possible variations in actual trade make a detailed formula approach impractical. The matter, therefore, may be considered from a different point of view, comprising:—

1. Comparison with total operational area of existing modern ports.
2. The physical requirements of port layout.
3. Probable future changes in port operation.

THE CHOICE OF PORT FOR COMPARISON

It is necessary to analyse a port system which represents modern industrial practice as fully as possible. This would have the advantage of avoiding the distortions which would be created by using a continental analysis, since European ports, with their large central land mass, serve not only the immediate hinterland, but population remote from the coast on a scale not found in Britain.

The suitability of South Wales for comparison purposes springs from the virtual total disappearance of the traditional trade—coal—and a large-scale commercial redevelopment which has replaced that trade by a better balanced and more modern and varied throughput, including raw materials in substantial tonnages. Because of land availability this throughput is largely handled by methods appropriate to modern port operation, including the use of deep transit areas on quays. The use of this example is, of course, based on the hypothesis that increasing ship size will be catered for as trade expands.

Alternative examples might be found if the trade balance indicated by a particular economic forecast shows the South Wales analysis to be unsuitable.

Similar results might be obtained from other former coal exporting ports. The original need for rail networks, usually at right angles to the quay, is the factor that makes these ports peculiarly suitable for conversion of operational zones to modern methods.

ANALYSIS OF EXISTING OPERATIONAL ZONES

A land use analysis of the South Wales ports in 1969 is given in *Table XXX*.

Excluding the new Tidal Harbour at Port Talbot, the operational and related use land of South Wales totalled 1,253 acres. In 1969 the total inwards trade was 10,422,383 tons and outwards trade 7,928,718 tons; in all 19,161,295 tons. In that year a strike at Abbey Steelworks, Port Talbot, lost an importation of about 1,150,000 tons of iron ore compared with the previous year.

Adjustment for this major item produces a figure of 20,310,000 tons. It will be noted that exports are approximately 75 per cent of imports and the high ratio of imports of iron ore (in national terms) is balanced by the low ratio of crude oil imports. The 1970 trade total was 20,534,388 tons.

The South Wales ratio of tonnage to land area for operational and related uses (categories 1–5 in *Table XIX*) is, therefore, 16,200 tons per acre based on corrected 1969 figures.

Table XXX.—South Wales Ports—Land Use Analysis

Port	Water River and Tidal	Impounded	Total Water	Land Operational	Related Uses	Non-related and Vacant	Total Land	Grand Total
Swansea	95	202	297	172	76	164	412	709
Port Talbot	32	128	160	40	41	203	284	444
Tidal Harbour	434		434	58	—	—	58	492 *
Barry	93	185	278	133	297	389	819	1,097
Cardiff	325	146	471	142	169	397	708	1,179 †
Penarth Harbour	80		80	2	4	44	50	130
Newport	96	148	244	111	66	362	539	783
	1,155	809	1,964	658	653	1,559	2,870	4,834

* Port Talbot Tidal Harbour did not become operational until March, 1970. These areas have, therefore, been omitted from the calculations.

† The closure of East Dock, Cardiff, means that the land/water ratio will change when reclamation is undertaken.

CORRECTION FOR BERTH UTILIZATION

In further consideration of this figure, evidence has been given of the extent of berth utilization in South Wales in 1966.*

	per cent
Newport	45
Cardiff	29
Barry	24
Port Talbot	50
Swansea	42
	or 38 on broad average.

It is, of course, a virtual impossibility to secure complete berth usage for reasons of cargo organization, ship delays, etc. It is suggested that a 25 per cent 'slack' would mean a heavily used port. Le Havre envisaged a 67 per cent berth utilization in 1970 and, on this basis, planned provision of six extra berths to accept the forecast increases in trade.† The six extra berths will bring down utilization to 57 per cent initially. On the assumption of 75 per cent berth utilization, each of the South Wales ports would still be able to offer surplus capacity as follows:—

	per cent
Newport	30
Cardiff	46
Barry	51
Port Talbot	25
Swansea	33
	or 37 on broad average.

In 1966 total trade was approximately 18,800,000 tons and the adjusted 1969 figure represents an increase of 1·5 million tons and, therefore, an increase in berth utilization of approximately 8 per cent, or use of 46 per cent capacity on broad average. The reduced figure of usable surplus capacity averaged over five ports to give 75 per cent utilization is, therefore, 29 per cent. In general terms this should mean that the ports could handle tonnage calculated by the formula:—

$$\frac{20\cdot31}{46} \times 75 = 33\cdot1 \text{ million tons}$$

but congestion and 'bunching' would affect efficiency.

The area used would not increase in the same proportion since the areas given in the first land column under 'operational land' (*Table XXX*) represent all quaysides including those underutilized. It is likely, however, that related uses

* Petition against the Bristol Corporation Bill. Evidence taken before Select Committee of the House of Lords, May, 1968.
† Lecture on French ports by M. Baudelaire, Cardiff, 1969.

will increase and, on the assumption that the same percentage applies, the related use area of 653 acres should increase to 1,065 acres, giving a new total of 1,665 acres. The average tonnage per acre would then almost be 20,000 tons per acre.

COMPARISON WITH ROTTERDAM

The throughput analysis for oil refining industry has already shown an Antwerp concentration twice that of Milford. Similarly, the analysis of general operational throughput per acre at Rotterdam (*Table XXXI*) shows much higher figures than 20,000 tons per acre but these should be compared with the examples analysed in *Table XXVII*.

Table XXXI.—ROTTERDAM: VOLUME OF TRADE AND ASSOCIATED UNIT LAND AREAS STORAGE AND TRANSIT, 1960–80

	1960		1980	
	Volume of Trade (tons × 10^6)	Annual Tonnage per acre	Volume of Trade (tons × 10^6)	Annual Tonnage per acre
Piece and bagged goods	19·4	44,500	45·7	50,600–52,750
Handled by grab	31·6	900,000	40·4	
Pneumatically handled	6·0	600,000	9·8	570,000
Petroleum and products	12·2	varies	54·8	240,000
Timber	1·7	12,000	1·6	12,000
Totals	70·9	—	152·3	—

(*Source*: *Zeehavennota Het Zeehavenbeleid van der Rijksoverheid S'Gravenhage*, Staatuitgeverij, 1966.)

Any increase at Rotterdam is due to an increase in average ship size, to the need to make more intensive use of land, and to other factors, such as the nature of the hinterland:—

1. The figures include crude oil, which in South Wales is mainly imported through Milford Haven, and much of this is afterwards pumped overland for considerable distances, e.g., to Amsterdam, Antwerp, Duisberg, and Frankfurt.
2. There is a considerable amount of overside discharge to barge for Rhine traffic where no land areas are involved. For example, grain is discharged simultaneously to silo and to 5,000-ton barges.
3. There is also a considerable degree of re-export by inland waterways and, as a result, many large inland industries are served from transit storage sites at Rotterdam (e.g., ores for the Ruhr).

In South Wales, with a theoretical 100 per cent berth utilization, the land area in operational and associated use should increase to 2,020 acres (600+1,420) excluding water and the throughput to 44·1 million tons or almost 22,000 tons per acre.

Table XXXII gives the comparative figures. It will be noted from this that any increase in average throughput is accompanied by a much larger percentage increase in area for related uses.

Table XXXII.—SOUTH WALES: VOLUME OF TRADE AND AREA/TONNAGE ANALYSIS, 1969

Berth Utilization (broad average) per cent	Projected Annual Trade (million tons)	Land (acres)		Throughput (tons/acre)
		Operational	Related Uses	
46	20·31	600	653	16,200
75	33·1	600	1,065	19,900
100	44·1	600	1,420	21,800

ADJUSTMENTS OF ANALYSIS

EFFECT OF MAJOR BULK TRADES

By excluding major bulk trades, it is possible to adjust the result of the general analysis to yield average figures which will be of value in assessing operational needs in transit ports. Since the container trade of South Wales is relatively small, the results will not be applicable to container berths, where traffic densities can be as high as with some major bulk trades.

If iron ore and refinery trade is excluded from the South Wales analysis the 1969 figures become:—

Inwards   4·204 million tons
Outwards   4·186 million tons

8·390 million tons

The existing port areas dedicated exclusively in 1969 to ore and refinery oil handling amount to 46·64 acres. Ore stockyards and crude oil storage were generally outside port areas.

The revised 1969 throughput, excluding ore and oil, is, therefore, 8·39 million tons over 1,206 acres or 6,950 tons per acre. The iron ore and oil berths have a high utilization factor. Other berths will have a lower percentage use with capacity for increasing occupation. Using the same principle of amending related use areas, the tonnage could double to become 16·78 million tons over 1,859 acres or 9,000 tons per acre for 75 per cent berth utilization in trades other than oil and ore.

Appendix II illustrates the balance of trade on which all these calculations are based. The average of 20,000 tons per acre can be seen to agree substantially with a number of specific averages in *Tables XXVII–XXIX*, notably those for grain, oil transit storage, and petrochemicals. In considering estimation of operational areas for a new industrial port, regard should be had to the way in which the economic forecast shows an imbalance in relation to the trade of the port analysed. Any increase in petroleum products (and the addition of crude oil), ore, or raw materials imports will alter the basis from which this average has been reached. Similarly, certain trades fall well below the average throughput. The adjusted 1969 tonnage for iron ore forms approximately 34 per cent of Welsh trade, and refinery trade inwards and outwards 23 per cent. It is a simple matter to revise calculations in direct proportion to the change in these or similar large throughput items using the averages relating to the particular commodity.

In estimating requirements for operational and portside uses, particular regard must be had to the proportion of the forecast represented by the lower tonnage trades, i.e., excluding oil and ore. The analyses in *Tables XXVII–XXIX* exclude land for communications, services, port operational areas, and so on, and the effect of these additional requirements can be seen by comparing the revised 1969 throughput, excluding ore and oil, of 6,950 tons per acre overall (p. 157) and the general average of 16,200 tons per acre, with the figures in *Table XXVII* for the buoyant trades. This comparison shows that analysis of the total area reduces the average throughput per acre.

The lower tonnage trades, if read in conjunction with an average throughput of 80–120,000 tons per annum per berth illustrate a considerable land requirement. *

Whilst recognizing the specialized nature of most South Wales berths, a modest throughput of 120,000 tons per berth at 6,950 tons (p. 157) would require a minimum average land allocation of over 17 acres per berth or 14·4 acres at 9,000 tons/acre. Ore and crude oil storage areas would be larger. Seen in conjunction with other standards of 17 acres per berth or more, the suggested current minimum need for 20 acres per berth for operational use is seen to be reasonable. In fact, with new developments, the individual requirement may be much higher because berth throughput is increasing with improved appliances and methods, and increasing ship size also affects the land requirement.

ADJUSTMENTS FOR AVERAGE SHIP SIZE AND AREA DISTORTIONS

A further major qualification is necessary. Adjustments have been made on the basis of berth utilization, but it should be emphasized that the whole of the preceding analysis has been carried out on the basis of existing trade. Not all vessels calling at the ports analysed would be of the latest type or optimum size; not all quayside operations are carried out by the latest methods. In order to use such an analysis to project ultimate land requirements of a future operational zone, it is essential that the basic assumption should include optimum ship size and maximum berth efficiency throughput.

* Portbury—Reasons for the Minister's Decision not to authorise the Construction of a New Dock at Portbury, Bristol (1966). London: H.M.S.O.

The total length of quays in South Wales is 101,161 ft. (equal to 165 berths of 600 ft. length). In 1969 ship arrivals totalled 11,621, with net registered tonnage of 10,748,116 tons or 925 tons per vessel on average. In 1970 the average tons per vessel was 1,133. This increase is due, in part, to the opening of Port Talbot Tidal Harbour, but it is significant that in 1970, 2,200 fewer ships carried 1·4 million tons more trade.

Net registered tonnage is not strictly comparable with deadweight tonnage and both are artificial measurements. The latter is the more realistic measurement for bulk trades such as ore and oil. 925 N.R.T. is roughly equivalent to 2,300 dwt. and 1,133 N.R.T. to 2,800 dwt.

An increase in average deadweight tonnage will lead to a corresponding increase in the total of potential trade. For the purpose of illustration, it is assumed that the relationship is arithmetical. If average vessel tonnage should approximately double with the same berth utilization, land requirements will also increase (see Fig. 29). A full analysis should include individual berth characteristics, and also related use area characteristics.

Table XXXIII.—South Wales: Volume of Trade and Area/Tonnage Analysis
Future Projection

Average Vessel Size		Projected Annual Trade (million tons)	Land (acres)		Throughput (tons/acre)
			Operational	*Related Uses*	
1969	2,300	33·1	600	1,065	19,900
Future	4,600	66·2	$\dfrac{600 \times 3}{2+\frac{1}{2}}$	$\dfrac{5}{3} \times 1,065$	
			$=720$ *	$=1,775$	26,600

* Desirable operational area (in acres) $=3x$

$\therefore 600 \text{ acres} = 2x + \dfrac{x}{2}$

$\therefore$ Area for future operational use $= \dfrac{600 \times 3}{2+\frac{1}{2}} = 720$ where $\dfrac{5x}{2}$ is the existing operational area.

A broad assumption based on a hypothesis that one-third of existing berths have only half the new operational area necessary for larger ship size may be counter-balanced, to some extent, by a present under-utilization of related use areas (see Table XXVII). Assuming one-third of these related use areas are only half used and can therefore deal with a doubling of trade, and starting from the result of a 75 per cent utilization analysis (Table XXXII), the final analysis could be that shown in Table XXXIII. From this point onwards, corrections to tonnage and acreage are made in direct ratio to increase in average ship tonnage. Land areas will only vary from this ratio as a result of technical improvements in utilization, which can also be measured.

PORT LAYOUT

It is necessary, as a consequence of the preceding analysis, to say something of the physical requirements of port layout and probable future changes in port operation. *Fig.* 27 (p. 129) has illustrated the change in depth of unloading 'aprons' and wharves over 70 years. These changes have been rendered necessary and possible by changes in ship size, the development of handling appliances, and the emphasis on quick turnround. Since the recent change in handling methods began, the handling depths on quay have increased for some commodities from a few hundred feet to over two thousand feet. Old limitations on economic distance for such machines as forklift trucks have changed with higher-speed appliances. The sheer size of site required by containers, for example, with perhaps 1,000 units outgoing and another 1,000 units incoming, has forced this deepening. In a new port it might be possible to limit any further similar tendencies by placing high-demand operations alongside low land-demand cargo such as oil, if the trades are compatible. Given a standard depth of operational zone, this would give the opportunity for sideways extension for high-demand cargo behind quays with low land-demand cargo and limiting long runs for expensive equipment. For planning reasons it is desirable that the operational zone should have a constant depth. This usually means relating depth to the more extensive uses. Such a practice will increase future flexibility to cope with operational and trade changes.

FUTURE CHANGE

Future changes affecting port operation must also be taken into account. The possibility of the discovery of large oil deposits in the North and Irish Seas might render some British quayside facilities redundant, as can the introduction of cross-country pipelines or offshore buoy moorings. The introduction of new methods of unloading crushed iron ore by pumping fines ashore can have similar effects. Any plan should, therefore, include provision for sufficient land to enable the port facility to be converted to a different use, and the constant depth proposal will assist in this. Because ore and oil unloading facilities (apart from buffer storage) do not require large port land areas, possible changes in handling these commodities have a particular effect on land reserve policies for replacement of trade.

Other changes likely, such as improved plant, increased stacking heights (as with packaged timber), and the conversion of more and more commodities to bulk handling methods will alter the extent of land use.

SUMMARY OF GENERAL OPERATIONAL ANALYSIS

The purpose of the analysis in Chapter VII has been to illustrate a method of calculating the size of a new operational zone by reference to an existing viable port system and calculating the relationship between trade and area. In summary, the method involves the following steps:—

1. Choice of a suitable port or port group for comparison.
2. Analysis, by area, of the appropriate land uses in the chosen port.
3. Corrections for percentage berth utilization.
4. Adjustments to allow for any changed balance of trade, based on relative characteristics of trade in terms of berth and land utilization.
5. Corrections for changes in average size of vessels and cargo.
6. Corrections for under-utilization or over-utilization of existing operational and related-use land areas.
7. Corrections for the proportion of unsatisfactory berths (in terms of capacity and area) in the existing port.
8. Correction for improvements in cargo handling productivity affecting intensity of land use.

It should be possible to devise an economic model to cover such a situation, but, just as the construction of a new industrial port is a problem of considerable magnitude, so is the investigation for this land use analysis. Land area plays such a central part in determining the potential of a new port that the labour involved should be justified.

The information produced by land use analysis is useful in all calculations for new port operational areas, but the principal statistics are those relating to proportions of land for different uses and, in particular, the average tonnage/area ratio. Having established the characteristics of the port to be constructed and reproduced these in the analysis, the appropriate tonnage/area ratio can be selected in conjunction with an economic forecast to estimate total operational area.

It must be emphasized that the result is conditional on the land being provided in the correct places in relation to berths and communications. This aspect is dealt with in Chapter VIII.

The choice of ratio must be governed by the conditions of land utilization envisaged. It is unwise to base land allocation on estimates gained from the most intensive land use ratio at maximum berth utilization when it would be preferable to have scope for increasing potential trade. Thus, the appropriate results of the analysis will be used to produce land estimates catering both for the realistic initial trade and giving ultimate capacity with maximum utilization.

LAND USE ANALYSIS: COMPARISON WITH DUTCH PROJECTIONS

Chapters V–VII have attempted to provide guidelines both for the overall estimation of land requirements and for the specific projects. Many more examples of the latter might be required in experience, but it is suggested that the methodology will not differ greatly. Hence, the analysis for maritime industry, together with that for the operational, portside, and service zones, will

Table XXXIV.—ROTTERDAM: PROJECTION OF LEASED AREAS BY LOCATION, 1970–2000,
GREATER DELTA REGION

(Additional areas required (in ha.))
(1 ha. = 2·47 acres approx.)

Land Location	1970	1980	1990	2000
With deep water facilities	740	2,480	3,800	4,850
Next to plants having deep water facilities	—	2,350	3,600	4,600
Adjacent to existing sites	—	170	260	330
Within 10 km. from existing sites	100	190	290	370
Within 25–30 km. from existing sites	—	1,300	1,980	2,540
Small users, scattered but mostly near Rotterdam	20	480	730	930
New refineries, with pipelines to oil port	—	900	1,380	1,760
Chemical and supporting industries near new refineries	60	1,500	2,300	2,940
Net land required	920	9,370	14,340	18,320
20 per cent external reserves	180	1,870	2,870	3,660
Total net	1,100	11,240	17,210	21,980
Total gross	2,200	22,480	34,420	43,960

(*Source*: Harris Report, 1968, and R. Ruiter, College of Europe, 1970.)

Table XXXV.—ROTTERDAM: PROJECTION OF LEASED AREAS BY INDUSTRY, 1970–2000,
GREATER DELTA REGION

(Additional areas required (in ha.))

	1970	1980	1990	2000
Refineries, including oil storage and terminals	140	1,100	1,680	2,140
Chemical industries	120	3,370	5,150	6,570
Metal industry (supporting chemical industries)	20	250	380	490
Basic steel, including direct support	500	1,250	1,910	2,430
Steel fabricating	—	2,750	4,210	5,350
Ship cleaning and repairs	100	300	460	590
General cargo and bulk handling (excluding ore)	40	230	350	450
Container handling	—	120	200	300
Net land	920	9,370	14,340	18,320
20 per cent external reserves	180	1,870	2,870	3,660
Total net	1,100	11,240	17,210	21,980
Total gross	2,200	22,480	34,420	43,960

(*Source*: Harris Report, 1968, and R. Ruiter, College of Europe, 1970.)

combine with the engineering scheme for the water areas of the port to provide a picture of the size of site which might be necessary, including reserves. It should also give satisfactory answers on a realistic basis of present trade levels as well as assisting in calculations of ultimate capacity.

For reasons of planning and amenity, it has been suggested that, in oil refinery calculation, the Milford Haven averages should be preferred to those of Antwerp, to enable landscaping, tree screening, and other ameliorating projects to be carried out, reducing the concentrations of polluting gases and improving the visual amenities.

It is important to emphasize again that the detailed methods suggested have other uses: to test the practicability of trade proposals; to examine the adequacy of sites for particular purposes; to examine the intensity of use of existing sites and show potential available for further exploitation; and to predict the potential of reserve and redevelopment areas.

As a contrast, one Dutch approach to the problem consists of a hypothesis, based on preliminary analysis, that an increase of 10 per cent in maritime industrial production, will mean an increase of 7 per cent in seaport area.* A further analysis, based on interviews with 12 principal port users covering 80 per cent of the port area, produced the forecast giving a breakdown of future land requirements for industrial leases by location and by industry (*Tables XXXIV, XXXV*).†

Whilst these tables, which were quoted at the Conference on the Future of European Ports at Bruges,‡ afford interesting comparisons with predictions from other analyses, neither method seems to commend itself for assessments in a British situation.

The first Dutch analysis may be true for limited projection, provided it is used for extension of an existing port with characteristics similar to Rotterdam. Beyond a limited projection, it will encounter a situation outside its possibilities. Such a situation is created by the need to provide additional communications and other major infrastructure at stages in port evolution to cope with any long-term or massive growth. This will show itself as a periodic 'jump' in land demands. Such 'abnormal' increases, which are really a normal feature of progress, will also be affected by technological advances in ship size and cargo-handling techniques.

The second method is probably too subjective for a 30-year projection since it relies on only 12 interviews. The value of these interviews depends on the accuracy of the information supplied by the industry analysed and a safeguard against this could only be provided by a much broader sample.

---

* Report of the Consultation Organisation for Seaport Development in South-West Netherlands, 1968.

† Harris Report, 1968.

‡ RUITER, R. (1970), 'Seaport Development in the Netherlands', *Report of the Conference on the Future of European Ports*, Bruges. College of Europe.

CHAPTER VIII

PORT PLANNING

THE potential for future port and industrial growth brings with it a need for a proper understanding of the shape which future industrial ports will take because of the size of the new unit and its effect on the region. The need for improved efficiency in smaller and more 'conventional' ports leads to the same requirement.

Although large areas of level land may be available, physical geography and the need to prevent sprawl make it essential that the best use should be made of every acre, not only for development but for conservation. Far too many mistaken or unsatisfactory schemes have been undertaken in Britain since 1945. Although European development is not perfect, there is a steady improvement in standards of planning which makes a study of such projects worth while.

In order to secure the best use of natural or acquired advantages, it is essential to consider the principles of port planning, both general and detailed, and to consider any lessons which may be learnt from recent port development and schemes.

The lesson of almost all major post-war port developments is of growth exceeding forecasts, particularly in Europe. As an example, consumption of oil products in Europe rose 14 per cent in the first six months of 1970 compared with a predicted increase of $6\frac{1}{2}$ per cent.* Some ports have experienced serious planning difficulties as a result and in the cure have been forced to produce plans which both distort the natural shape of port development and impose high and sometimes crippling financial burdens in coping with the changed prospects. Others have yet to experience this problem, but, if growth comes, the prospect must be faced. Essentially, therefore, the main aims of a plan must be to provide flexibility in layout, to enable changes to be accommodated, to preserve the economic investment, and to avoid the serious problems which would arise should the development become locked in by other development.

The possibility implies a close association between Government and port and local planning authorities, to secure that growth is possible and that decisions are not taken by Government or Local Planning Authority that will inhibit port growth and, therefore, hinterland prosperity.

There is sometimes an attitude in ports that planning tends to be the responsibility of a single discipline. Nothing could be farther from the truth. The experience of Planning Authorities generally is that multi-disciplinary teams are essential to cope with the complexities of the present time. Although port

* *The Times* Business News, 26 August, 1970.

planning is a highly specialized part of the whole, the number of disciplines able to contribute to the plan is still many and these should form part of any team. To advocate the concentration of planning in the hands of any one discipline can only be harmful to the port and ultimately to the national economy.

Where ports have been successful in redeveloping in recent years, it will be found that planning has not only been treated as a multi-disciplinary task but has taken into account the opinions of the respective port users.

GENERAL PLANNING PRINCIPLES

Once the location of a new port has been decided on economic, social, or political criteria, or a combination of all three, a number of basic principles will require consideration.

The quayside is an interface between sea and land transport. In the future the sea vehicle could include ships of all sizes, hovercraft, hydrofoils, towed containers, submersible containers and barges from the BOB, LASH, and other systems. The water approach must, therefore, be capable of dealing with all these sea transport methods and of adaptation to new demands. The land transport can be rail, road, pipeline, or conveyor. The advent of the 'jumbo' jet could lead to a desirable relationship and proximity between airport and industrial port for export of secondary manufactures.

All the land and water areas in the port have a relationship to the interface—the point at which the transport systems meet and cargo transfers take place.

The requirements in planning a port are variable and sometimes incompatible. The port operation is a commercial activity and the port must, therefore, be designed to handle cargo at the minimum cost consistent with port efficiency. It must also be designed to allow of flexibility in use and to permit development to cope with growth, with changes in trade, industry, and in transport modes. It must be concerned with amenity for its workers.

Where industrial port development is involved, maritime and portside industries are concerned with the economics of their own processes. This concern can lead to universal demand for quayside locations and guaranteed berths which the port may be unable to provide.

Local Government (including Planning) is concerned with a larger area and wider considerations; with the availability of land for differing uses, including other industry; with location of residential areas for port and industries; with education; with demand on communications, and, above all, with the quality of life of the community. Hence, it can be expected to try to achieve a balance between port and community and to be especially concerned with amenity, including landscaping and the control and reduction of pollution.

Government has the widest responsibility and power; its interest should count the social and economic cost (and saving) in national terms as well as the port's profitability. Its power should be used wisely since the competing political demands of different areas can lead to the imposition of artificial controls or encouragements distorting the shape and prospects of the port in ways which might be impossible to forecast.

All these and other competing interests must have an effect on the plan. It would, however, be illogical to attempt to approach the solution from every viewpoint at once, since some could prove to be incompatible. The port authority will be charged with the responsibility of building and operating the port. Its revenue depends solely upon its efficiency and not upon taxation. It will have the largest 'risk' investment in the particular project. Planning should, therefore, commence with consideration of the port operators' requirements. To this can then be added modifications which could be justified in meeting other requirements, thereby producing the plan which provides the best solution for the competing demands.

Reference has been made (p. 103) to the need for a further industrial classification for land suitable for maritime industry, which ought not to be frittered away on unrelated projects. Equally the planning of that land for industrial port purposes requires the most careful consideration to avoid the waste of a scarce national resource.

THE PROVISIONAL PLAN

The port operator's requirements, in planning, stated briefly, are:—
1. Economy,
2. Efficiency,
3. Flexibility,
4. Space for expansion,
5. Amenity.

In order to achieve the best results, it is essential that the port planning organization should be formed on the basis resulting from the Schuster Report* and consist of a team comprising all the major skills needed in dock construction, management, and development.

Planning, construction, development, and operation of a port involve:—
1. Commercial management,
2. Economics and land economics,
3. Civil engineering and hydraulics,
4. Port operations,
5. Shipping control,
6. Land transport,
7. Finance,
8. Staff management,
9. Law,
10. Tele-communications.

* Report of the Committee on Qualifications of Planners, Cmd. 8059 (1950). London: H.M.S.O.

It is suggested that the planning team should embrace:—
Commercial management and operating specialists,
Civil engineers,
Surveyors and land economists,
Financial experts and general economists,
with other skills represented on an *ad hoc* basis.

Table XXXVI shows how different skills might play a part in port development, with some explanation of the lesser known functions involved in applied land economics.

1. ECONOMY

In considering a new port from the point of view of economy, regard should be had to minimizing the capital expenditure in port development to match the economic trade forecast. With quay walls of only 35 ft. depth costing £2,000 or more per foot run, a berth for a 600-ft. ship could cost £1·2 million. Should a large lock be necessary, an additional cost in excess of £10 million could be incurred. The dredging of approach channels and turning areas increase the cost. It is, therefore, desirable that the design should enable the new port to be so constructed that berths, especially for deeper ships, are limited to the demand, but the port should be capable of being expanded to keep pace with growth at minimum cost. Dredged materials should be used for reclamation wherever possible.

In the Golfe de Fos development being carried out by the Port of Marseilles, this situation, in a practically tideless sea, is achieved by means of a three-pronged development, each prong being dedicated to a different class of use (*see Fig.* 35). Where locks, with their high cost, are necessary another solution must be found. Even the non-tidal problem could be solved in a more economic way by following the principles set out later.

The need for keeping capital works to a level capable of being serviced by port income in a competitive world is, therefore, accompanied by a need to cater for future expansion, or stage-by-stage development.

In order to assist in keeping capital investment low, it should be recognized that port-related and portside industry, whether transport, storage, prime or secondary, cannot all be offered prime locations. This infers zoning of sites according to type of industry.

2. EFFICIENCY

This requires a port design which lends itself to the rapid handling of cargo. Because of the pressure for quick turnround of ships, space is a prime requirement. The location of sufficient areas for cargo handling close to quays is of the greatest importance. Industry also requires a location which has regard to the ease and cost of handling the raw materials it requires.

These conditions imply segregation of uses to avoid the muddles of some older port layouts and the development of specialized berths with zoning of cargo

167

Table XXXVI.—Functions and Processes in Dock Projects

Skill	Conception	Research	Planning	Statutory Powers	Purchase	Construction	Operation	Development
General management	XX	X	XX	XX	X	XX	X	X
Commercial management	XX	XX	X	X	X	X	XX	XX
Operational management	X	XX	XX	X		X	XX	X
Engineering	X	XX	XX	X	X	XX	XX	X
Finance	X	XX	X	X	X	X	XX	X
Personnel management	X		X	X		X	XX	
Legal	X	X	X	XX	XX			X
Economics	X	XX						XX
Land economy	X	XX	XX	X	XX	XX		XX
	For early assessment of land availability	For land use estimates and land income	Physical land planning and statutory requirements affecting land	Referencing owners and estimates of land costs	For purchase of land interests	Seeking development projects and assessment of future developments		Planning negotiations developing and land management

XX, Executive Action; X, Advice or Liaison

classes both in relation to quay length and land areas in the major operational zone. Dry cargo berths should be kept together, as far as possible, as should liquid cargo berths. Provision must be made for separating 'clean cargo' zones from 'dirty cargo' zones; and cargoes subject to tainting (such as food) from

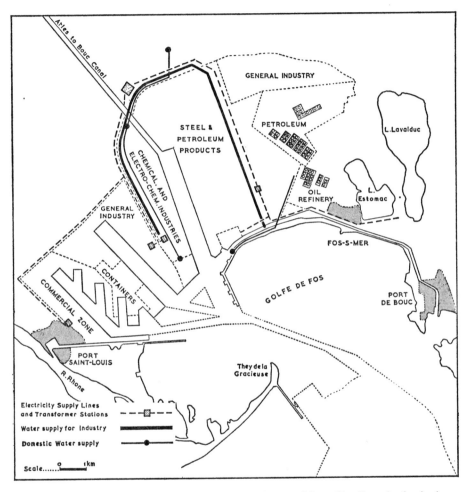

Fig. 35.—Golfe de Fos. New port layout. (*Source*: Marseilles Port Authority.)

cargoes which can cause tainting. The handling of inflammable or dangerous goods needs special attention.

Each individual use within the operational zone must receive attention in relation to shape, size, location, internal layout, and its relationship to the external pattern. Specialized berths must also have locations which relate to the situation of the industry or hinterland served.

Industry itself is sited with due regard to the problems of handling its raw materials and to its effect on adjoining uses.

Adequate communications add to efficiency and the road/rail and pipeline/cable layouts, together with national network connexions need special care.

Efficiency is also increased in very large industrial ports by the inclusion of sites for services, such as petrol stations and vehicle maintenance, normally found outside port areas.

3. FLEXIBILITY

The pace of change in port handling and trade is increasing ever more rapidly. Iron ore, handled in 1970 by grab and conveyor, has been suggested as a suitable commodity for handling by pipeline. The coal exporting island of Britain is now importing foreign coal. The last decade has shown tremendous growth in through-transport systems such as the use of containers—a protective box for general cargo, for carriage in the larger mobile box, the ship. This development is being supplemented and, perhaps in some trades, will be replaced by the LASH and BOB ships, which, in essence, consist of floating segmented boxes.

Many other systems suggest the same need for flexibility in port planning to preserve the capital investment for its economic life. Logic suggests that the best way of achieving this is to design the basic part of the port—water for ships and land for cargo and industry—on the simplest possible shape so that the superstructures can be developed and redeveloped as long as waterborne transport exists. Where surplus land in the operational zone is developed for unrelated purposes, the land contract must be paced to coincide with the forecast for the existing berth usage. It is important to ensure that surplus areas can be brought back into operational use when port trade changes. Similar practices must be followed for maritime industrial land.

4. EXPANSION

The need to provide against urban or industrial strangulation is emphasized by the fate of many ports throughout the country. The new investments needed to overcome the problems created by the restrictions of old congested sites, even where old berths are of adequate depth, provide sufficient economic reasons for ensuring that modern port policy and technology should see, as far as possible, that similar situations do not arise again. Had foresight in port land planning matched that of the engineer dock designers of the nineteenth century, Liverpool, London, and Bristol, to name only three ports, would not be seeking to invest on the scale that now seems necessary. It is particularly important not to allow the new type ports to be encircled by unrelated development and to retain the ability for the port authority to redevelop land areas once obsolescence is reached.

5. AMENITY

The picture of the port of the eighteenth and nineteenth centuries is of bustle and activity, but as the phrase 'sights and sounds of Eastern markets' never conjured up the smell, the nineteenth century picture of ports omits much unpleasantness. Accounts of the South Wales ports in Edwardian times rarely mention the dense clouds of coal dust affecting their neighbourhoods on dry and windy days. The airborne and waterborne pollution of modern industry can be far more noxious than coal dust, if more insidious. The density of population and industry is also much greater than a hundred years ago. Universal education has created a much wider realization of the effects of uncontrolled pollution and, therefore, has increased public pressure for control. The days are gone when match manufacturers, for example, treated phossy jaw as a normal, if unwelcome, incident of employment.

The creation of large housing areas adjacent to steelworks, with a high incidence of chest ailments, is hopefully a thing of the past. On a less injurious scale, the interest in the amenities includes a respectable regard for appearance, for factory design, and for locations which will be least harmful to the appearance of the environment. Conservation is not only concerned with chemical damage to plant and animal life, but also with changes in the natural habitat. In Rotterdam, recent realization of these needs has led to extensive tree planting, both for screening and for reducing the ill-effect of atmospheric pollution, and to the creation of the attractive Brielsemeer on the fringe of a major industrial area.

Apart from the general requirements, modern standards require that port and industrial employees should have working conditions free from atmospheric and other dangers and high standards of amenities for cleanliness and relaxation between work periods.

In Antwerp the port is aided in the fight against pollution of all types by the Pollution Committee, including the City Chemist, a University Professor of Toxicology, and representatives of the City and Central Government (*see* pps. 20, 21, 56).

This Committee examines each industrial proposal, both in regard to its own problems and to the global effect of the industrial group in which it will fall. It prescribes limits which can vary according to these two aspects and will also recommend changes in location. The port authority regards the Dutch policy of a common standard as being too rigid and considers that interspersing low-pollution industries between heavier-pollution plants can enable the port to be more flexible in its industrial policy and hence increase the attraction of Antwerp in relation to its competitors.

In France central government prescribes permitted levels of atmospheric and water pollution, but the port of Le Havre has it own more stringent rules and, moreover, takes its own samples with a view to enforcement.

LAYOUT OF THE INDUSTRIAL PORT

The planning of a new port, therefore, is an immense task, requiring a wide range of expertise, and dealing with an equally wide range of considerations. The shape of the port will be affected by these as much as by the geography of the site. The suggestions which follow are purely in outline, putting forward possible solutions to the problem of the basic shape.

Simplicity in layout, so far as this can be contrived, is to be recommended. A simple shape reduces cost, waste of unusable corners of water or land, and improves flexibility. In 1914 John Macaulay, General Manager of the Alexandra Dock and Railway Company, wrote:—

'Perhaps the most convenient form for a dock is the rectangular; and there is no doubt that continuous quays in docks of this kind are preferable and more efficient in every way than those with breaks in them; since in the former case, advantage can be taken of the whole of the quay space, whatever the size of the vessel may be that requires a berth'.*

When these words were written, port construction was on a different scale to that of today but the conclusions embodied in them are just as true now. In the replanning and redevelopment of John Macaulay's docks, less problems were found and less compromises were necessary than in many other ports. Similar views were also expressed by Sir Frederick Palmer (1862–1934) who had been Chief Engineer at the ports of Calcutta and London. Evolution towards the continuous quay is dramatically illustrated by the series of schemes prepared by the Port of Gothenburg over recent years. The earliest was for a complex inset dock design. Continuous modifications resulted finally in a straight line quay development.

In 1970 the shape of water area which lends itself to maritime industrial development is the ship canal, which can also be constructed in stages, with minimum capital investment, to keep pace with development. This shape is found at Rotterdam (Europort), Antwerp (Kanaldok), and Le Havre.

ZONING OF ACTIVITIES

In order to reduce the capital costs of new port construction to an economic level, especially where lock construction is essential, it is suggested that the principle of zoning development according to the nature of the activity should be adopted. Zones segregating different classes of traffic and portside industry are shown on the master plans of some existing ports. Proper practice is designed to take account of the equipment needs of the various zones, putting traffic using the same appliances in the same zone; separating clean from dirty and inflammable from non-inflammable. Easily handled goods, such as bulk liquids, are encouraged to settle farther from quays.

Developing the same principle in the industrial port, similar zones should be allocated to different types of industry, nearness to quay being determined by scale of traffic and difficulty of 'handling'. Location of site might also be determined by amenity considerations. The proposed dimensions which follow are, of course, those suggested by experience, but these could be altered to suit the

* BIRD, JAMES (1963), *Major Seaports of the United Kingdom*, p. 227. London: Hutchinson.

varying needs of trades or industries which are attracted. The various zones would be separated by communications and amenity belts (*Fig.* 36).

The principal zones are:—

1. Port operational zone for cargo handling and portside industry.
2. Port related industry using dry bulk cargo.
3. Port related industry using liquid bulk cargo.
4. Port service industry and communications.

1. The port operational zone approximates to the areas forming the present-day transit ports of South Wales. It will accommodate warehouses, transit areas, container bases, bulk and buffer storage; prime processing for such industries

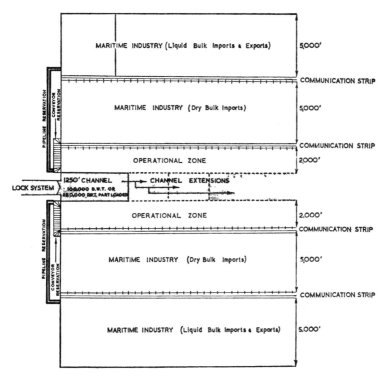

Fig. 36.—The industrial port. Zone diagram showing M.I.D.A. layout to achieve economy in port costs.

as grain milling; and will take account of the need for specialized berths. The depth of the port zone is primarily determined by the economic working distance of mobile appliances, but it must also provide the desirable berth/land ratio (*see* Chapters VI and VII). As development of the second zone will create a rigid boundary, it is also essential that the depth of port zone should take account of the fact that the berth/land ratio increases on a cube basis in relation to increases in ship size. The maximum depth for this zone in British ports studied, is approximately 2,000 ft. This compares with the Antwerp minimum standard of 1,200 ft. depth, giving at least 18 acres per 600 ft. berth, the Rotterdam figure of 25–30 acres, and the Bremen figure of 34 acres (*see* p. 132). At 2,000 ft. depth, a berth of 600 ft. fronts a land area of about 30 acres. Whilst this is only 50 per cent higher than some present-day standards, other factors, such as allocation of a proportion of berths for bulk liquid, increase the ratio considerably since where cargo is pumped direct from quay to industrial zone, the berth activity generates no land requirements. The Antwerp, Rotterdam, and Bremen standards have been calculated with full knowledge of the trends in port layout.

2. The second zone is particularly suited to industry, such as steel and non-ferrous metals and other dry bulk using industry where conveyor feeding, combined sometimes with buffer storage in the first zone, can be located. It is thought that a suitable depth for this zone is 5,000 ft.

3. Such a depth would also suggest itself for the third zone where industries using bulk liquids (such as oil refining, petrochemicals, and chemicals) might be located.

The second and third zones might also be considered together where, for example, dry bulk industrial development takes place at a slower pace than that for industries using bulk liquids. *Fig.* 37 shows how use of the two zones can be interchanged to avoid premature investment in dock extension.

4. Port service industry and communications require substantial land reservations. The location of service industry will vary according to its function, but apart from ship repairing it is desirable to locate this away from the water frontage to avoid interfering with cargo operations. Most port service industry plant can be taken to site by road and the flexibility of road transport permits location of depots at any point well situated for access to a wide part of the port area. Port maintenance services will, of course, frequently require central location, because of the need to provide for speedy action in emergencies, and this may mean a prime site, but other service industry (which is labour intensive) could well be sited at convenient locations for access by employees from residential areas, as well as work access.

In the chapter on the assessment of requirements, it is shown that communications can take 20 per cent or more of an operational zone. Main port communications should be located in an identifiable strip and this strip may also perform the function of separating zones. Internal access is required along quays for operational purposes. Transport access should be given along the rear of the port operational zone with entries to the quayside. This access can also provide limited access to the second zone for industries requiring dry bulk material. A similar strip between dry and liquid bulk industry will provide access to both of these zones and should be regarded as the main industrial access.

It is generally desirable to segregate traffic connected with shipping from industrial traffic since these have different patterns and can interfere heavily with each other. Accordingly, particular emphasis should be placed on the segregation of routes, including those for employees' vehicles. This will lead to the placing of employees' car parks adjacent to those main roads dealing with the employing industry. Industrial access to port operational zone roadways should, therefore, be sited at points inconvenient for unofficial use by others of port workers' car parks.

The argument in favour of 5,000 ft. zones is suggested by a frequent size, in site enquiries for maritime industries, of 400–500 acres. With a depth of 5,000 ft.

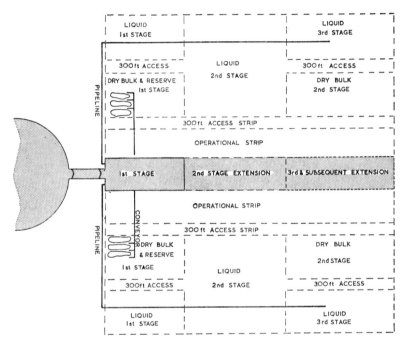

Fig. 37.—The industrial port. Zone diagram showing variations in bulk liquid zones.

the frontage of a 400-acre site is approximately 3,200 ft. and a 500-acre site just over 4,000 ft. In other words, in a 5,000-ft. strip, the frontage of a typical site is rather less than the depth. The site shape is near enough to a square to be economic in development and the narrower frontage improves the economy in quay construction suggested in the diagrams. Furthermore, liquid bulk industry would be located rather more than 7,000 ft. from the quay, the actual distance depending on the width of communications and amenity belts. The rear of the third zone would be over 12,000 ft. from the quay. Although oil is easily handled, pumping costs increase in proportion to distance and a maximum pumping distance of 2–2½ miles is considered a reasonable limit for a port site.

175

Fig. 36 shows such a layout. A water frontage of 4,000 ft. serves a port operational zone of about 200 acres and two industrial sites of about 500 acres, and this is repeated on the other side of the dock. The quay frontage will accommodate from 3 to 6–7 berths according to the size of vessels. Those berths provided for bulk liquid cargo will have only a limited operational land requirement adjacent to the quay, which permits backing land to be used for other

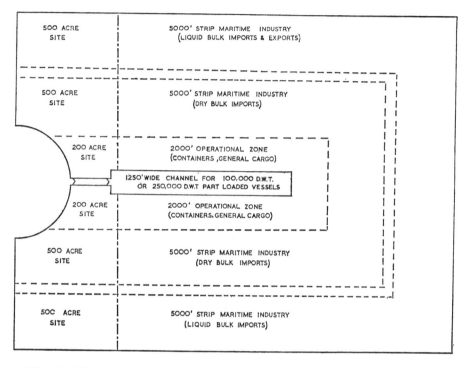

Fig. 38.—The industrial port. Restrictive effect if no extension strip is reserved.

purposes, since any surplus capacity for other trade in the oil berth will have a land requirement below that for general purpose quays. The surplus land behind berths, such as oil discharge quays, in the 2,000-ft. operational zone, therefore becomes available for use in conjunction with other berths or for portside industry. Dry bulk berths will generally require stockyards in the port zone, but these should never exceed the width of the berth frontage. If (usually with non-ferrous ores) there is not full berth utilization, the stockyard should be sited to permit other use of the berth. This usually means a narrow frontage of stock-piles or, alternatively, location of stockyards away from quay. On the other hand, high traffic densities in major bulk trades may mean berth elaboration. In this case, the design should attempt to concentrate additional berths, perhaps by jetty or mole construction, on the allocated frontage. The possibility of future trade changes implies the need for economy in construction, and also makes it necessary to plan for future obsolescence and conversion to other trading uses.

Fig. 38 shows the results of allowing the three zones to form a perimeter around the water area. The effect of this layout is to restrict future expansion in the same way that urban development has affected older ports and should not be permitted. A corridor reservation is essential, within the limits of geography, to permit full exploitation. This corridor should also include the port operational zone. Such a reservation does not mean sterilization because there are always short-term uses available in an active port, which do not require heavy capital investment and which enable land to be utilized. Short-term uses could include scrap sorting and preparation, crushing plants for converting scoria to road making materials, standage for road vehicles and trailers, stockyards for construction and maintenance materials, stockpiles of breakwater repair material, and so on. Short-term uses assist in consolidation of the ground and also produce revenue.

The port, if successful, will attract vessels of various sizes. Whilst a large-capacity entrance is the essential factor in modern industrial port development, excessive traffic in small vessels can prove an embarrassment by causing congestion if a lock is needed. It can be uneconomic to use a large dock for a small vessel. Not only are the units of cargo and ship size lower (and, therefore, the income less), but with a smaller displacement, the water used up in locking operations can be greater, especially as a result of arrivals at lower states of the tide. Provision should, therefore, be made for an extra lock or series of locks of varying sizes when traffic demand and port income justify this. The Port Autonome du Havre is, in fact, planning for a battery of three locks in the port extensions, the largest and first being for ships up to 250,000 dwt.

Similarly, the demand for large berths inside the port is likely to be less than for other classes of vessel, and it would be financial folly to provide a port water area of uniform depth over the whole area. The high cost of excavation makes it essential to provide the deepest berths as near as possible to the entrance and *Fig.* 39 shows a solution to the problem. The deep water area, which also includes space for ships to turn, is located immediately inside the lock. The variation in depths of industrial zones on one side is intended to relate berth provision to the scale of industrial sites usually supplied by berths of that draught.

Fig. 39 also illustrates a way of dealing with a site of limited overall width, whilst retaining the industrial zone principle. Planning factors include the size of vessel serving industry and the size of industrial site. All industries using 'small' vessels—say, below 30–40,000 dwt.—and which are usually on a smaller scale than refineries and steelworks, could be located on one side of the water area which is divided into port zone, dry bulk, and liquid bulk areas as before. The opposite water frontage is developed by those industries served by large vessels. Extension of deeper berths is possible by dredging a strip of deep water along the same side as the original deep berths, with a dredging slope (shown in the section as lying in the centre of the water area). Extra demand for deep water berths in the long term could be catered for by dredging to full width for the necessary distance in any future extension. This type of layout can also be used to provide for industrial location on the basis of amenity or pollution considerations, higher pollution activities being confined to one side of the water area.

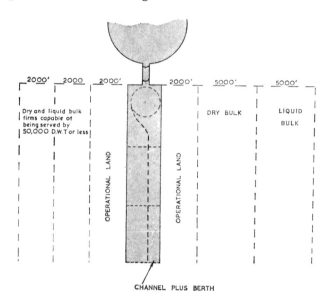

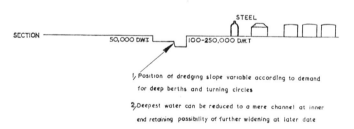

Fig. 39.—The industrial port. Variations in zones and draughts.

Whilst lock size must be determined on the fullest investigation, current financial problems in Britain suggest that any new locks should have an upper draught limit of about 55–60 ft. Vessels of greater draught—usually tankers— should enter part laden or discharge at lower cost installations, such as single-buoy moorings. This recommendation will not exclude other tankers from docks since part laden or 'small' vessels still trade in considerable numbers. It seems wiser in present circumstances to avoid the extremely high costs implicit in the Le Havre solution wherever possible, although land provision could be made for future lock development of this sort.

The variations possible in port layout are of course legion, but at all times the finance of port operation is a central consideration. For this reason, industrial zoning and segregation will be a necessity.

REPLANNING AN EXISTING PORT: CASE STUDY

Many port authorities will be concerned to obtain an extension of life for existing structures, but are frustrated in their desire by the expense of operating and maintaining an old layout. Nevertheless, successful conversions have been made, and, in one case, the reshaping was carried out, in the words of the Port Director, T. S. Roberts, by 'cutting out the deadwood and good housekeeping'. The surgical operation concerned physical replanning and, since the original was haphazard in layout, a brief description may be of value.

The port of Cardiff, before recent redevelopment, was extremely complicated in plan (*Fig.* 40). In chronological order, the works comprised:—

1. West Dock, Basin and locks (1830)
2. East Dock, Basin and locks (1855–59)
3a. Roath Basin (1874)
   b. Roath Dock (1887)
4. Queen Alexandra Dock (1907).

The later docks were fine docks but all were open to shipping until 1964, when West Dock was closed. East Dock was closed in 1970. Before 1964 Cardiff suffered from chronic financial difficulties.

West and East Docks were parallel to each other, and linked by a junction lock (used as a dry dock).

Roath Dock and Basin lie almost at right angles to East Dock to which Roath Basin is connected by a junction lock. The basin has a junction passage connecting to Roath Dock. Queen Alexandra Dock is parallel to Roath Dock and Basin but is offset to the south-west and linked to Roath Dock by a communication passage.

Each of the four main works had its own sea lock, together with road and rail layouts to each side. The first three works also had inner locks. There were, in all, 4 sea locks, 3 inner locks, 3 communication locks or passages, 7 swingbridges, 5 road/rail layouts, and numerous other expensive works to serve a water area of 165 acres. In addition the parallel layouts of dock areas imposed a rigid limit on redevelopment of land areas backing the old quays. Perhaps the saving factor, once coal exports fell, was the construction of the East Moors Steelworks, with its need for imported iron ore, in the angle between East Dock and Roath Dock.

179

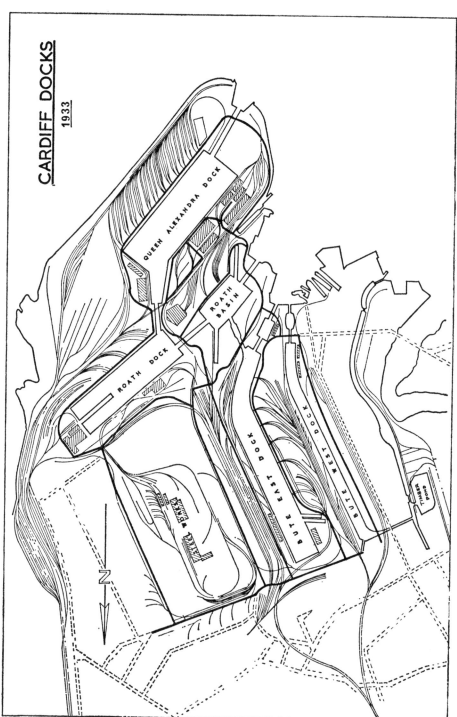

Fig. 40.—Cardiff Docks, 1933. (*Source:* The Great Western Railway.)

Most of the disadvantages imposed by the plan have been removed. In 1963 a decision was taken to transfer the declining coal trade to Barry. The two oldest docks were then closed and their trade transferred to the deep-water docks, with careful zoning of cargoes to avoid the need for providing expensive appliances at too many quays. The plan was helped by the shape of the remaining docks. Whilst a canal shape has not been achieved, the result shows an east/west alinement of berths and the ability to develop in depth to north and south. The land areas are being reclaimed, or cleared of old rail/road layouts and buildings to provide a deep operational zone. The port became profitable, on a commercial basis, in 1967 (*Fig.* 41).

INDUSTRIAL PORT PLANNING: CASE STUDY

Development within zones will depend on the type of projects attracted by the industrial port. These will naturally vary from port to port as a result of the varying economic advantages and disadvantages. In detailed planning each project will need to be examined from the port aspect as well as from the industrial aspect. The best results will be obtained when it is possible to satisfy both points of view, but in practice the ideal is rarely attainable.

When there is a conflict, the solution will be dictated by the overall port situation. If, for example, land use analysis shows too small a throughput to justify a prime site, although berth investment may be involved, then the port financial appraisal will imply a less valuable location from the industrial viewpoint in order to allow space for other use of the same berth. On the other hand, there may be cases where industrial needs will be so important that an intrusion into the port operational zone is a necessity. A difficult case is illustrated at Port Talbot Harbour (*Fig.* 42) where the ore stockyard and blending activities lie within 2,000 ft. of the jetty. This location was dictated by physical circumstances, the hills lying very close to the coastline and most of the coastal strip being occupied by steelworks and urban development. Too great a distance between jetty and stockyard would also have eaten into the cost advantage gained by harbour construction. With such a large throughput as the raw material for Abbey Steelworks, the loss of part of the port operational zone is offset by the quantities of ore to be handled through the harbour.

The logical future development of the tidal harbour is also illustrative of a different solution to port planning and shows how the general principles can be applied to an extremely difficult site.

Because a tidal harbour had been proved to be the best way of providing a large ship facility for this location, it was not possible to construct an impounded canal dock with industrial zones on either side. Existing development contours, and the narrow coastal strip, also make such a proposition impracticable.

The harbour itself has a jetty which can be developed to give two ore berths and is capable of holding up to four additional berths alongside the eastern

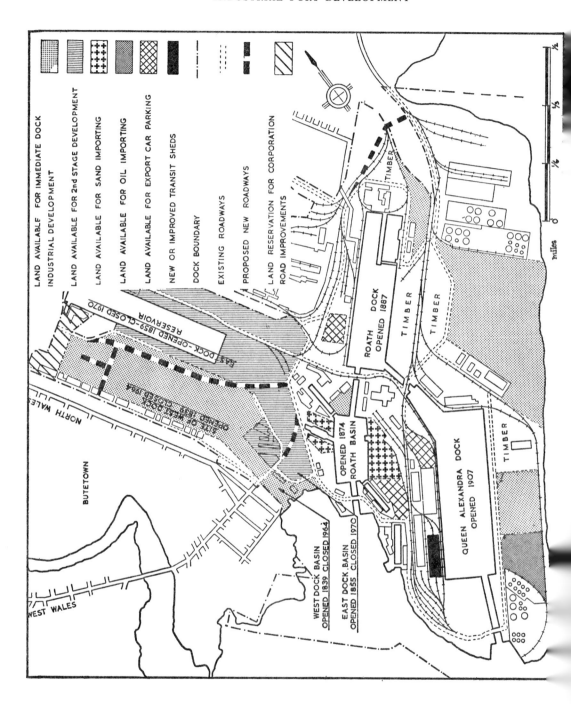

LAND AVAILABLE FOR IMMEDIATE DOCK INDUSTRIAL DEVELOPMENT

LAND AVAILABLE FOR 2nd STAGE DEVELOPMENT

LAND AVAILABLE FOR SAND IMPORTING

LAND AVAILABLE FOR OIL IMPORTING

LAND AVAILABLE FOR EXPORT CAR PARKING

NEW OR IMPROVED TRANSIT SHEDS

DOCK BOUNDARY

EXISTING ROADWAYS

PROPOSED NEW ROADWAYS

LAND RESERVATION FOR CORPORATION ROAD IMPROVEMENTS

NORTH WALES

WEST WALES

BUTETOWN

RESERVOIR

EAST DOCK · OPENED 1859 · CLOSED 1970

WEST DOCK BASIN OPENED 1839 CLOSED 1964

EAST DOCK BASIN OPENED 1855 CLOSED 1970

OPENED 1874 ROATH BASIN

ROATH DOCK OPENED 1887

TIMBER

TIMBER

TIMBER

TIMBER

QUEEN ALEXANDRA DOCK OPENED 1907

miles

breakwater. The breakwater design, as well as the position of the turning space, might prevent further berth development west of the jetty, because of the direction of the prevailing winds.

In order to provide the type of industrial land necessary for M.I.D.A. development, it is essential that this should be provided along the coastal strip to the south-east of the harbour, including reclamation. Because part of this strip is of interest to naturalists and is unlikely to be made available for industrial use, the extension of industrial development can only continue on the coast as far as the River Kenfig, where it may again change direction inland to provide a sufficient reserve.

The layout shows some of the characteristics of the triple zone proposed for a canal dock but with industrial zones of greater depth and only on one side of the port. If the area north-west of the port were available and berths could be constructed on this side, the layout could be duplicated.

A similar master plan has been prepared for Zeebrugge in Belgium where, because of physical characteristics, the industrial strip can run inland almost at right angles to the coast. There is also a canal from the outer harbour running along the industrial strip. Such a canal could not be provided at Port Talbot, partly because of the configuration of the land and partly because no inland water-ways system exists to provide a communications network for a larger hinterland.

In general, the detailed planning of industrial zones should present no insuperable difficulties provided that the general principles of land transport economy and port economy are borne in mind.

DETAILED PLANNING: PORT OPERATIONAL ZONE

Great difficulties of detailed planning arise in the port operational zone. One major difficulty is often not that of planning except in a broad sense. In a land-hungry economy tremendous pressures to develop land can be expected in every developing industrial area and this is true of ports as much as elsewhere. With the trend towards the construction of speculative industrial estates provided in advance of demand, sometimes linked with inadequate provision in past town planning schemes of sufficient industrial land in suitable locations, pressures can be expected from many quarters to release land in existing ports as well as new ports for general industrial development, sometimes with flimsy port-related arguments. To give in to pressure is fatal for the port authority. Enough evidence has been produced of the trends in port development to show the importance of adequate land reserves. The loss to the port by surrender of the principle of proper location of industry is not confined to land revenue. The land use analysis indicates the sort of tonnages per acre which are at stake. When these are considered, together with the scale of existing or future investment in port infrastructure and facilities, the folly of weakness in resisting unrelated land demands is fully revealed.

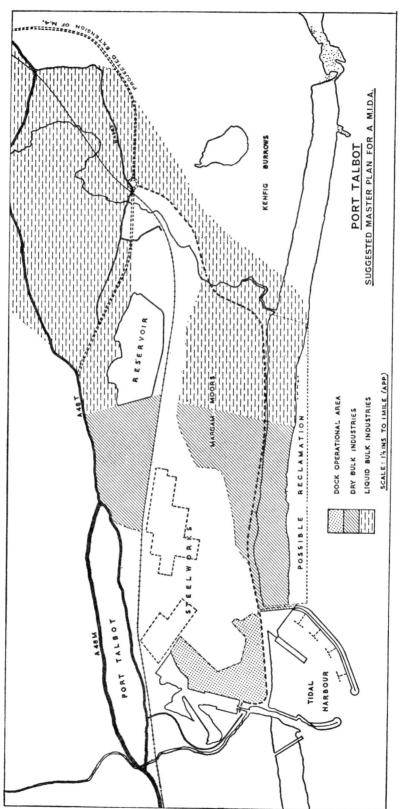

Fig. 42.—Port Talbot. Suggested master plan for a M.I.D.A.

In considering detailed planning of port operational zones, the following functional land uses must be kept in mind:—

1. Quays; berthing; access to vessels; landing and loading facilities; pipelines; crane and rail tracks; transfer of cargo to vehicle (short or long haul).
2. Cargo areas; sorting cargo; short-term storage areas for incoming and outgoing cargo; gear storage.

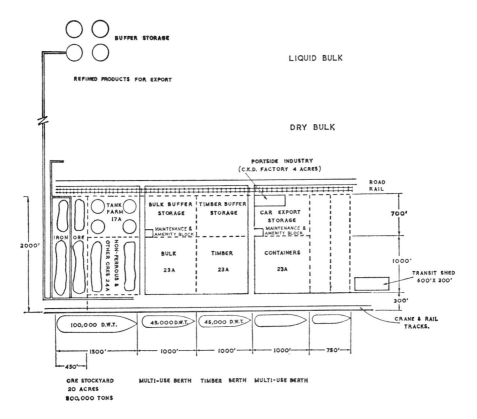

Fig. 43.—Port operational zone. Detailed plan.

3. Transit storage areas; transit sheds; buffer storage for phased deliveries to market, e.g., tank farms; hopper storage; timber yards; cold stores.
4. Portside industry; necessary for reduce bulk processes, e.g., grain mills.
5. Port-related industry (small units only).
6. Staff facilities including offices, call stands, canteens, changing rooms, rest rooms, medical centres.

185

7. Port maintenance services, including workshops, stockyards, yards for specialized plant and equipment.
8. Port service industry requiring prime locations, e.g., dry docks, emergency ship repair services, ship supplies, specialist engineering services.
9. Transport yards for standby vehicles, rail or road.
10. Employees' car parks.
11. Major communications; road, rail, pipelines.

The essential considerations can be summarized:—

1. Ship turn round and cargo handling must take priority.
2. Development must be properly sited both as to uses, including contamination characteristics, and as to length of security granted to occupier.
3. All development, except that concerned with ship and cargo handling, must be kept behind short-term storage areas.
4. Construction of an expensive and permanent nature (other than transit sheds) should be located at the rear of the operational zone.
5. All other developments (apart from cargo handling) based on mobile units should be sited at tactical or strategic locations at the rear of the operational zone.

Fig. 43 shows a layout in which these principles have been observed and which shows how a cellular concept has been applied to internal divisions within the port operational zone.

PLANNING TRENDS IN BRITISH PORTS

Britain has been one of the leading maritime nations of the world since the time of Elizabeth I. It has had the largest fleet and has carried the largest proportion of world trade. After the coming of the industrial revolution the growth in industry and population increased the dependence of Britain's economy on these factors. With the changes in sources of raw materials for energy and manufacture, Britain has become almost totally dependent, even for an almost stagnant economy, on sea trade and imported raw materials for most industries.

In these circumstances it is sad to report that almost every new concept in recent port development is of overseas origin. It is true that the consulting civil engineers of Britain are among the foremost in the world, but the opportunities for their employment in Britain are limited and major port developments are principally found overseas. Recent developments in British ports show examples of *ad hoc* solutions and limited projects as at Immingham and Port Talbot and, until the National Ports Council Report for 1966, few ports had appreciated the extent of the changes in port opportunities and development.

Since then there has been a gradual realization of the nature of the changes, but there are far too many current examples of port development which ignore or only partially accept the principles of lineal quayage and adequate land provision which have been identified for some time. For this reason it would be well to consider briefly British developments and proposals which seem to illustrate problems that can arise.

LONDON AND FOULNESS

The pressures on land space with increasing ship size have meant that the older London Docks are closing or are under pressure to close. The consequent release of extremely valuable land in the heart of London as a result of this trend has certainly helped London in meeting its present financial crisis, but this has been almost accidental.

Fig. 44 shows the new dock development known as Tilbury Docks Extension. * This is really an extended inset dock and is based on the proposals of Sir Frederick Palmer, Chief Engineer of the port 60 years ago. The map clearly shows the limitations placed on development by the River Thames and a freight-liner terminal. Although the latter can be moved, at a cost, the land between dock and river is permanently restricted and, moreover, means limitation of river frontage berths in order to make the maximum possible area available for dock development. The backing areas for dock berths vary from 9·4 to 22 acres per berth, with even smaller areas for mill sites adjoining the river. As the discussion in Chapters V–VII will show, a minimum average requirement today ought to be at least 20 acres per berth, in order to provide for flexibility and intensity of use, and only two Tilbury berths exceed this basis. The corner berths at the junction with the main dock provide an even more extreme example of restriction on potential use.

The 'Forest Products' maximum of 22 acres per berth compares, for example, with a 33-acre site at the Newport Timber Terminal—which still has further reserve land behind, and a potential 30 acre backing to the container terminal. Whilst such sites can undoubtedly operate with smaller areas, the price is high intensity working, or high level stacking, necessarily at a cost, and ultimately loss of versatility in coping with trade changes. The plan shows little or no potential for associated industrial development within reasonable distance of berths.

It must be acknowledged that, apart from some success at Tilbury, the Port of London has been active for some time in investigating the possibilities of industrial port development in association with a proposed airport. It has joined a consortium, forming the Thames Estuary Development Co., with Southend Corporation, Shell Petroleum Co., John Howard & Co., John Mowlem & Co., and the Rio Tinto-Zinc Corporation. Another consortium, the Thames Aeroport Group, is investigating the airport project.

The area which is the centre of interest is Maplin Sands, off Foulness, which belongs to the Ministry of Defence and is used as a firing range. The sands occupy about 45 square miles and lie to the north of the deep water approaches to the Port of London. It is proposed at present to reclaim an area of 18,000 acres,

* FOGARTY, BRIGHT, COODE, McGAREY, ORDMAN, and WILLIAMS (1969), 'Land for port development', P.I.A.N.C., 22nd International Navigation Congress, Paris.

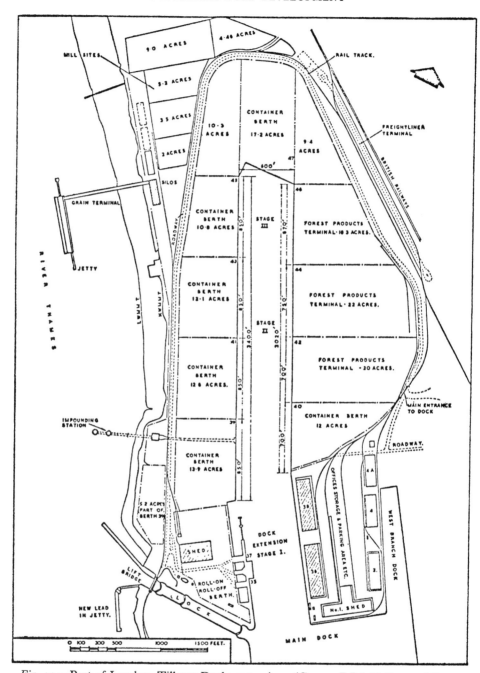

Fig. 44.—Port of London, Tilbury Docks extension. (*Source*: P.I.A.N.C., 22nd International Navigational Congress, Paris, 1969.)

of which 7,000 acres would be used for a four-runway airport and 8,000 acres for the industrial port.

The port scheme (*see Fig.* 45) has a number of variants but all illustrate tidal berths with a high-water draught, in the approaches, of 90 ft. The port and industrial area are separated from Foulness and the mainland by the airport. Because of the need for a site near deep water, the port lies 13 miles from South-end and this seems a typical minimum distance from existing infrastructure and for travel to work. It requires a 34 miles approach channel.

The airport scheme is one of four examined by the Roskill Commission* which finally recommended the Cublington site. The others were Thurleigh (Bedfordshire) and Nuthampstead (Hertforshire). One member of the Commission, Professor Buchanan, preferred Foulness for the airport but even he described it as the difference between a severe loss and a disaster. Other members of the Commission felt that the choice of Cublington meant environmental gains at Foulness as well as a more acceptable economic cost (a saving of £150 million). The Essex and North Kent coasts would continue unharmed and would become available to a wider public once the Ministry firing range is closed. The Report emphasized that airport and industrial port development at Foulness could only be achieved by major urban development north of the River Crouch, causing environmental damage to Essex, comparable with that likely at Nuthampstead, one of the rejected sites. The argument is, therefore, rather more than Stewkley Church versus the dark-bellied Brent goose.

In these circumstances it seems right to question whether an alternative to a third major London airport should be sought. The Government has been under pressure to consider what effect regional airports in places like Manchester and the Severn might have in reducing pressure on the London airports and their approaches. Other proposals are for a complete alternative to Foulness, such as Lydd, Hurn, Dengia Flats, or a site in the 'Essex Gap'. All these were excluded from final consideration because there was insufficent space for four runways; yet Roskill showed a third runway would not be completed until 1998 and a fourth runway would not be required before 2010.† The form of transport at such a distant date may well have undergone a complete change.

Such considerations, together with the fairly rapid development of STOL aircraft, might lead to the conclusion that London's third airport should be limited to two runways and thus only entail a very limited amount of reclamation of Maplin Sands if it were sited at Foulness. In spite of these arguments, the Government announced on April 26, 1971, that it had selected Foulness. Without the extensive reclamation for the airport, the port costs might be un-acceptably high because of the need to construct berths close to deep water. A change in decision in favour of a limited airport at Foulness would also have a similar effect.

* *Report of the Commission on the Third London Airport* (1971). London: H.M.S.O.
† *Guardian*, 28 April, 1971, p. 12.

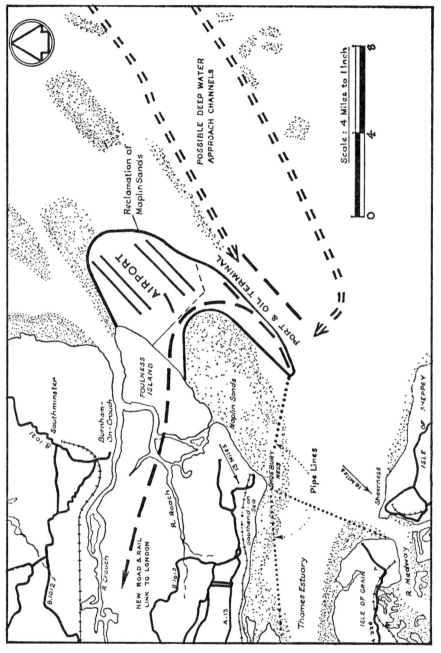

Fig. 45.—Map showing projected development of airport, port, and marine oil terminal at Foulness. (*Source*: Thames Estuary Development Co., 1970.)

The strictures of the Commission on environmental damage to Essex are answered by supporters of the port scheme with a proposal for selection of those types of facilities and industries for the port area which are capital intensive, in order to limit employment growth. This policy, of course, would be most difficult to enforce in the face of temptation by large traffic flows. It would certainly deny to the nation's economy the advantages to be gained from the agglomeration effects of industrial port development. The attraction of a steelworks to the site would bring a substantial labour force, but this possibility might be judged in the light of the industry's actual site examinations in the past (see pp. 95–97) and the problems of adequate fresh water supplies.

The port layout also shows other limitations. Intensive aircraft use will inhibit expansion of the industrial area because of the tall stacks or chimneys common to maritime industry.* The tidal berths avoid the heavy expense of a lock but, with a tidal rise of about 17 ft., make it more difficult for the port to diversify because of the effect of tidal movements on handling cargo from smaller vessels. The plan also prevents 'double frontage' development. The berths appear to be close to the main approach channel for Thames traffic, which might lead to navigational problems. A later plan (the 'TAG' scheme) bears a striking resemblance to the French development at Golfe de Fos, without the advantage of an almost tideless sea.

Finally, the site falls within the 'red' area shown in the Oceanspan report and is subject to the strictures implicit in the land bridge argument. Nonetheless, it is in harmony with modern trends and has the advantage of provisional support from at least two merchant bankers. Perhaps the most outstanding criticism is the apparent assumption that this is the only possible site for a U.K. M.I.D.A. It would seem that a simple consideration of the statistics in *Table XI* should dispel this view.

THE MEDWAY

Like South-East Wales and Humberside, the Medway was one of the three listed sites in the Halcrow Report, meeting all the criteria. Kent County Council has carried out considerable research into the project, using the Economist Intelligence Unit for an economic report. Obviously, the extent of this economic study was limited by the time and money available for the study. An excellent planning study has been published by the County Planning Officer (R. G. Clarke) but unfortunately only a summary of the economic study has been released.† Further examination is taking place and the Council has not committed itself to the project.

* In announcing provisional approval for scheme preparation the Secretary for the Environment announced (*Lloyds List*, 3 February, 1972) that no industry would be located at the port. This means that Foulness will not be a M.I.D.A., but another *ad hoc* installation.

† CLARKE, R. G. (1970), *The Potential of the Medway Estuary as a Maritime Industrial Development Area.* Kent County Council.

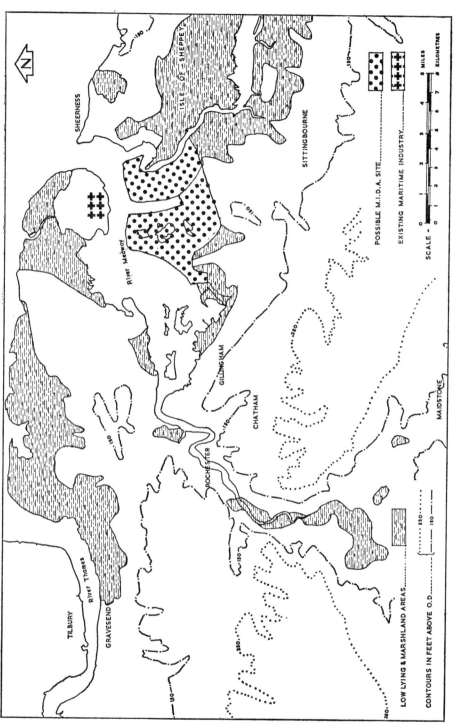

Fig. 46.—Suggested M.I.D.A. on the Medway. (*Source:* R. G. Clarke, Kent County Council, 1970.)

The proposed site is approached along the River Medway and its estuary between Sheerness and the Isle of Grain (*Fig.* 46). Isobaths show depths of 5 and 10 fathoms with a sandbank off the Isle of Grain. The total area of flat and reclaimable land is about 23,000 acres, with 6,000 acres investigated for development by 1991. The eventual harbour would be sheltered. Depths of channels have not been investigated beyond 60 ft.

One serious disadvantage of the site lies in the fact that it is physically separated from other major industrial concentrations of Britain by the large urban mass of London.* This is a strategic planning problem which offsets natural locational advantages offered by the South-East. The site proposed is also on the opposite bank of the Medway from that which already has port installations of the M.I.D.A. type, and will thus increase the tendency towards industrial sprawl.

From the critical point of view, the unsound parts of the investigation rest on the general and unsupported assumptions which appear to have been made in the economic study. The Economist Intelligence Unit did not examine the alternative sites in detail, but reported that 'the Medway appeared to be by far the best site among those suggested for a M.I.D.A. in the United Kingdom, it makes sense in national economic terms and would be cheaper to establish than most other sites'.

Generalizations like this are misleading to those who do not possess the specialist knowledge of port operators, but who may make the important decisions. They are dangerous to developers who have capital at risk and may perhaps have to compete with other M.I.D.A.s.

LIVERPOOL

This ancient port has grown along the banks of the Mersey, being extended again and again as the trade of the port increased.

Many ports show characteristics in the way in which they develop and the dominating characteristic of Liverpool is branch dock development. This form of layout has only one major advantage; the ability to provide the maximum length of quay in any given area. Similar principles are displayed in the finger piers of New York Harbour. The two principal disadvantages of branch dock development are the loss of ability to cope economically with changes in size of vessels, and the rigidity of the land/berth ratio. Comments on the desirability of continuous quays have already been referred to (p. 172) while *Fig.* 49 shows up the land problem. With parallel branch docks the available land between them is fixed and incapable of extension to meet increasing demands. Land problems become more acute at the reverse corners of branch docks where two berths will need the same land area to serve them. Sometimes the best palliative is to abandon alternative branch docks and reclaim the water areas.

There is a much higher proportion of dead water frontage at Liverpool than in most other ports and this is mainly due to branch dock development and the resulting land starvation.

* CLARKE, R. G. (1970), *op. cit.*, p. 8.

The port of Liverpool, like London and others, is now hemmed in by urban development and cannot be redeveloped to provide for modern land requirements except at great social and financial cost. The port authority has therefore sought to develop a new installation downstream at Seaforth.

The new dock is based on a land and water area of about 500 acres and was to provide 10–12 new berths laid out as shown in *Fig.* 47. The average net land area per berth is probably about 30–35 acres and this is adequate for operational

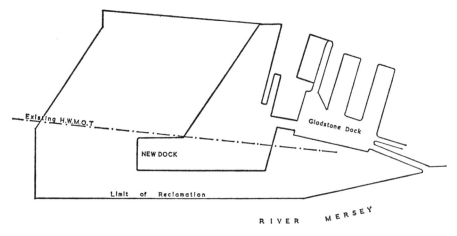

Fig. 47.—Liverpool. Development at Seaforth. (*Source*: Mersey Docks and Harbour Board.)

zone uses at the present time. Unfortunately, no provision seems to have been made for maritime industry, which is surprising in view of the proposal to cater for vessels up to 75,000 dwt. By this token, the port has not catered for the most likely form of future development and has instead been content to restrict operations to those common to ports in the past. This increases the vulnerability of the investment.

The plan also has shortcomings. It resembles the development pattern of the past, with a branch dock and an involved approach through Gladstone Dock, whilst the shape of the boundary suggests that a further branch dock is to be constructed when Seaforth is extended. The dock layout is improved to some extent by the need to provide a turning area for vessels of 75,000 dwt. and this has resulted in greater lengths of straight quays, but there will still be berths lacking sufficient land, such as those on reverse corners, whilst the berths backing on the Gladstone Container Terminal are extremely restricted in land area. A similar restriction will apply to those berths serving the strip between dock and river. At costs of £2,000 and more per ft. run, the waste in berth frontage, due to inadequate land provision and reduction in flexibility caused by changes in direction of quays, can have fundamental effects on viability.

In connexion with the financial difficulties of the port, the Shipping Correspondent of *The Times*, Michael Baily, said:* 'In spite of the £38 million Seaforth project, which in cold logic should probably never have been embarked upon, much of its traditional deep-sea traffic is moving to Tilbury, Southampton, and Felixstowe, and short sea traffic to east coast ports'.

For the sake of Britain's second port, it is hoped that this view is wrong, but the inclusion of planning features which lead to the restriction of potential in some berths and the lack of provision for maritime industry can only make recovery more difficult.

BRISTOL

The port of Bristol with its principal installation at Avonmouth has long been an important British port. Reputedly in the early 1950s its then General Manager, F. D. Arney, C.B.E., a past member of the National Ports Council, proposed the idea of a new dock on the opposite bank of the Avon, at Portbury Wharf. The Port Authority purchased land in this area in 1959 and now claims that approximately 2,000 acres are available.

The foresight shown by this step was to some extent offset by a transfer back to the Corporation of some 300 acres near Avonmouth immediately before port nationalization proposals were published. It was not until May, 1964, that a scheme was submitted for approval of the Minister of Transport, anticipating the provisions of the Harbours Act passed in June, 1964. Consent to the scheme was refused in 1966† after it had been recommended by the National Ports Council.

It seems obvious from the reasons given by the Minister that refusal was strongly influenced by the Martech Report,‡ conclusions of which had been known in official circles before publication. It was believed that the Port of London was concerned about the Portbury proposals, which publicity described as an answer to Rotterdam. A subsequent scheme—West Dock—was likewise submitted and refused after being supported in the House of Lords in the face of formal objection by the South Wales Ports. The major arguments in opposition were that the trade growth available would not support a new but limited port venture such as this and that the geographical position of Bristol militated against any possibility of attracting entrepôt trade from Western Europe.

In 1970 a further scheme—West Dock II—had been prepared, pruning capital costs and revising estimates of trade. Both schemes proposed a period of 80 years for repayment of capital expended on dock structures.

By 1970 the pressure on Bristol had grown severe. The city had retained the oldest part of its undertaking—City Docks—far past the date of obsolescence,

* *The Times*, 14 November, 1970.

† *Portbury—Reasons for the Minister's Decision not to authorise the Construction of a New Dock at Portbury, Bristol* (1966). London: H.M.S.O.

‡ Britain's Ports: The facts and the future: A pioneer analysis of overseas trade: P.L.A. and Martech, July, 1966.

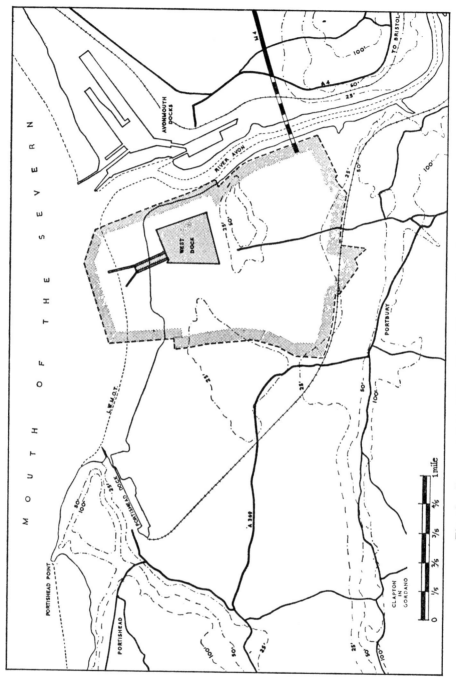

Fig. 48.—Proposed Bristol West Dock. (*Source*: Port of Bristol Authority.)

reporting, in 1969, an annual loss of about £250,000 for that system. Avonmouth's redevelopment was hampered by multi-storey development right up to the quay aprons, with the only land areas capable of redevelopment at reasonable cost lying to the rear and separated from the berths. Only expensive demolition could rectify the situation and quayside development was taking place after the new pattern of port layout and development became apparent in Europe. Unfortunately for Bristol, preoccupation with the refusals of the new schemes seemed to have obscured the need for extensive redevelopment at Avonmouth and thus delayed action.

This was the situation when the new Minister of Transport announced in a written answer that the scheme could go ahead.* At the same time, during the long periods between conception and submission and those of Ministerial examination, the scale of maritime port development changed, both in ships and land.

The proposed development includes provision of a lock measuring 1,200 ft. × 140 ft. and 45 ft. draught for vessels of 65–80,000 dwt. at the upper reaches of the Severn tideway (*Fig.* 48). This compares with Antwerp's new draught of 57 ft. With the rapid rise and fall of the second highest tide in the world, time for access by the biggest class of ships from the deep water off Barry (*see* p. 60) will be extremely limited. This suggests that if growth of maritime industry served by large vessels should result, other locks would be necessary for smaller vessels and the economics of operation would be altered. On the other hand, the basis of the fastest growing industry—oil refining—has moved into a class of bulk carrier which is too big for the new lock.

Whatever trade can still be attracted to the site, atmospheric pollution will create a problem. Portbury lies to the west of Bristol and the prevailing winds blow from the south-west or west. Furthermore, the area of 2,000 acres, about the size of the 'Zones Portuaires' of Nantes-St. Nazaire, is capable of only limited expansion, being hemmed in by the hills running from Clevedon to Bristol. It may be that the tidal conditions will prevent the lock from serving a much greater area but it would certainly seem wiser, given the evidence available in 1970, to have considered a new development elsewhere in the estuary, where suitable land is physically available in quantity and atmospheric pollution over large residential areas would be avoided.

The new development cannot be considered an adequate M.I.D.A. if carried out. In the House of Commons on the 4 July, 1968, the Minister of Transport stated in a written answer that Consultants (Halcrow) had reported there was insufficient industrial land at Portbury. The lock cannot even accommodate the larger dry bulk carriers. After allowing for water area, operational zone, dock service industry, communications and storage areas, there will only be room for a comparatively small amount of port-related industry. It is said that great hopes rest on chemicals and petrochemicals. The land use analysis (pp. 115–117) shows

* *The Times* Business News, 18 November, 1970, p. 1.

anaverage production tonnage (not imports) for even 2,000 acres, of 4·5 million tons of petrochemicals or 3·4 million tons of chemicals when fully developed; but petrochemical plants are more and more tending to grow in association with a refinery (e.g., Baglan Bay, Swansea), not least because of the supply of feedstock from refinery and the return of fuel gas and cracked spirit. Continental petrochemical plants exist in association with refineries and the operation is affected by length of pipeline connexion to port (*see* p. 73). A completely detached plant will be correspondingly more vulnerable. In addition, feedstock or raw materials for chemicals or petrochemicals may be more economically carried to the area by rail in 100-ton tankers on a freightliner service if they originate in Great Britain or are imported in vessels which are too large for the West Dock. This situation has already emerged at one or two isolated petrochemical plants based on ports.

The plan submitted for Parliamentary approval suffers from defects which will prevent maximum exploitation of the capital investment. It also seems from previous submissions and public statements that great difficulty has been experienced in producing a scheme with a sufficient rate of interest to justify investment. This has resulted in pruning of civil engineering costs and reductions in the size of the scheme.

The degree to which this pruning has resulted in adoption of lower or novel construction standards is not known, but must be considered in association with the powers sought to write off capital for works over 80 years as against 60 years for land purchase costs. This is an exceptionally long period in any case, particularly as the rate of change in the economic life of port structures has speeded up.

The dock has been sited in the angle between the Rivers Avon and Severn, with sea access from the latter. Its position leaves only narrow strips of land between the dock and river frontages. The widest strip adjoins the Avon and is between 800 and 900 ft. deep, which would only provide a potential land area of between 12 and 13·5 acres per 600 ft. berth on this side. Considerable extension of the dock in either direction is necessary before even a modest increase in this land ratio is possible. This inferior location may well have been imposed as a result of geological conditions.

The layout has four principal defects: First, it dictates that only two out of four faces of the new dock give a reasonable depth for berth development. The remaining two faces represent a very high proportion of dead frontage. Secondly, if extension is in mind, only one of the remaining two frontages can be developed. In this event the initial investment only provides one dock face capable of reasonable development and almost halves the period after which further investment becomes necessary. Thirdly, the choice of face to be developed determines the direction in which future extension will take place. If this direction must be changed, it will increase the cost and lessen the flexibility of berth allocation as a result of changes in direction of the dock wall.

Finally, the location of the dock in relation to the industrial area reduces flexibility of planning for industrial sites importing 'difficult' cargoes.

The effect of this development on the estuary might be to delay proper development or distort the natural evolution, although the latter is doubtful. The real point is that, for planning and economic reasons, it will produce a port half-way between the old order and the new and will absorb a considerable proportion of port investment in the process.

The chequered history of the scheme and its outcome illustrates the need for estuarial development to be considered as a whole and divorced from the political arena.

London and Liverpool are the two principal ports of Britain. In the major projects of Tilbury and Seaforth each has ignored the trend to maritime and port-located industry on the grounds of insufficient land provision. The port designs also, apart from draught, closely resemble the designs of the great Victorian engineers. Tilbury, in fact, is a development along the lines proposed by Sir Frederick Palmer in 1910. There is a case, often a very strong one, for re-developing 'Victorian' ports of sufficient size, provided they have the land for adequate exploitation but there can be no real case for reproducing a nineteenth century design at twentieth century prices.

Although London has been active more recently in connexion with Foulness, only Bristol, of the major independent ports, has worked for long to develop an industrial port and, even here, the march of progress has overtaken a conception limited by geography and the failure to apply new planning principles.

PLANNING PROBLEMS AT ROTTERDAM

The port of Rotterdam with its rapid growth since the last war now occupies an almost continuous strip on the South Bank of the Maas about 25 miles long, with other port areas on the North Bank. Intruding into this strip are the two towns or suburbs of Pernis and Rozenburg, and both are surrounded by maritime installations and industry. To the south of the industrial strip lies a chain of other towns and villages, such as Hoogvliet, Spijkenisse, Geervliet, Heenvliet, Zwartewaal, and the ancient, moated and walled town of Brielle, birthplace of Admiral van Tromp. Most of these lie outside the Municipality of Rotterdam (see Fig. 9).

These are the keys to the problems created. Firstly, the extremely rapid growth of trade—from 24,500,000 tons in 1938 to 160,000,000 tons by 1968—caused tremendous expansion of the port area. This expansion, because of the attraction of port-based industry, was faster in terms of land development than a trade/land ratio obtained from analysis of the pre-war port could have suggested. Secondly, the political problems arising from the pressure for land outside the Municipality could not be solved quickly enough for an ideal plan to be put into effect. It was, of course, an achievement to keep as close to demand as was the case. Hence, the port area comprises a relatively narrow strip, 25 miles long and usually less than 2 miles wide, with heavy pollution in the earlier post-war developments. Since industrial development is principally of the oil and petro-chemical type and land intensive, the result has been an extensive water frontage in relation to the number of berths required.

Increasing traffic on the Nieuw Waterweg has also led to the construction of the Caland Canal to separate shipping for the Europort areas from the main river shipping lanes. *Fig.* 49 shows one result. The narrowness of the strip has meant location of refinery and petrochemical development at the water's edge.

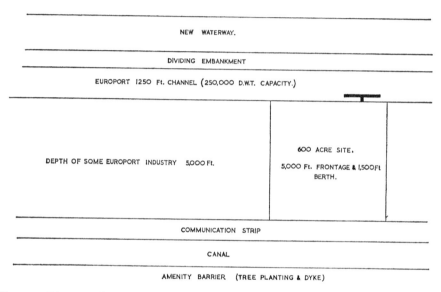

Fig. 49.—Diagram of Europort showing restrictive nature of site and effect on layout and economic land use.

A typical 600-acre site, therefore, occupies a water frontage of 5,000 ft. and may only require one berth of 1,500 ft. The remaining frontage of 3,500 ft. is largely unused or only capable of limited berth development. In addition, the embankment between Europort and the New Waterway is incapable of extensive exploitation for most of its length. This expensive canal for ships up to 250,000 dwt. tons is, therefore, starved of the land for full development.

The planners of Rotterdam realize this fully and their *Plan 2000+; Development, of the Northern Delta*—only one of a number of studies in depth—shows a much more comprehensive approach to port planning. The dangers remain that the rate of increase in trade may not leave sufficient time for the problems associated with this vast project to be fully resolved; and compromise may again spoil the result.

CHAPTER IX

LAND VALUATION IN PORT AREAS

REVENUE FROM LAND

THE principal income of a port operator is derived from dues on ships and goods. With the changes in cargo handling methods and the changing character of ports, land revenue is forming an increasing proportion of the port's revenue. The land revenue of the British Transport Docks Board in 1970 amounted to £3,458,674* and this item has shown substantial increase every year since the Board took over the nationalized ports in 1963. The industrial port of the future may have a land revenue of even greater relative size, since it would contain the major industrial sites. Le Havre already claims that 25 per cent of its revenue is derived from land.

The problem of land valuation in port areas is extremely complex. Although principles establishing the basis of value are those of general application, the specific factors which apply in port areas differ from those with which the surveying profession is generally familiar. For this reason, many professional criticisms of the level of port land values are not informed. It is frequently argued that the proximity of deep water and expensive berthing facilities does not justify higher values for land since the port is able to charge dues on ships and goods.

This argument is difficult to understand. Industries with major transport fleets pay heavy licence fees but still find added value in sites near motorways and major road connexions. In fact, dues in ports are levied for specific services provided by the port and are independent of leased areas in that port. Many users do not have such leased areas.

Ships dues are levied for services rendered to the ship, like dredging, use of approach channels, locks, and berth. Wharfage on goods is in respect of the provision of quay and wharf with lighting and access. Other port services, such as cranes and use of sheds, attract additional charges.

Many industries and potential tenants find an added value in a site close to dock facilities.

CONTINENTAL PRACTICE

The practice in some continental countries differs from that in Britain. Rents for land in both Antwerp and the major French ports are related to the cost of providing the land and not to its market value. The method of calculation is similar in each case. French practice is to add to the basic value of land—usually

* B.T.D.B. Report and Accounts, 1970, House of Commons Paper No. 406.

agricultural or nominal—the cost of reclaiming, raising levels, or levelling, together with the cost of providing necessary services, such as roads, rail, drains, etc. In 1970 rents were assessed at approximately 9 per cent of the total capital cost of making land available.

The purely artificial level of value achieved by this calculation was then modified in order to provide an attraction to port using industry. The rather complicated formula is subject to a maximum reduction of 15 per cent of the port dues accruing.

Example

Standard rent	= 1 franc per sq. metre
Area let	= 100 hectares = 1,000,000 sq. metres
Dues payable	= 500,000 fr. (say, 1m. tons at 50 centimes)
	= 500 fr. per 1,000 sq. metres
15 per cent of 500 fr.	= 75 fr.
Allowance	= $\frac{75}{1000}$ fr. per sq. metre = 0·075 fr.
Therefore rent	= 0·925 fr. per sq. metre.

The disadvantage of an artificial method of assessment is that it loses for the port the income which a market value basis would provide for prime sites. On the other hand bad sites and bad port locations could be penalized by high rentals. The theoretical advantage of covering costs is negated in the latter case, if the land cannot be let. In the end it could lead to abandonment of the standard and the introduction of 'subsidized' assessments. Once these have been introduced for poor locations, it is only a short step to substandard levels for good locations. The most equitable principle of land assessment is market value, yielding a fair return for the port and a just payment for the developer.

Port competition will undoubtedly lead to inducements and these would be best dealt with by commercial adjustments to dues, which would also cover trade in which port land occupation is not involved. The end-result of an artificial valuation policy is distortion of the level of values in an area or industry which could, in extreme cases, have an effect on the economics of industrial location. It can also obscure the profitability of port activities, as where the inducement is contained in the rent and shown in a different part of port accounts.

Market value assessments form the basic policy at Rotterdam, although such values may be adjusted to take account of trade volume.

NORMAL FACTORS

As in all valuation, the principal factor is location. Urban location values vary according to the activity. A shopping centre will have its optimum frontage, which is different from that of an office, warehouse, or residential centre. The requirements of each are different. The same variations appear in port valuation. Careful analysis of port development areas will reveal a number of peak values arising for different reasons. The most obvious peak, and usually the most valuable, concerns the area adjacent to deep-water berths.

General purpose wharves apart, industry using deep-draughted shipping will find a particular advantage in a good port location for buffer storage and transport installations. Shipping lines have a similar interest in transit sheds near berths for the build-up of ship's cargo, although this demand is being affected by the growth in container traffic. The peak area will vary according to the class of berth required and its availability. It will also vary according to the land route of the maximum flow. An industry sited to the west of the port will not favour a berth in the east of the port.

Dock service industry will have different requirements. Ship repairing needs a water frontage for dry docks, but will prefer a site with a minimum of in-dock towage since many ships attracted for repair may not use the port for cargo. If total dry dock hire costs, including towage, can be reduced by an optimum site near the lock, the site value is higher. Other service industry will require a central location where all parts of the dock are equally accessible.

Commercial services, such as shipping offices, agents, and ships' stores, may have interests connected with the commercial centres of the town and the port management, as well as the berths. These perhaps conflicting requirements will determine yet another peak area.

In assessing port land values it is essential first to analyse the development to establish the varying needs of operation and the activities with which it is involved. Berth requirements; storage and transit characteristics; commodity properties, such as fire risk; direction of traffic flows or the related industrial locations; compatibility with other cargoes; the saving in transport costs attributable to locations; all these and other occasional factors need to be analysed in relation to valuation as well as site allocation.

The result of an examination will reveal to the experienced valuer the economic attraction of a particular site and hence its value. On a market value basis, the actual amount of rent is determined by a comparison with values of similar sites and similar uses, correcting for advantages and disadvantages of the sites.

LAND ACQUISITION

An important aspect of port land valuation is related to the purchase of land for new port construction. In the past the major part of port construction has taken place on land areas in private ownership. The evolving law of compulsory acquisition culminating in the six principles contained in Section 5 of the Land Compensation Act, 1961, has meant that port authorities have been able to acquire land at favourable prices. Apart from the favoured treatment which these rules provide (for example, special value for a particular purpose is excluded), it is possible to take disputes to an independent tribunal—the Lands Tribunal—composed of prominent members of the professions of law and land.

Evidence can be produced and advocacy practised with the certainty of an impartial and independent hearing.

Deeper-draughted ships, restriction on land space by built-up areas, the need for large flat land areas, sometimes gained by reclamation, and extensive sea protection works, have all led to a tendency for new port developments to move seawards. In general, all land below highwater mark belongs to the Crown. Occasionally, land between high and low water mark can belong to a private owner, as when it forms part of the original grant of a manor. Below low water mark, private ownership is only recognized if created by a direct grant from the Crown. So rigid is this rule that Crown agents can claim ownership of some land which has fallen below low water mark as a result of erosion by the sea. In one case, a pier was constructed at the turn of the century on part of a strip of land, between high and low water marks, purchased from a private estate. Fifty years later, the sea and the elements had made repair essential and, to preserve the new works, cast concrete forms were placed round the base to break up the wave force. Unfortunately, successive Admiralty charts since the nineteenth century showed a shorewards movement of the low water mark and by the time of reconstruction a short length of the pier projected beyond low water mark. Although the cast concrete forms were to be placed on land originally purchased from the private estate, the Crown was able to claim that the land, apart from that physically occupied by the pier (and projecting above the waves) had reverted to rts ownership. The port authority, therefore, purchased the same area twice as a iesult of circumstances—the encroachment of the sea—over which they had no real control.

THE CROWN ESTATE ACT, 1961

Before 1961 this rule was relatively unimportant. Crown lands were administered by the Crown Estate Commissioners. Sale prices of foreshores were low and often nominal. In that year, the basis for the valuation of Crown lands was changed. The Crown Estate Act, 1961, adversely affected the interests of port authorities in obliging the Crown Estate to seek the best price which could reasonably be obtained. At the same time, responsibility for advice on values and negotiation passed to the Inland Revenue Valuation Department.

Superficially this reorganization contained little to complain about. The Crown Estate Act (Section 3 (1)) specifically excludes monopoly value. The Inland Revenue Department Valuation Office is an independent service of high reputation. In fact, when originally established in the early part of the century, it had the effect of creating confidence in private individuals that their just dues were being fairly assessed.

Problems came about, reputedly, after the Acquisition of Land (Assessment of Compensation) Act, 1919, following an earlier attempt to deal with the problem of betterment value and which provided new rules for assessment for public purchase. The practice of paying the professional fees of surveyors retained by persons affected by compulsory land purchase, meant that official valuers faced a member of their own profession instead of a layman. In transactions with laymen they had been able to act as arbitrators. Now, the revelation of their case at the first stage of negotiations became a weakness. Out of this situation arose the familiar pattern of today; the sides adopt an attitude of advocacy with, frequently, wide differences between offer and claim. All this is far from the vision of the early days. Today, the final resource in compulsory purchase is to the Lands Tribunal. The original 'arbitrator' is now subject to arbitration.

The Crown Estate Act permits assessment of value for dock purposes on a nominal basis (Section 4 (1) (b)) but, in practice, it has not been possible to obtain this. Ports throughout Britain have found that the only basis for land purchase from the Crown is to reach agreement with the District Valuer. If terra firma is involved, agreement is still not difficult. Special value to the purchaser can be claimed but, if a settlement is based on open market evidence, there can be no unfairness. Evidence is available from a variety of private transactions and these often include special value. In these cases the major drawback is sometimes a rather long period of negotiation. This is inevitable with the attitudes created by universal employment of professional surveyors on both sides and the pressures caused by the work load on the Valuation Office. The very independence of the District Valuer encourages delay, since he is concerned with public funds and must be certain of his settlement.

Below high water mark a different situation exists. There is no general market for this land and below low water mark there is only one owner. Port development requires statutory powers and this, in turn, means one possible purchaser in any single area. Such other transactions as have been effected in respect of land lying between high and low water have usually been on a compulsory basis covered by the special rules. In this climate negotiations for Crown land below high water must leave the realm of informed assessment for that of speculation.

Two aspects of the problem of assessment under the Crown Estate Act rules react unfavourably on port authorities. First, expertise in land valuation in relation to ports is very limited. Specialists, who in 1963 numbered 15,* are employed by port authorities and in that year no expertise in this field existed within the Valuation Office of the Inland Revenue Department. The sole experience of this body springs from the Crown Estate Act and, since the Crown is the sole owner, it has been necessary to try to devise a satisfactory basis of assessment.

Secondly, the nature of sub-aqua land is such that before it can have real value, extremely expensive processes, including dredging, piling, breakwater construction, reclamation, and other harbour engineering works, are necessary. Furthermore, when these works are carried out, much of the land is not administered in a way which will show a value. Breakwaters, channels, turning areas and ship room merely contribute to the value of land elsewhere and are themselves

* Royal Institution of Chartered Surveyors: List of Members.

expensive to maintain. An analysis of expenditure at Port Talbot Tidal Harbour has shown that the need (due to land problems) to construct in a seawards direction, increased costs. Breakwater costs increased with depth faster than dredging costs increased in the opposite direction.

It is theoretically possible to arrive at a value by a method known as the 'residual value basis'. This involves valuing the undertaking in its completed state and deducting the cost of putting it into that state. Perhaps to the relief of those concerned in negotiation, this laborious method has not shown itself as attractive to the Valuation Service: but the methods proposed in its place are much less attractive to a commercial port. Opinions have been expressed in discussions between members of the Dock and Harbour Authorities Association that the strategy adopted has been to negotiate the best value possible for the early post-1961 negotiations and afterwards to improve upon it in each successive case. Since port authorities have to follow an elaborate and time-consuming procedure before they can start port construction, it is obvious that the time factor is extremely important. The port provides a service to the economic community and the interests of this community cannot often accommodate long delays in land negotiation. In these circumstances port authorities faced with negotiating delays, settle 'under protest'. It is understandable if they feel as if a starter's pistol has been levelled at their heads. In attempts to solve the problem of assessment, valuation proposals have included the use of formulae which have no practical relevance to the economics of port operation. A basis for payment of x shillings per deadweight ton of the class of vessel for which a berth is constructed fails to recognize that doubling the tonnage of a vessel usually means halving the number of ships and increasing capital and dredging costs. A ratio between value and construction expenditure ignores the fact that expenditure increases as basic advantages of site decrease. The existence of so many miles of coastline in Britain reacts against the conception of high scarcity values.

Offers by port authorities have not often met with much success. Even detailed comparisons with earlier settlements have been rejected in some cases. Port authorities seriously consider that pre-1961 settlements with the Crown Estate Commissioners for land below low water represented fair assessments.

The national tragedy of this situation is that most port authorities are public bodies and the application of effort by highly trained and qualified staff is dedicated to what is almost an internal balance sheet transaction. As a final comment on the claim for high values (and up to £4,000 per acre for land below low water mark has been reported), most port authorities in Britain fail to make a profit on a commercial accountancy basis.

This situation is not one in which blame should be apportioned. The Inland Revenue Valuation Department and port authorities have been given an almost impossible task; to apply a conception resembling market value, which assumes a variety of vendors and purchasers, to a situation where only one vendor and, by the selection of statute, only one purchaser exist; and to carry this out in a 'market' in which there is an extreme shortage of expertise.

If the conception of market value is to continue, then the only remedy can be the insertion of arbitration provisions. The presentation of evidence and arguments by both sides can then be weighed by a semi-judicial panel. The presence of a number of independent tribunal members will to some extent compensate for the lack of a market. Although the results will still be theoretical, it is felt that the port industry will feel more confidence in settlements than in the past.

Ideally, the problem should be settled by recognizing the public nature of port investments, the benefits they create for the community, and the service to the nation which they provide. If, as in France, the independent port were regarded as a national rather than a private asset, the same practice of land allocation at nominal value could apply and the machinery for this already exists in Section 4 (1) (b) of the Crown Estate Act, 1961.

PART III

BRITAIN AND LONG-TERM GROWTH

CHAPTER X

THE NEED FOR DECISION

'MONEY IN MOTION'

BROOKS ADAMS, writing of the industrial revolution, said: 'In themselves, inventions are passive, many of the most important having laid dormant for centuries, waiting for a sufficient store of force to have accumulated to set them working. That store must always take the shape of money, not hoarded, but, in motion'. *

Just as with inventions, the undeveloped assets of nations lie dormant waiting for the investment which will set them in motion. These assets should combine with inventiveness drawn from the more recent continental port examples.

The idea of maritime industry is not new and is an important component of the British industrial pattern. What must be new is the combination of future maritime developments in much larger schemes and their integration in a national port development plan. This situation has been brought about by the ever-spiralling costs of port development, caused mainly by the increasing size and complexity of the installations; by the increasing pressures of population on land space, and the need, not only to make the most effective use of every developed acre, but also to preserve those few outstanding safety values of natural beauty which still remain; by the need to squeeze each possible economy from the industrial chain of processes in transport terms; and by the necessity to take heed of the economic advantages of industrial concentration and co-ordination so evident in continental port areas.

The year 1970 was not a good one for British ports with considerable losses reported by London, Hull, Bristol, Southampton, and the Forth. Liverpool was brought almost to bankruptcy. Most had indulged in large investments in an intermediate class of port development. The danger lying before Britain is that private industry might go ahead at an increasing pace, in penny packets, with maritime industrial development, unless there is firm guidance from the centre, purely because of the need to remain competitive in the face of world competition. Worse, many developments could move to continental and other sites so that Brooks Adams' 'money in motion' will be seen to be in reverse gear and Britain's industry, once a world leader, will enter a period of decline.

If the conclusions in this account are correct, Britain's future, therefore, hangs to a considerable extent on the direction chosen by Government. Without positive direction there will undoubtedly be scattered growth in port-related industry, but, unless opportunity occurs for existing port authorities to

* BROOKS ADAMS (1921 Edition), *The Law of Civilisation and Decay*, p. 314.

participate in the creation of the general pattern, this may produce as many problems in the long term as it solves. Comprehensive development is essential if a viable and workable pattern is to emerge.

FORECASTING DIFFICULTIES

Attempts to forecast future development have the disadvantage that posterity can judge the projection against the reality. Few forecasts, indeed, achieve truth; most, mercifully, are forgotten before the time arrives.

The risk lies in the still primitive methods which are used in projection. These entail use of present-day techniques and knowledge to analyse the way in which existing techniques can change. Unfortunately, not only can future events fail to conform to a known pattern, but evolution of any sort is such a complex affair that there is an inherent incapability of human comprehension to encompass sufficient facts and variables for complete accuracy.

In the practice of land surveying, the ideal is to create a surveyed framework surrounding the area of interest. When this is practicable, projections from control positions are inwards; the normal errors in the framework are thereby reduced. Where projections take place outside the framework, these errors increase in proportion to the distance projected.

A forecast of the future shape of ports would, therefore, suffer from this defect, as well as the problems of uncertainty concerning the future.

PAST AND FUTURE

The past can be represented as a series of relatively stable periods of development. The early use of rivers by prehistoric man was followed by a few centuries of Roman control. Rivers were used in that period as a means of supply to Roman garrisons and for exploitation of conquered countries. Wharves were built as at Caerleon and Portskewett, and the Pax Romana encouraged a period of stable trade for the benefit of Empire. The decline of Roman power and the effect of piratical use of British waters shattered the trading position and reduced maritime progress to a period of furtive use by shipping. Viking names of islands and towns and the tradition of piracy connected with many inlets and harbours are relics of these times.

The restoration of stable government enabled regular trade to resume and grow. For centuries there was a picture of steady growth of riverside wharves and trade. Ships developed until long journeys could be made, but the vessels remained small. In the time of Elizabeth I one of the largest ships was *The Revenge* of 500 tons. The East Indies trade, involving a voyage of 10,000 miles, started with a vessel of 600 tons, reaching a vessel size of 1,100 tons by 1610. *The Mayflower* was only 180 tons and had previously been engaged in the wine trade between English and Mediterranean ports. *

* TREVELYAN, G. M. (1944), *English Social History*, p. 232. London: Longmans.

This stage was ended by the industrial revolution, including the improvements in communications and the discovery of coal reserves and technical improvements in its use, culminating in the steam age. The period eventually saw an entirely new development of artificial floating docks. The original floating docks were primarily constructed to increase berth capacity at the various ports and catered for similar vessels to those using tidal berths. West Dock, Cardiff, had a maximum depth of 19 ft., and 12 ft. at the inner end. As ship technology advanced, the inherent advantages of wet docks were used to accommodate longer and larger ships which would have been unable to use a tidal berth.

In South Wales, the Tees, and the Tyne the major spur was the demand for coal exports. The new period, with the rapid expansion of ports and port-related industry has been experienced in continental Europe since about 1950. It stems from the practical realization of very large ships and the attendant economies of sea trade. These facts emphasize that coastal location is of prime importance for most major industrial activities.

Some ports have already entered this period, with the development of specialized berths. They have been enabled to do so, on a significant scale for Britain, as a result of the early development of nineteenth century industries like coastal steelworks and the more recent creation of major coastal strip mills and other maritime industries. This situation, however, arises from the decisions of private industrialists and an enlightened policy in local port management.

It seems that the time is opportune for a comprehensive national approach to be made to the question of the suitability of various British sites for a new-style industrial port complex.

Prospects for the future depend on an objective assessment of the potential. It is the Author's opinion that such an assessment would justify the conclusions of this examination, but it should be emphasized that in any final selections for British industrial ports, lack of objectivity in determining locations will have a rapid and adverse economic effect, which will escalate in direct proportion to the relationship between cost of development and the disadvantages of a bad site.

In considering future development, the examination must not be limited by the more restrictive conceptions of the past, since modern technology is capable of a relative step in the scale of port development similar to that which occurred between the eighteenth and nineteenth centuries.

STRATEGY FOR THE FUTURE

During the course of the research leading to this account of port development, political interest in Maritime Industrial Development Areas has fluctuated. Such a sound economic conception should be independent of political sponsorship since it is based on the facts of transport costs and their influence on manufacture. Nevertheless, because the concept depends upon port facilities and the extent of these on vessel size, the scale of investment to produce a satisfactory development needs government support by way of loans and statutory powers. Likewise, the spread of development is more likely to affect a wide area than port development in the past and the support of local as well as central government is required.

The new form of industrial port development is apparent in Europe and its planned extension in Britain cannot be long delayed if she is to remain a force in world trade. There are no indications that it will change in its basic form except insofar as ship design alters the berthing requirements. Novel forms of transport, such as hydrofoil and hovercraft, are unlikely to enter the large bulk carrier class.

It is unlikely that shore installations will be provided for the largest tankers, although they are likely for large ore carriers. Because of the uncertainty of ultimate tanker size, and the relative ease of handling liquid cargoes, it is better to handle this commodity at offshore facilities, connected by pipeline to the shore. This will avoid the heavy expense of providing harbours, perhaps including lock gates, with expensive dredging, and increase flexibility by permitting re-siting of equipment like single-buoy moorings when ship size renders anchorages obsolete. The much lower cost of these moorings should also be attractive with the prospect of more oil discoveries off British shores, since this may drastically alter the scale of crude oil imports.

There are a number of sites in Britain with capacity for shipping and industrial port development, and the potential of South Wales has been outlined as an example. Some of these sites are well located for British markets and for land bridge development.

Entry to the Common Market will greatly expand the size of the market which could be served by British industry, whilst the conditions existing in the English Channel indicate a need for reappraisal of the sea approaches to the enlarged Market. Inevitably, this will affect the distribution and nature of new port developments.

Although Britain could be criticized for its piecemeal approach to past port development, the lack of excessively high capital commitment to outdated port schemes could be an advantage. When the time comes to match the scale of continental investment, the clearer vision of future trends could mean wiser investment, whilst study of recent European ports could produce better designs.

The economic study must be the guide to the scale of development; further studies will infer locations; wise planning will help by enabling investment to be made at realistic rates to keep pace with trade, whilst preserving scope for expansion.

If these visions prove correct, the opportunities for Britain could resemble those which have been seized so surely by Rotterdam in the past. In this event, the development, now, of techniques for port planning, for conservation and prevention of pollution, have an urgent importance. It is no idle speculation to assert that research in the field of industrial port development could earn for Britain a reputation equal to that gained in the sphere of New Towns.

This, then, is the prime need in port development; for the identification of those techniques which will enable the nation to squeeze the maximum economic, social, and environmental returns from such investments. Economic historians may well say that the failure of Britain to realize the importance of a new ports strategy at an early stage was one of the causes of the economic stagnation of the 1950s and 1960s. It should not be a criticism of the 1970s and 1980s.

The planned development of maritime industry would be of benefit to the nation; it would naturally prove of infinitely greater value to areas like South Wales and the Clyde. It could provide an economic reason for self-generating growth similar to that which attracted the industrial population of the nineteenth century.

Growth produces wealth and it is for Britain to use that wealth for the benefit of future generations. Maritime industry through its related secondary industry could produce a new justification for communities in declining areas. Above all, twentieth century wealth could remove the nineteenth century scars, whilst twentieth century technology could prevent similar accusations being levelled at the creators of a new industrial port.

The study deals specifically with the proverbial 'tip of the iceberg', but it will perhaps stimulate interest in ports, their problems and developments. By so doing, the author is confident that it will help in establishing the basis for a better standard of living.

Appendix I.—Traffic Figures for Estuaries, 1969 (in million tons)

Location		Foreign			Coastwise			Total			1968
		Imports	Exports	Total	Imports	Exports	Total	Imports	Exports	Total	Total
Thames (including Medway)	(a)	13·5	4·2	17·7	1·8	·5	2·3	15·3	4·7	20·0	20·0
	(b)	33·1	6·9	40·0	13·4	7·0	20·4	46·5	13·9	60·4	62·0
		46·6	11·1	57·7	15·2	7·5	22·7	61·8	18·6	80·4	82·0
Severn (including Milford Haven and Bristol)	(a)	11·5	1·9	13·4	·2	·3	·5	11·7	2·2	13·9	14·5
	(b)	25·4	6·7	32·1	6·3	14·3	20·6	31·7	21·0	52·7	40·5
		36·9	8·6	45·5	6·5	14·6	21·1	43·4	23·2	66·6	55·0
Mersey	(a)	11·8	5·8	17·6	·8	·5	1·3	12·6	6·3	18·9	19·5
	(b)	15·9	·9	16·8	5·9	2·7	8·6	21·8	3·6	25·4	25·5
		27·7	6·7	34·4	6·7	3·2	9·9	34·4	9·9	44·3	45·0
Southampton Water (including Fawley)	(a)	1·0	·5	1·5	—	·1	·1	1·0	·6	1·6	2·0
	(b)	16·2	·9	17·1	2·0	7·9	9·9	18·2	8·8	27·0	26·0
		17·2	1·4	18·6	2·0	8·0	10·0	19·2	9·4	28·6	28·0
Humber	(a)	8·6	2·2	10·8	·2	·2	·4	8·8	2·4	11·2	10·0
	(b)	5·2	2·2	7·4	2·8	4·4	7·2	8·0	6·6	14·6	11·0
		13·8	4·4	18·2	3·0	4·6	7·6	16·8	9·0	25·8	21·0
Clyde	(a)	4·8	·6	5·4	·3	·1	·4	5·1	·7	5·8	6·0
	(b)	5·3	—	5·3	1·8	·3	2·1	7·1	·3	7·4	7·0
		10·1	·6	10·7	2·1	·4	2·5	12·2	1·0	13·2	13·0
Forth	(a)	2·3	·7	3·0	·3	·3	·6	2·6	1·0	3·6	3·5
	(b)	·8	·4	1·2	1·1	2·0	3·1	1·9	2·4	4·3	4·5
		3·1	1·1	4·2	1·4	2·3	3·7	4·5	3·4	7·9	8·0

Appendix II.—SOUTH WALES GROUP. TOTAL TRADE 1969/1970

Traffic	1969	1970
Net Register Tonnage of Shipping Entering and Leaving	21,468,119	21,443,250

	Tons	Tons
Inwards		
Cereals (including flour)	132,521	147,000
Fish (landings from fishing vessels)	337	731
Fruit and vegetables	277,700	246,983
Other foodstuffs	46,491	58,271
Timber	283,729	356,686
Iron ore	5,608,177	6,858,640
Non-ferrous ores	347,601	305,246
Crude fertilizers and minerals	53,746	26,232
Sand and gravel (dredged)	646,626	659,204
Oil seeds and nuts	—	250
Wool and other textile fibres	558	1,399
Wood pulp and waste paper	40,708	43,271
Other raw materials (including scrap)	144,015	62,466
Petroleum (including products)	2,360,827	2,388,972
Iron and steel	744,879	720,479
Machinery, vehicles, and metal goods	223,287	247,061
Other manufactured goods	147,304	183,247
Other commodities	10,840	15,296
Total Inwards	11,069,346	12,321,434
Outwards		
Cereals (including flour)	2,649	219
Other foodstuffs	19,045	22,899
Crude minerals	73,775	59,147
Other raw materials (including scrap)	53,770	73,000
Coal and coke	1,775,938	1,778,160
Petroleum	4,662,011	4,963,991
Manufactured chemicals and fertilizers	34,782	35,756
Iron and steel	1,153,396	1,020,980
Metal manufactures (including non-ferrous metals)	51,857	47,445
Machinery and vehicles	64,573	47,357
Other manufactured goods	26,043	32,294
Other commodities	10,878	11,433
Bunker fuel	162,234	169,994
Total Outwards	8,090,951	8,262,675
Grand Total	19,160,297	20,584,109
	No.	No.
Motor vehicles and trailers not for import or export	28,430	29,209
Passengers	170,160	199,520

(*Source*: British Transport Docks Board: Published Commodity and Traffic Statistics.)

Appendix III.—ANTWERP: PORT INDUSTRIES—LAND USE ANALYSIS, JANUARY, 1969

(*Source*: Published statistics of the Port of Antwerp)

Industry	Products	Annual Production Capacity (tons)	Employment	Area (HA)	Area (acres)	Tons per HA	Tons per Acre	Employees per HA	Starting Dates
Oil Refining									
S.I.B. des petroles	All petroleum products	14,000,000	860	192·7	481	72,900	29,160	4·5	1951
Esso Belgium	All petroleum products	5,000,000	350	130	325	38,500	15,400	2·7	1953
Raffinerie belge	All petroleum products	2,400,000 (4,400,000 in 1970)	625	30·1	75	80,000	32,000	21	1934
International oil	All petroleum products	1,000,000	250	5·1	12·7	19,600	7,874	50	1935
Albatros	All petroleum products	2,250,000	270	120	300	18,750	7,500	2·25	1968
Anglo Belge	Intermediate products	40,000	100	2·3	5·75	17,400	6,960	44	1925
		24,690,000	2,455	480·2	1,200	53,500	21,400	5·1	
Petrochemicals									
Petrochim	Ethylene-oxide	20,000	650	30·4	76	11,900		4	1951–68
	Ethylene-glycol	12,700							
	Cumene	30,000							
	Dodecyl-benzene	8,500							
	Propylene	100,000							
	Ethylene	500,000							
	Aromatics	159,000							
	Cyclohexanes	85,000							
		906,200							
	Synthetic rubber S.B.R. and polybutadiene	55,000		14·7	36·5	3,800	1,520		1968

Union Carbide	Polyethylene (low density)	100,000	383	10·1	25·3	16,000	6,400		1962–68
	Ethylene-oxide Glycols, etc.	62,000							
	Polyoxylalkylene-glycols and polyols	120,000	250	35	87·5	3,430	1,370		1968
	Acetic acid esters								
	Industrial gases O₂, N₂, Argon								
		282,000							
Amoco Fina	Lubr. additives Polyisobutylene	6,000	50	10·1	25·3	600	240		1961
Distrigas	Cracking plant and storage of gas	6,000	80	6·0	15	1,000	400	13	1958
Polyolefins	Polyethylene resins (high density) Manolene resins Marlex resins	30,000	75	6·0	15	5,000	2,000	12·5	1968
Polysar Belgium	Butylrubber	27,000	250	9·9	24·7	2,725	1,090	25	1962
U.S.I. Europe	Polyethylene (low density)	50,000	270	12·0	30	775	310	10	1968 second phase
			380	53·0	132				
		1,362,200	2,388	187·2	467·3	5,670	2,918	13	
Chemicals									
Bayer	Caprolactam	70,000	600	180 (only 36 built upon)	450 (90)	2,470 (gross)	988 (gross)	3·3	1967
	Ammonium sulphate	350,000							
	Sulphuric acid	180,000				12,400 (net)	4,960 (net)		
	Perlon fibre	7,000							1968
		607,000							

[see over

*Appendix III.—*Antwerp : Port Industries—Land Use Analysis, January, 1969—*continued*

Industry	Products	Annual Production Capacity (tons)	Employment	Area (HA)	Area (acres)	Tons per HA	Tons per Acre	Employees per HA	Starting Dates
B.A.S.F.	Caprolactam	60,000	1,500	455 (200 built over)	1,137 (500)	3,500 (gross) 7,900 (net)	1,400 (gross) 3,160 (net)	3·3	1967/8
	Ammonium sulphate	150,000							
	Nitrophoska	600,000							
	Vinoflex	50,000							
	Lupolen	30,000							
	Polyethylene (low density)	30,000							
	Nitric acid	325,000							
	Sulphuric acid	145,000							
	Vinyl chloride	110,000							
	Chlorine	80,000							
		1,580,000							
Monsanto Europe	Plasticizers Breach preventers Rubber chemicals		80	102	255			0·8	
Quaker furans	Furfurol	11,000	25	1·6	4	6,870	2,750	16	1968
Solvay	Chlorine	65,000	—	100	250	1,650	660		1970
	Caustic soda	100,000	—						
Degussa	Decolourizers Hydrocyanic acid White fillers		800	109	272	—	—	7·4	1970
		2,363,000	3,005	947·6 (548·6)	2,368 (1,371)	4,300	1,700	5·5	
Motorcar Industry (various)	Cars	280,000			573		690 cars per acre	56	
	Tractors	30,000	13,000		231·9		1,070 tractors per acre		
	Radiators								

(*Source*: Published statistics of the Port of Le Havre)

Industry	Date of Commencement	Area occupied	Employees 1.1.1970	Employees per HA	Employees per Acre
West of Junction Canal:					
Nickel treatment plant	April, 1964	7 ha. 40 a. 30 ca. plus option on 1 ha. 54 a. 13 ca.	—		
Metal coatings, shot-blasting and boilermaking	April, 1964	32 a. 20 ca.	12	37·5	15
Petrochemical plant	Sept, 1966	26 a. 19 ca.	21	8·0	32
Timber wharf and stockyard	Nov., 1966	1 ha. 29 a. plus Bassin Stockage 1 ha. 66 a. 02 ca.	6	4·5	1·8
Chemical plant (titanium oxide)	End, 1957	19 ha. 87 a. 44 ca.	520	26	10·5
Timber wharf. Tropical hardwoods including treatment	April, 1962	17 ha. 69 a. 76 ca. plus timber pond 2 ha. 52 a. 27 ca.	576	32·5 (excl. pond)	13
Ship and industrial woodwork	End, 1962	16 a. 54 ca.	25	150	60
Mechanical workshops (industry and shipping)	1957	70 a. 32 ca.	70	100	40
Tank cleaning plant	1959	1 ha. 39 a. 68 ca.	20	14·5	6
Chemical plant (sulphuric acid)	End, 1957	14 ha. 82 a. 54 ca.	43	2·9	1·2
Tank farm: petroleum products	1947	11 ha. 02 a. 48 ca.	87	8	3·2
Central generator	April, 1968 End, 1969	32 ha.	185	5·8	2·4
Public warehouses	1930	5 ha. 20 a.	720	138	56
Cold stores	1928	1 ha. 75 a. approx.	79	45	18
Ship repairing	(a) 1959 (b) 1962	27 a. 50 ca. / 21 a. 94 ca.	309	790	320
Tank farm: Latex and animal and vegetable oils	1947	3 ha. 07 a. 42 ca.	41	13	5·3
Mechanical workshops	July, 1968	2 a. 40 ca.	23	950	380
Liquid natural gas storage and re-gasification	1965	9 ha. 80 a. plus 6 ha. 75 a.	32	1·9	0·8
Tank farm: petroleum products	1949	(a) land 87 ha. 67 a. 30 ca. (b) water 31 ha. 13 a. 70 ca.	264	3 (excl. water)	1·2
West of Bridge 8 and North of Tancarville Canal:					
Fitting out workshops	1952	3 ha. 66 a. 60 ca.	302	80	32

[see over

Appendix IV.—Le Havre: Industrial Development: Areas and Employment—10 February, 1970—continued

Industry	Date of Commencement	Area occupied	Employees 1.1.1970	Employees per HA	Employees per Acre
East of Junction Canal and North of Industrial Route:					
Butane and propane bottle filling centre	July, 1952	3 ha. 22 a. 75 ca.	79	24	10
Storage and distribution of liquid petroleum gas	1954	1 ha. 45 a. 94 ca.	1	0·66	0·27
Fuel oil storage	1966	1 ha. 11 a. 55 ca.	—		
Petrochemicals	Dec., 1958	18 ha. 98 a. 56 ca.	252	13	5·3
Petrochemicals and lubrication additives	Dec., 1958	18 ha. 58 a. 30 ca.	245	13	5·3
Refinery and petrochemicals	1933	421 ha. 70 a. 43 ca. (1968: 33 ha per million tons) (1970: 30 ha per million tons)	1,765	4	1·6
Petrochemicals	July, 1969	24 ha. 83 a.	15	0·6	0·24
Petroleum storage and blending	1970	5 ha. 97 a. plus option on 6 ha. 10 a.	—		
Storage of materials and ferroconcrete	Oct., 1969	3 ha. 06 a.	3	1	0·4
Storage of materials	Oct., 1969	99 a.	1	1	0·4
Chemicals (synthetic rubber)	April, 1963	21 ha. 97 a. 69 ca.	156	7	2·8
Car assembly	Jan., 1965	155 ha. after extension	5,452	35	14
Pipe warehouse	Sept., 1967	1 ha. 15 a.	35	30	12
Distribution centre. Brewery warehouse	May, 1969	2 ha. 04 a. 22 ca.	64	31	12·4
East of Junction Canal and South of Industrial Route:					
Metal wrapping and packing factory	Sept., 1958	2 ha. 41 a. 99 ca.	156	64	26
Petroleum products storage	1971	8 ha. 82 a. 40 ca. plus option on 10 ha. 91 a. 72 ca.	—		
Chemicals and fertilizers	1970	42 ha. 21 a. plus option on 25 ha.	257	6	2·4
Liquid gas storage	1970	5 ha. 06 a.	—		
Chemical storage	Jan., 1970	3 ha. 08 a. 50 ca. plus option on 3 ha. 95 a. 50 ca.	—		
Petrochemicals	1970	65 ha. 76 a. plus option on 43 ha. 24 a.	7	2·3	0·9
Cement works	1969	40 ha. 64 a. 63 ca. plus option on 19 ha. 35 a.	100	2·5	1
Grand total (all four areas)		1,067 ha. 42 a. 77 ca.	11,923	11·17	4·5

222

Appendix V.—FINANCIAL INDUCEMENTS FOR NEW INDUSTRIAL INVESTMENTS
IN EUROPE, 1970

Country	Attitude to Foreign Investments	Capital Incentives	Capital Restrictions	Special Tax Allowances
Belgium	Favourable, special considerations, formal programme regional incentives	Formal subsidies* on fixed assets (20 per cent), materials (7·5 per cent) and on interests	None†	Depreciation rate double normal for 3 years, property and registration exemption 10 years, local tax allowances vary, no tax on regional subsidies
France	Ambivalent, no special considerations, regional incentives informal	Subsidies up to 25 per cent of investment in fixed assets, low interest loans, land price reductions	Not on earnings or disinvestment but on ownership	Extraordinary depreciation rate of 25 per cent of investments in some areas, property exemption,* reduced licence tax,* local tax allowances 50–100 per cent,* for up to 5 years
Luxembourg	Favourable, special considerations, regional incentives informal	Subsidies up to 15 per cent of investments, loan assistance and subsidy on interest	None†	Accelerated depreciation for 5 years, local tax exemption for 3–5 years, business taxation reduced by 25 per cent for 8 years
The Netherlands	Neutral, no special considerations, formal programme regional incentives	Reduced interest advances, with loan guarantees,* formal subsidies* up to 35 per cent of capital invested	None	Accelerated depreciation rates on one-third of fixed assets except in west of country
West Germany	Neutral, no special considerations, formal programme regional incentives	Loan guarantees* with reduced interest loans,* up to 15 per cent subsidy of investment	None‡	Depreciation rate 50 per cent in the first year on equipment and 30 per cent on buildings for 3 years

* Relating to regional incentives.
† Essentially none but administrative procedures tend to introduce minimal restraints.
‡ Except in regard to natural resources.

(*Source*: *The Amsterdam Port Areas*, 1970, p. 79. Inbucon Ltd.)

Appendix VI.

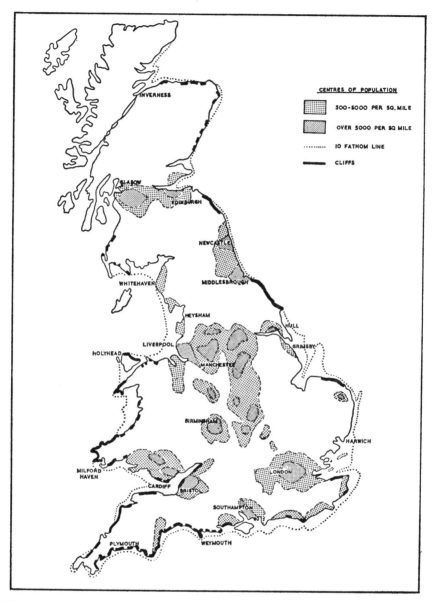

Natural deep water and coastal features in relation to population centres, United Kingdom. (*Source*: National Ports Council *Annual Report*, 1966.)

Appendix VII.

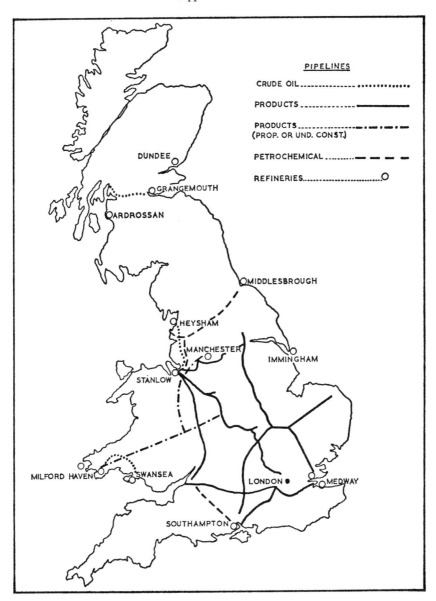

Pipe lines and refineries in the United Kingdom. (*Source*: National Ports Council, *Port Progress Report*, 1969.)

AGGLOMERATION EFFECT. The aggregate of all results of a development including additional economic growth arising from that development which is not the specific growth for which the scheme of development was designed: used to describe the fact that large-scale prime industrial growth will also attract secondary and service industries and commercial and other growth connected with the original industry and its workers.

ALIENATION OF USE. Term used in this book to illustrate the effect of changes in land use in port areas to uses inconsistent with the nature and function of a port.

BEAM. The measurement (usually in feet) of the widest part of the vessel.

BERTH ELABORATION. Departure from the simple outline (in plan) of the single wharf or early quays: term often used to describe complicated berth layouts such as inset docks, jetties, and moles, as opposed to continuous quays.

BULK/VALUE RATIO. The ratio between the bulk of a commodity and its value: of importance in development of maritime areas since imports of high bulk and low value are restricted in market area to the immediate vicinity of a port.

CONSERVATION. Used (in contrast to preservation) to describe planning provisions in control of new development to conserve what is especially interesting, rare, or outstanding of the original environment, e.g., flora and fauna, scenery, open spaces, and resources.

DEAD WEIGHT TONNAGE (DWT). The actual weight of cargo carried: the difference between loaded and light displacement.

DIRTY CARGO. Cargo which has unpleasant characteristics such as smell, dust, or contaminating effects: usually more expensive in labour costs because of additional payments to dock workers as compensation.

DRAUGHT OR DRAFT. The vertical distance in feet from the waterline of a vessel to the lowest point of the keel.

ENVIRONMENTAL POLLUTION. Literally destruction of the purity of the environment—air, water, flora, fauna, or landscape: normally used in the widest sense to describe the effects of industrial development on the natural habitat.

FLASHPOINT. The temperature at which volatile liquids in particular are liable to flash or explode if exposed to sparks or naked flame. By regulation all material with a low flashpoint (below 73° F.) must only be handled under stringent rules and precautions.

GOLDEN DELTA. Popular name for the Rhine Delta, reflecting the economic growth attracted to this area over the past 25 years. It owes a large part of its attraction to the character of the Rhine waterway and its connexions for distribution to the western European hinterland.

226

GROSS TONNAGE. Measurement of total ship capacity: calculated by measuring the cubic capacity (in cubic feet) of all spaces available for cargo, stores, crew, passengers, and engines and dividing by 100.

INFRASTRUCTURE. Literally the 'structure below': used in town planning to describe the fixed installations supporting community life, such as roads, commercial and administrative centres, drainage, water supply, etc.

In ports the term usually refers to common user facilities for shipping, such as entrance channels, locks, dock water areas, breakwaters, etc.

INSET DOCK. A rectangular water area inserted into a line of quay frontage to increase the number of berths in a given area.

INTERFACE. The point where two or more transport systems meet: in maritime parlance, generally, the port area; more specifically, the quay at which cargo transfer takes place.

INTERMODAL. Ability to be transferred between transport modes without breaking bulk. The term is used especially to describe systems such as containers, which are designed to be carried by rail, road, or ship; or LASH, where the container is also a barge capable of being towed along inland water networks.

ISOBATH. A line on a chart joining all points of equal depth below the surface of the sea. The depths of successive isobaths are all measured from an arbitrary point known as 'chart datum', which is based on the position of low water at mean Spring tides.

KNOT. Speed measurement in standard nautical miles per hour.

LAND USE ANALYSIS. Technique widely used in planning and land economics to obtain practical information from specific projects in a form which can be used to provide data for other projects.

LIGHT DISPLACEMENT. Weight of ship in an unloaded condition (in tons or tonnes).

LOAD DISPLACEMENT. Actual weight of ship, cargo, stores, fuel, etc. (in tons or tonnes).

MARITIME INDUSTRY. Port-related industry.

NET REGISTERED TONNAGE (NRT). Derived from gross tonnage by deducting the space used for crew accommodation, navigation, engines, fuel, and water ballast ('deducted spaces').

PORT-ORIENTED INDUSTRY. Port-related industry.

PORT-RELATED INDUSTRY. Industry which, by reason of imported raw materials, substantial exports, or its connexion with other port-related industries, finds an economic advantage in a site in or near a port.

PORTSIDE INDUSTRY. Port-related industry which, for special reasons (e.g. difficulty and expense in handling raw material from ships; needing early reduce-bulk processes), requires a site close to a berth.

PRIME INDUSTRY. Industry performing the first industrial process on raw material, e.g., steelmaking, oil refining. In countries importing raw materials, prime industry is usually maritime industry.

SECONDARY INDUSTRY. Industry which uses the products of prime industry as its raw material.

SPECIALIZED BERTHS. Berths specially equipped and laid out to handle a bulk flow of a particular type of cargo or cargoes with similar handling characteristics. The term is sometimes used in substitution for 'bulk cargo berth' to distinguish it from a berth which may have equipment for handling a number of different types of bulk cargo flows.

SPIN-OFF. Term used in economics to describe incidental effects on adjoining areas resulting from specific development.

STANDARD NAUTICAL MILE. 6080 feet (1852 metres): Based on the average length of a minute of arc of a meridian, rounded off to the nearest 10 feet.

SUPERSTRUCTURE. Term used in ports to describe installations for specific port purposes such as quays, cranes, and warehouses.

UNITS OF MEASUREMENT

Fathom.	Unit of depth=6 feet	1·8288 metres
Mile.	1760 yards or 5280 feet	1·60934 kilometres
Yard.	3 feet or 36 inches	0·9144 metres
Foot.	12 inches	0·3048 metres
Inch.		25·40 millimetres
Kilometre.	1000 metres	0·621371 mile
Metre.	1000 millimetres	1·09361 yards
Acre.	4840 square yards	4046·86 square metres=0·4047 HA
Hectare.	10,000 square metres	or 2·47105 acres
Square mile.	640 acres	2·58999 square kilometres
Square kilometre.	247·105 acres	100 hectares
Ton.	2240 pounds (lb.) or	1,016·05 kilogrammes
Tonne.	1000 kilogrammes	2204·62 pounds (lb.)

VISUAL AMENITIES. Term describing standards of appearance, outlook, or view in relation to the standards of new development, the general appearance of an estate, and the conservation of natural features of beauty.

BIBLIOGRAPHY

ATKINS, W. S., and PARTNERS (1964), *A Preliminary Study of the Future Port Requirements of the Severn Estuary*. Epsom: W. S. Atkins.

ATKINS, W. S., and PARTNERS (1967), *Notes on W. S. Atkins and Partners' Proposals for an International Airport, Deep Water Port and Reservoirs on Reclaimed Land in the Severn Estuary*. Cardiff: W. S. Atkins.

Atlas of Britain and Northern Ireland. Oxford: Clarendon Press.

BIRD, JAMES (1963), *Major Seaports of the United Kingdom*. London: Hutchinson.

BLACK, J. N. (1970), 'Potential Aspects of Development', Foulness Conference. Thames Estuary Development Co.

BRITISH TRANSPORT DOCKS BOARD, *Annual Reports, 1963–1970*.

BROOKS ADAMS (1895), *The Law of Civilization and Decay*. London: Sonnenschein.

BUREAU D'ÉTUDES ET DE DOCUMENTATION (1970), *Les Ports maritimes et Fluviaux français*. Paris: Cerex.

CLARKE, R. G. (1970), *The Potential of the Medway Estuary as a Maritime Industrial Development Area*. Maidstone: Kent County Council.

COLLEGE OF EUROPE, *Report of Conference on the Future of European Ports* (Bruges, April, 1970):
> The Function of Maritime Ports: T. Thorburn.
> Future Development of Maritime Transports: R. Regul.
> Evolution of Demand in Petrol: A. Lefebvre.
> Evolution of Demand, Iron Ore and Coal: O. Becker and R. Denckewitz.
> The Industrial Function of Ports: H. Aujac.
> Principles determining Localization of Refineries and Petrochemical Industry: J. Burchard.
> Principles determining Localization of Steelworks: A. Capanna.
> Port Comparison:
>> Hamburg: H. Sobisch.
>> Wilhelmshafen: G. Eickmeier
>> Belgium: M. Anselin.
>> France: M. Brossier.
>> Great Britain: D. Perkins and M. Gifford.
>> Italy: G. Dagnino.
>> Netherlands: R. Ruiter.
>> Scandinavia: N. Heggemsnes.
> Macro-economic Evaluation of Port Investments: N. Vanhove.
> Size of Ships: R. O. Goss.
> Development of Traffic by Containers: P. Kendall.

CONSULTATION ORGANISATION FOR SEAPORT DEVELOPMENT IN SOUTH-WEST NETHERLANDS (1968), Report, *Exploration of Some Aspects of the Development Possibilities for Seaports in the Delta Region* ('The Green Book'). Rotterdam: Consultation Organisation.

COTTRELL, LEONARD (1957), *Lost Cities*. London: Robert Hale.

DALE, R. N., and MASON, D. F. (1970), 'Ore Handling Equipment at Port Talbot Tidal Harbour', *Proceedings of the Institution of Civil Engineers*, vol. 45, pp. 627–640. *The Dock and Harbour Authority*, 1967, July.

FREEMAN, T. W. (1967), *Geography and Planning*. London: Hutchinson.

FULLER, J. F. C. (1970), *The Decisive Battles of the Western World*, 1792–1944. London: Paladin.

HALLETT, G. (1970), 'How not to plan M.I.D.A.s, *Loughborough Journal of Social Studies*, No. 10, p. 41.

HALLETT, G., and RANDALL, P. (1970), *Maritime Industry and Port Development in South Wales*. Cardiff: University College.

HARRIS, F. R., and COMPANY (1968), *The Greater Delta Region: An Evaluation of Development and Administration* ('The Blue Book'). Rotterdam City Council.

HEAVER, TREVOR D. (1968), *The Economics of Vessel Size*. National Harbours Board of Canada.

HOOKER, A. V. (1970), 'Severnside of the Future', *Proceedings of the Institution of Civil Engineers*, vol. 47, pp. 337–348.

INBUCON B. V. and PORT OF AMSTERDAM (1970), *The Amsterdam Port Areas*. Amsterdam.

INSTITUTE OF NAVIGATION (1968/69), *Annual Report*.

INTERNATIONAL ASSOCIATION OF PORTS AND HARBOURS, Melbourne Conference, 1969: The Economic Impact of Ports and the Regions they serve and the Role of Industrial Development: R. Vleugels.

KING, W. G., and TAKEL, R. E. (1971), 'The Port of Swansea', *Swansea and its Region*, Chap. XX, pp. 287–301. Swansea: University College of Swansea on behalf of Local Executive Committee of the British Association.

LANGEFELD, J. M. (1969), 'Offshore Tanker Terminal', *Symposium on Tanker and Bulk Carrier Terminals*. London: Institution of Civil Engineers.

MALKIN, BENJAMIN (1809), *The Scenery, Antiquities and Biography of South Wales*.

MANNERS, GERALD (ed.) (1964), *South Wales in the Sixties*. Oxford: Pergamon.

MANNERS, GERALD (1966), *Some Planning Needs and Opportunities in South Wales*. Swansea: Gerald Manners.

MEREDITH, W. G., and WORDSWORTH, C. (1966), 'Size of Ore Carriers for the New Port Talbot Harbour', *Journal of the Iron and Steel Institute*, vol. 204, pp. 1075–1078.

MINISTÈRE DE L'ÉQUIPEMENT ET DU LOGEMENT (1970), *Résultats de l'Exploitation des Ports maritimes*. Paris.

MINISTRY OF HOUSING AND LOCAL GOVERNMENT (1967), *Planning Bulletin No. 8*. London: H.M.S.O.

NATIONAL PORTS COUNCIL:
Digest of Port Statistics, 1969.
Ports Progress Report, 1969.
Annual Reports and Accounts, 1966–1970.

Maritime Industrial Development Areas (M. H. Peston and R. Rees), 1970.

A Comparison of the Costs of Continental and United Kingdom Ports (Touche, Ross and Co.), 1970.

NORTH, F. J. (1964), *The Evolution of the Bristol Channel.* Cardiff: National Museum of Wales.

OFFORD, R. S. (1970), 'Water Supply: Distribution and Resources'. *Proceedings of a Conference on 'Civil Engineering Problems of the South Wales Valleys'*, Cardiff, 1969. London: Institution of Civil Engineers.

PERMANENT INTERNATIONAL ASSOCIATION OF NAVIGATION CONGRESSES (P.I.A.N.C.). 22ND INTERNATIONAL NAVIGATION CONGRESS (Section II, Subject 6), Paris, 1969:
Germany: Dr. Ing R. Lutz and Baudirektor G. Thode.
Belgium: M. Van Cauwenberge and F. A. Deweirdt.
Spain: M. V. Gonzales, E. A. Minon, and R. C. Perez.
United States of America: R. Q. Palmer, M. E. Lepine, S. H. Froid, B. E. Nutter, and A. D. Quinn.
France: M. Barillon, M. Mandray, and M. Boissereinq.
Japan: K. Ukena.
Poland: A. Tubielewicz, A. Kienits, and R. Karbowski.
United Kingdom: Miss Susan W. Fogarty, D. J. Bright, D. C. Coode, D. G. McGarey, N. N. B. Ordman, and J. T. Williams.
Sweden: A. Waldemarson.
International Commission on Irrigation and Drainage: Captain G. C. Dawson.
General Report: Henri Babinet.

POLLOCK, E., and TAKEL, R. E. (1967), *Severnside: Report on an Economic Study.* British Transport Docks Board.

POLLOCK, E., and TAKEL, R. E. (1968), *Ports and Development in South-West Wales.* British Transport Docks Board.

PORT OF LONDON AUTHORITY and MARTECH (1966), *Britain's Ports: The Facts and the Future.*

Portbury: Reasons for the Minister's Decision not to authorise the Construction of a New Dock at Portbury, Bristol (1966). Code No. 55–432. London: H.M.S.O.

The Protection of the Environment, Cmd. 4373 (1970). London: H.M.S.O.

RADWAY, E. R. (1970), *Barry Docks Approaches: An Appreciation of Various Schemes for handling 35,000–200,000 dwt. Tankers.* British Transport Docks Board.

Report of the Committee of Inquiry into the Major Ports of Great Britain, Cmd. 1824 (1962). London: H.M.S.O.

Report of the Committee on the Qualifications of Planners, Cmd. 8059 (1950). London: H.M.S.O.

Report of the Severn Barrage Committee (1933). (London: H.M.S.O. Departmental Report.)

Report on the Severn Barrage Scheme (1945). (London: H.M.S.O. Departmental Report.)

ROBERTS, T. S., and TAKEL, R. E. (1970), 'The South Wales Ports and the Economic Community, 1969,' *Proceedings of a Conference on 'Civil Engineering Problems of the South Wales Valleys'*, Paper No. 5, pp. 55–65. London: Institution of Civil Engineers.

ROTTERDAM CITY COUNCIL (1965), *Exploration of Future Employment in the Port and Industrial Region of Rotterdam* ('The Orange Book').

ROTTERDAM CITY COUNCIL (1969), *Plan 2000+: Development of the Northern Delta* ('The Yellow Book').

SCOTTISH COUNCIL (DEVELOPMENT AND INDUSTRY), (1970), *Oceanspan, A Maritime based Strategy for a European Scotland*. Edinburgh.

SCOTTISH COUNCIL (DEVELOPMENT AND INDUSTRY) and VERENIGDE BEDRIJVEN BREDERO N.V. (1971), *Oceanspan II, A Study of Port and Industrial Development in Western Europe*. Edinburgh.

SERETES (1966), *Fonctions portuaires et Devéloppement urbain dans quelques Grands Ports européens*. Paris: Seretes.

SOUTH WALES ELECTRICITY BOARD, *Annual Reports*, 1966–1970.

SUSSAMS, J. E. (1968), 'Some Problems associated with the Distribution of Consumer Products', *Operational Research Quarterly*, Vol. 19, No. 2, pp. 162–163.

THAMES ESTUARY DEVELOPMENT CO. (1970), *The Case for Foulness*.

TREVELYAN, G. M. (1944), *English Social History*. London: Longmans Green.

TUGENDHAT, C. (1968), *Oil: The Biggest Business*. London: Eyre & Spottiswoode.

VLEUGELS, R. (1973), 'Port Economy in the European Economic Community,' *Chartered Institute of Transport Journal*, March.

WATTS, D. G. (1970), 'Milford Haven and Its Oil Industry, 1958–1969', *Geography*, Vol. IV, Pt. 1, January, pp. 64–72.

WHITE, SIR BRUCE, WOLFE BARRY, and PARTNERS (1965), *Report on the Proposed Development of the Port of Cardiff*. Cardiff: Cardiff Corporation.

WILSON, E. M. (1966), 'A Multipurpose Barrage on the Bristol Channel', Paper given at a joint meeting of the South Western Associations of the Institution of Civil Engineers and the Institution of Electrical Engineering, Bristol, January, 1966.

World Bulk Carriers and Review (1970). Oslo: Fearnley & Egers Chartering Co.

World Tanker Fleet Review (1967). London: John I. Jacobs & Co.

Zeehavennota her Zeehavenbeleid van der Rijksouerheid, S'Gravenhage, Staatsvitgeverij (1966). The Hague: Ministeries van Verkeer en Waterstaat, Volkhuisvesting, Ruimtelijke Ordening en Economische Zaken.